History and Contribution of the Zamindars in Visakhapatnam Region (A.D. 1611-1949)

History and Contribution of the Zamindars in Visakhapatnam Region (A.D. 1611-1949)

Dr B. Anjani Kumari

GYAN

This book is published with the Financial Assistance given by the Indian Council of Historical Research, New Delhi.

ISBN : 978-81-212-1339-4

Price : ₹ 485

First Published, 2017

Published by

Gyan Publishing House
5, Ansari Road
Daryaganj, New Delhi-110002
Phone: 9811692060
E-mail: books@gyanbooks.com

Printed at: G. Print Process, Delhi.

Cataloging in Publication Data—DK
Courtesy: D.K. Agencies (P) Ltd. <docinfo@dkagencies.com>

Anjani Kumari, author.
History and contribution of the zamindars in Visakhapatnam region AD 1611 1949 / Dr Anjani Kumari.
pages cm
Includes bibliographical references.
ISBN 9788121213394

1. Landlords—India—Vishākhapatnam (District)—History. 2. Landlords—India—Vishākhapatnam (District)—Social conditions. 3. Landlords—India—Vishākhapatnam (District)—Economic conditions. 4. Landlords—India—Vishākhapatnam (District)—Social life and customs. 5. Poets, Telugu—India—Vishākhapatnam (District)—History. I. Title.

HD1331.I4K86 2016 DDC 333.54095485 23

Contents

Foreword

Dr Badarala Anjani Kumari has made a contribution to the history of modern northern Andhra by attempting a study of the History and Contribution of the Zamindars in Visakhapatnam Region. She has succeeded in presenting an exhaustive account of the Zamindars and their political and cultural contributions. She has discussed the problems pertaining the geneology and chronology of the Zamindari families and has come to conclusions which are judicious. The utilisation of the archival records along with the literary works for the reconstruction of the social, economic and the religious conditions of the period is noteworthy.

I hope that Dr Anjani Kumari will follow up the work by attempting a critical study of the British – Zamindari relations and the Impact of the Zamindari regime on the economic life of northern Andhra.

Kolluru Suryanarayana
Former Professor and Head,
Dept of History and Archaeology,
Andhra University.
VISAKHAPATNAM.

Preface

In the following pages, an attempt is made to reconstruct the history and contribution of the zamindars in the Visakhapatnam region. This subject still remains largely a virgin field. From the last few decades the focus of interest of researchers has been clearly on studies related to the personalities, struggle for freedom and different movements related to socio-economic aspects of particular regions. The role of the elite and sub-altern classes in those movements and struggles have been no doubt covered in such studies. But there are some aspects which have not completely drawn the attention of the scholars, or some of them need further study in the light of new focus on the source materials as well as in the shift in the ideologies. The province of Visakhapatnam deserves special study as it acted as a link between two different politico-cultural zones, viz., Andhra and Orissa. Even from the early historical periods it shows its unique nature and significance as evident from a number of sources. Later, it became a centre of political activity and turned as a buffer zone between different political powers in different centuries. In the late medieval period, which is during the advent of the Muslims as well as Europeans into this land, it came into the authority of the local chiefs and zamindars. They dominated administratively and strengthened themselves. It is interesting to know that out of the four hundred and forty eight zamindaris in Andhra, more than fifty two zamindaris are located in the then Visakhapatnam District.

As a link between medieval and modern periods, some of the families traced their origin from the earliest centuries and gradually evolved as local fiefs and zamindars in this province. Under different circumstances in different periods they received land chief either from the Sultans of Golkonda or from the ruling chiefs of Orissa. As this area is geographically a link between Andhra and Orissa, different ruling families and zamindars connected themselves and stated their lineages either from the Orissan Chiefs or from the Sultans of Golkonda who expanded their territories eastwards. The zamindar is of the Kakarlapudis of Anakapalli, the Pusapatis of Vizianagaram, etc., were established under the Sultans of Golkonda, where as the zamindaris of Madugula, Golugonda and Gudem were established under the authority of the Orissan chiefs. In addition to the above two, some of the zamindaris originated under the rule of English East India Company. The Gode zamindars showed their thorough impact on the areas of Visakhapatnam and Anakapalli emerged as zamindars under English East India Company. Thus began zamindari families exercised their authority in this Visakhapatnam area for certain period and showed their impact on this province.

So far, no considerable effort has been made to study the history and contribution of those zamindari families of this area. No doubt, some scholars like A.Vadivelu, G.R. Varma, M.S.R. Anjaneyulu, Y. Sudershan Rao, T.S.N. Murthi, and T. Donappa attempted to study some aspects related to the above zamindars. But the objectives of their work were entirely different, and only sketch of some of the families were found in them rather than a detailed discussion of problems in their study. Great is my debt to the authors of those works, who enriched the subject.

M.S.R. Anjaneyulu touched upon this subject in his monograph Vizagapatam District (1769-1834). But as Mamidipudi Venkatarangaiya noticed, M.S.R. Anjaneyulu used the sources only for the purpose of delimiting the relations between the Company and the zamindars. But they deserve to be studied for the light they have thrown on the socio-economic and religio-cultural conditions of the zamindari period in this province. More or less same is the case with the work of Y. Sudershan Rao Andhra Between the Empires. The objective of those works is different and hence not covered the history and contribution of these zamindars.

In fact, this is a study of the transition of a polity, which was essentially medieval in character to what may be called a modern polity. The Nizam who claimed sovereignty over the Northern Sircars of which the area under study was a part, was not in a position to exercise control over the zamindars who fought among themselves and allowed them to act accordingly in various matters. The primary duty of the maintenance of law and order was also neglected which resulted in chaos and anarchy. When the central authority became very weak, naturally the local representatives exercise their powers, which favoured the French and the British to intervene into the political affairs of this province. The French were the first to gain political ascendency over the Nizam; but later the English due to their various resources ousted the French and established themselves in power over the sircars of by A.D. 1769, with the kind support of the Pusapatis of this province.

The English Company came from a country whose political culture was entirely different from that of this part of India during that period. Until then, they witnessed in England the passing away completely of the decentralised political culture of the middle-ages, and the rise of modern centralised political culture. It was with this new tradition of centralised political culture, East India Company tried to exercise their authority, which was naturally resented by the zamindars.

The zamindars in general, of this province in particular wished to deal with the Company in the same manner as they dealt with the Nizam earlier. But the limited resources of the zamindars were not enough to control the Company. The Company put down with a high hand all the rebellious zamindars. With the introduction of new administrative policies for agency and plains, to the maximum extent, administration was systematised and modernised.

The micro-level political analysis of the Visakhapatnam region during the troubled period between the fading away of the Muslim power and the emerging as well as established British power became a necessary requisite to understand the political dynamics of the British diplomacy. Evidently, this was the significant region to put up resistance to the expansion and consolidation of the British authority both from the petty tribal chiefs as well as zamindars. This region eventually suffered the British Rule for the longest period in our country. Again this region was first to react favourably to the impact of Western culture and ideas through its social reform. The present Visakhapatnam, the significant city of this region is referred to as Visakhapatnam, Kulottunga - Cholapatam, Vizag, Waltair etc., in different phases of history. But for convenience in the study, the name Visakhapatnam is used throughout. The subject matter is divided into six chapters.

Chapter – I deals with the Introduction, source materials, physiological and historical information of the province. Origin, growth and development of the zamindari system in the Muslim and European periods is discussed in this chapter. Various sources that deal with the History, Socio-Economic as well as Religio-Cultural aspects of the period are focussed in this. The literature, that produced and patronised by the zamindars, village kaifiyats and the European sources are utilised to the maximum possible extent. The data of the few inscriptions issued by the family members of the zamindars at places like Simhachalam, and Visakhapatnam are also utilised in interpreting the facts. The construction activity as well as the endowments by those families are also utilised to the suitable extent.

This chapter also deals with the geography, climate, nature of the soil, ranges of mountains, rainfall rate, river systems and tanks that irrigate the plain lands of this province. The political antecedents that witnessed by this province in the ancient and medieval times are briefly touched upon in this context. Begin with the Satavahana power, in different centuries how a number of ruling dynasties showed their impact on this province, and how they left their traces in this tract, is briefly narrated in this chapter. Growth of different religious ideologies and their important worshipping centres in this area are also recollected in this context. Significant religious monuments of different faiths like Bojjannakondalu and Simhachalam comes under this study.

Chapter – II is the study on the history of the zamindaris that existed in the province of Visakhapatnam at different stages of time. Begin with the advent of the Qutb Sahis of Golkonda, until the abolition of the Zamindari Act, the history of the ruling chiefs, zamindars, estatedars, and Muttadars that exercised their authority in this province is elaborately discussed in this chapter. The entry of the Kakarlapudi family into these areas as military officers (Payaks) under the Qutb Shahis, their political activity at places like Anakapalli and Satyavaram, their cordial as well as hostile relations with the contemporary powerful Pusapati chiefs, hill zamindars and the English Company are discussed in detail. The Bhupathi families at Madugula, Golugonda and Gudem located in the hill regions of this province, which got those estates through the Chiefs of Orissa played a significant role in creating troubles to the Company Government and its allies like Pusapatis. Such revolts which continued for years together created a lot of troubles to the Company Government, and all such revolts are incorporated in this chapter. The Gode and Ankitam families which showed their thorough impact for generations together on this province in general and on Visakhapatnam and Anakapalli estates in particular, is highlighted in this chapter. The Western education, Western scientific outlook of those families made them different from the other zamindars; and that factor made them closer to the English people and English Company. The important major Zamindari of the Pusapatis which originally belongs to Vizianagaram thoroughly extended their authority in the entire Province and their activities in controlling the remaining zamindaris, is also discussed in this chapter. Besides, a number of small zamindaris like those located at places like Kasimkota, Uratla, Kondakarla, Melipaka, Barnikam, Rayavaram, etc., are also discussed in this chapter.

Chapter – III deals with the inter-relations of the zamindars in the Visakhapatnam province. The friendly as well as the hostile relations that have taken place in between the various zamindars is the subject matter of this chapter. Owing to their personal causes some zamindari families either supported or joined hands with the English authority under certain circumstances and as a result they were forced to fight against the rebellious zamindars. This instance can be seen in the English-Pusapati alliance in suppressing the rebellious zamindari families like the Bhupathis of Madugula, Golugonda, Gudem and Kakarlapudis of Anakapalli. Under certain circumstances, some of the zamindars of this province joined hands either in protesting the Sultans of Golkonda, or the French. In the changing circumstances, to protect the interests of their zamindaris, how they acted accordingly is studied in this chapter. The treacherous acts of treatments or punishments levied on such rebellious zamindars or chiefs who challenged the English Company, is discussed in this context.

Chapter – IV is a discussion on the society and economy under the zamindaris in the area under study. Social aspects like education, customs and other allied items are briefly touched upon in this context. Various other charities like the establishment of choultries, poor feeding houses, hospitals, establishment of highest seat of learnings like college and university is focused. Interestingly, the establishment of Astronomical Observatory which is equipped with all types of modern tools of the then times at Visakhapatnam, under the Gode and Ankitam families is highlighted in this chapter. Position of agriculture, new methods of agriculture, introduction of new varieties of crops, growth in the rate of production of commercial crops etc., are discussed in this context. Promotion of irrigation facilities, construction of the canals and tanks etc., are also appended in this chapter. Land tenures, Haveli lands, Srotriams, Kowle lands, peasant problems and implementation of Permanent Land Revenue settlement in these areas are focussed in this context. Problems of agriculture droughts and famines, relief measures, etc., are also discussed here. Different crafts, small scale industries like toys of Etikoppaka and large scale industries like sugar, salt, jute, trade and commerce, transport, ports at places like Visakhapatnam, Bhimilipatnam, etc. are briefly focussed in this chapter.

Chapter – V is a discussion on religo-cultural conditions. Construction and patronage of different temples that belongs to different faiths, charities and constructions, tutillary deities like Niukalamma, and Sattemma of the Kakarlapudis, Modakondamma of the tribal chiefs, etc., are discussed in this context. Grants and donations issued by some of the zamindari family members are brought to light in this chapter by utilising the inscriptional data at places like Simhachalam.

Chapter – VI is a study on the patronage of the zamindars towards literature. Some of the zamindars as well as their family members are poets and enriched literature by their contributions. Besides they patronaged and encouraged a number of poets and scholars, who composed vast literature in different types and styles. Bhupathi Zamindari at Madugula and Gode Zamindari at Visakhapatnam became very familiar for their liberal patronage. They have donated largely for the promotion of literature both of Sanskrit and Telugu. It is interesting to note that some of the ladies of these zamindari families produced more than a number of works. A number of Satakas, devotional songs, puranic stories and dandakas were composed under these zamindars. As this is the period of gradual expansion of Christianity the efforts of the missionaries in promoting literature for their religious purpose is also included in this.

Conclusion is the sum-up of the entire date discussed in the earlier chapters.

I wish to express my deep sense of gratitude to my teacher and research supervisor, Dr Kolluru Suryanarayana, Professor, Department of History and Archaeology, whose constant encouragement, useful suggestions and guidance played the most important role in the completion of the present work. He has kindly placed at my disposal his personal library for my use.

I am grateful to Professor M. Krishna Kumari, former Head of the Department of History and Archaeology, Andhra University and to Professor P. Sivunnaidu, present Head of the Department for the encouragement and parental care they have taken in providing various facilities during the period of my research.

I am also obliged to Dr A.V.D. Sharma, Rector, MANSAS, Vizianagaram, for providing a number of important books and other information for my purpose.

I am grateful to Professor S. Girija, Chairman Board of studies and to all the staff members in the Department of History and Archaeology, for their valuable suggestions during the period of my research.

I also express my earnest thanks to Professor C. Somasundara Rao, former Professor in the Department of History and Archaeology, for his valuable help and suggestions at various stages of this work. I am thankful to Mr K. Narayana Kiran for his help at the typing stage of this work. I am obliged to the University authorities for providing all facilities for my research work.

I am extremely thankful to the Indian Council of Historical Research, New Delhi, for providing Junior Research Fellowship, during the tenure of my research. I am thankful to many institutions for permitting me to consult their libraries; The Librarian, Dr V.S. Krishna Memorial Library, Andhra University, Waltair; Assistant Director, Regional Office of A.P. State Archives, Visakhapatnam; Director, A.P. State Archives, Hyderabad; Director, Tamil Nadu State Archives, Chennai; The Librarians of the Libraries at places like Vetapalem, Kumudavalli and Anakapalli.

I am also thankful to a number of scholars and elders who permitted me to utilise their personal libraries. I extend my heartfelt regards to my father late Sri Badarala Durga Rao, who encouraged and initiated me into the field of research in History.

Finally, I acknowledged the services of Sri Malisetty Suri Babu and of Sri Madabathula Appa Rao, who typed this thesis neatly with utmost care and responsibility.

Ugadi
Nandana

Anjani Kumari

Abbreviations

A.P.H.C	: Andhra Pradesh History Congress
A.R.E	: Annual Report of Epigraphy
A.S.P.P	: Andhra Sahitya Parishat Patrika
B.O.R	: Board of Revenue
B.O.R.C	: Board of Revenue Consultations
Epi Andhrica	: Epigraphia Andhrica
E.I	: Epigraphia Indica
H.E	: His Excellency
J.A.H.R.S	: Journal of the Andhra Historical Research Society
K.C.I.E	: Knight Commander of the Most Eminent Order of the Indian Empire
M.C	: Military Consultations
M.R.O	: Madras Records Office
Mss	: Manuscripts
RC	: Revenue Consultations
RFSG	: Dispatches Records of Fort St. George: Dispatches to England
RFSG Dairy	: Records of Fort St. George: Dairy and Consultations Books
RFSG: Letters from FSG	: Records of Fort St. George: Letters from Fort St. George
S.I.I	: South Indian Inscriptions
V.D.G	: Vizagapatam District Gazetteer
V.D.R	: Vizag District Records.

Chapter - 1

Introduction and Sources

The Visakhapatnam Province consists of a beautiful, picturesque landscape surrounded with the hilly tracts that situated in the Northern part of the Madras Presidency. With a chain of Eastern Ghats with higher peaks of ranges more than 5000 feet high above the sea level, this district lies between 17-10°–18-25° longitude and 88-55°– 83-40° latitude covering an extent of 11.161 square kilometers, which consists 4.06 per cent in the extent of Andhra Pradesh.[1] In the earlier period, prior to its partition with the neighbouring districts like Vizianagaram, it was the largest district covering over an area of 47,511 sq.km and with a coastline of more than 176 kilometers. Once it was bounded on the north by the district of Ganjam and the Central Provinces (Madhya Pradesh); on the east by Ganjam and the sea; on the south by the sea and the Godavari district; and on the west by the Central Provinces. The mountain slopes which covered the large areas in the district flourished with vegetation consisting of tall forest trees and other plants. The mountain named *Sankara* of about 1,615 meters right near Sringavarapukota, on the way to Araku, is the highest mountain in this district.[2]

The hill portion of the Golugonda taluk is all within the agency and forms the southern most corner of the '3,000 feet plateau'. It drains northwards, mainly through the Paleru river, into the Sileru. It consists of a jumble of steep and broken hills, which is average about 2,500 feet, contain some fair plateaus at about that level, run up in many places to 4,000 feet and over, and produce the heaviest jungle of any part of the plateau. Some of that is moist ever-green growth and includes tree-ferns, orchids and many varieties of the smaller ferns. The maddi and gall-nut trees are numerous. The tops of the higher hills are usually bare, their sides and the lower hills carrying most of the forest, while the more level country is often covered with large stretches of grassland dotted with scattered trees gnarled and twisted by the annual jungle fires. The outer Southern slopes are clothed with good forest which is seldom burnt, and at the foot of them, especially round Kondasanta, are masses of splendid bamboos.[3]

The people, who all speak Telugu, consist chiefly of Bagatas (immigrants from the plains and the aristocracy to which belong the muttadars), Konda Doras, and Konda Malas or 'Hill paraiyans'. The last are a pushing set of traders who are rapidly acquiring wealth and exalted notions. The Konda Doras and to a less extent the Bagatas are the cultivators. Raagi or chollu is their favourite crop. Their methods of cultivation are very casual. The soil is undoubtedly rich, but the people go in for 'podu' cultivation or till the ground carelessly, making scant use of the irrigation possible from the numerous hill streams. Rather than toil at cultivation, they prefer to live by the natural products of the hills. There are very numerous and include limes, particularly sweet oranges, guavas, mangoes, tamarind, Jack fruit, gall-nuts, turmeric, long pepper, mustard, wax, horns, honey and so on.

The local Konda Doras, the people believe, have some religious powers and such feelings drove them yet times, to revolt against their enemical governments. In 1886, excited by the preachings of several Konda Dora priests, who had been travelling round the hills for months, declaring that the hill gods had directed a fituri, a gang of about 30 men got together, went to Gudem and Chintapalli, and burnt and looted police stations there.[4] In the later decades, Alluri Sitarama Raju influenced the tribals by his religious spirituality and prepared them to an armed fight against the English Government, in the agency of this province.[5]

The hill ranges in the district giving rise to a number of rivulets and streams. Rivers like Sarada, Varaha, Tandava, Machkand (Muchi-kunda), Champavathi, Sileru, Gosthani, etc., originated in the hill regions and merge in the Bay of Bengal irrigating the maximum plains in the province.

To the North of the district in the Palakonda hills, and also to the South-West, in the Golugonda and Madugula hill ranges, there were thick forests. The deltas formed at the mouths of those rivers contain rich alluvial deposits facilitating a high yield of variety of agricultural products. Its potential for enormous surplus productions, the agricultural and the industrial sectors and the well-knitted roads in the later stages contributed to the flourishment of trade and commerce in this region. Several places were developed as the centres of industries, both of agricultural and non-agricultural. The geographical location of the province was more favourable and allowing easy access between North and South, and thus paving way for the amalgamation of different cultures.

The geographical nature of the province has given rise to different climates ranging from place to place. In the coast it is moist, in the plain areas it is hotter and drier, and in the hill ranges it is wettest and coldest. The most prevalent disease is malaria, whose intensity varies according to locality.[6] It is very difficult for anybody to remain in the hilly regions of the district, particularly in the rainy season, due to their unhealthy climate. The mountain ranges made the forest region in the district impregnable and that id why in the historical periods it is called as Trikalingatavi.[7] Owing to such geographical conditions it became very difficult for any sovereign authority to control effectively the hill chiefs of that region. In the later centuries, the revolts of the tribal chiefs and their 'fituries' forced the zamindars and the chiefs to spend huge amounts on frequent expeditions, sometimes with the assistance of the troops of East India Company.[8]

In 1863, in view of the changed circumstances then existing, Vizianagaram, Bobbili, and Palakonda were excluded from the limits of the agency, and a further formation of those, upto the base of the hills, took place in 1865. The agency tract, however, still includes 12,622 sq. miles, or 10 per cent of the total areas of the district.[9]

In 1907, Visakhapatnam was India's largest district having an area of 17,222 sq. miles and it was also the most populous district of the Madras Presidency. Consequent on the formation of Orissa Province with effect from April 1, 1936, there has been a radical change in the geographical figuration and size of the district. Nine agency taluks of the old Visakhapatnam district, viz., Koraput, Pottangi, Padwa,

Malkanagiri, Nowrangapur, Jeypore, Raigada, Bissem-Cuttack and Gunupur have been excluded from the district and Chicacole division consisting of Chicacole (including Narasannapeta sub-taluk), Sompeta, Ichchapur, Tekkali and Patapatmam taluks of old Ganjam district have been added to this district.[10] For administrative purposes, the district is divided into five divisions under the control of the Divisional Officers and Taluks under Tahsildar and Deputy Tahsildars as shown below.

1. Vizagapatam Division	–	Vizagapatam, Anakapalli and Srungavarapu Kota Taluks
2. Vizianagaram Division	–	Vizianagaram, Chipurupalli and Bhimilipatnam Taluks
3. Narsipatnam Division	–	Viravalli, Sarvasiddhi, Gudem and Golugonda Taluks
4. Parvatipur Division	–	Parvatipur, Bobbili, Salur and Palakonda Taluks
5. Chicacole Division	–	Chicacole Taluk, Narasannapeta Sub-Taluk, Patapatnam, Sompeta and Ichchapur Taluks

In course of time, due to later consequences and formation of new districts in this province some divisions became parts of Srikakulam district and still later some became parts of the Vizianagaram district.

Thus, the largest populous district of Visakhapatnam, of the old Madras Presidency, has been gradually reduced to the present day size.

Regarding the historical background of this Visakhapatnam province, much have to be stated. That area has a continuous history from times immemorial. A number of evidences of pre-historical cultures are noticed in this province. From the periods of the Stone-age, existence of human culture is noticed at Lankelapalem, Marigavalasa, Sarada river valley, and at the hilly regions of the district.[11] The availability of a number of Stone-age sites, stone tools, urn-burrials, and megalithic burrials clearly inform us the existence of pre-historical cultures in the vicinity of Visakhapatnam.[12]

Coming to the historical periods, almost all the prominent dynasties that ruled the Andhra country in different periods of history either held sway or struggled hard to bring this province under their strong control. In those centuries that province forms an important sub-division in the Kalinga country known as *Madhyama Kalinga,* i.e., the middle part of the Kalinga country. The early historical ruling dynasties like the Mauryas seem to have brought this province also into their control. Mighty powers like the Satavahanas held their sway and exercised control in those areas. Later, this land was occupied by Matharas and Pitri Bhaktas.[13] Samudra Gupta, the greatest emperor in the Gupta dynasty, conquered that tract, which is known by then as *Deva Rashtra* in his Southern campaign as was described in his Allahabad Pillar Inscription.[14] In the entire South-India, the only gold coin of Samudra Gupta is found at Bojjanna Kondalu very nearer to Anakapalli. Almost all the ruling powers in the early centuries of Andhra history such as the Salankayanas, Vishnukundins and Durjayas brought that province into their control. Chikkulla Inscription of Vikramendra Varma of Vishnukundin dynasty, found near Payakaraopeta, Ramathirtham Inscription of Indra Varma of the same dynasty, found near Vizianagaram[15]; and the coins of the same dynasty found at places like Sarvasiddhi, and Bojjanna Konda clearly indicate the influence of the Vishnukundins in that province.

Early Chalukyas who started their political career at Badami in Karnataka, conquered major parts of South India, went upto river Narmada, sub-dued the powers in the Central Provinces; entered into *Trikalinga* and *Vengidesa* which is no other than the area under study. Kubja Vishnuvardhana of that family established a separate dynasty known as Vengi Chalukyan dynasty which continued in Andhra history for more than four and a half centuries.[16] Andhra literature and Andhra culture which the Andhras claim with great respect and pride, was originally their legacy. The area under study owes much to that Chalukyan family as their early occupation was in that area. They left their foot prints on that tract and their early inscriptions are found only in that province; The Chipurupalli inscription of Kubja Vishnuvardhana refers to the grant of a village by name Kaluva Konda (present Kalaval apalli) near Dimili in the Visakhapatnam area.[17] Ela-manchili, an ancient village in the Visakhapatnam district is referred to in their records; and some of the villages like Sarvasiddhi in this district were constructed in their names during their period. Dandin in his *Dasakumara Charitra* refers to a naval battle (*ambusamara*) that was fought between the

Andhra and Kalinga powers on the sea adjacent to the coast of the present Visakhapatnam area.[18]

From the Northern side, Ganga rulers were struggling hard to occupy that area. The Ganga records at Simhachalam refer to a number of villages of that province for the first time. Anakapalli, Kasimkota, Munagapaka, Nagulapalli, and Pisinikada, etc., are referred to in the inscription of Parvathi Devi and Narasimha Deva IV of the Eastern Gangas.[19]

In the succeeding centuries that area has gone into the hands of the Chalukya, Chola power.[20] It is during that period for the first time the name of Visakhapatnam appeared. In an inscription dated 1068 A.D. in the Bhimesvara temple at Draksharama in the East Godavari District, the name of Visakhapatnam is referred to[21]. During the period of the Chalukya-Cholas that succeeded the Vengi-Chalukyas in that area, an attempt was done by the Tamil merchants to change the name of Visakhapatnam as *'Kulottunga Chola Patnam'* in the name of the Chalukya Chola emperor, Kulottunga Rajendra Chola.[22] The suffix 'pattana', itself indicates that Visakhapatnam emerged as a trading centre which is connected with searoute, i.e., a port town. In the succeeding centuries the Velanati Chiefs, the Kakatiyas, the Reddis and the Velmas frequently fought among themselves for the supremacy over the present Visakhapatnam areas, as evident by a number of inscriptions and literary citations.[23] *Kanyakapuranam* otherwise known as *Vaisyapuranam,* the family history of the Vaisyas of the medieval centuries claims Visakhapatnam (Visakhanagara) as one of the centres of their trading activity.[24] The area of Visakhapatnam became a bone of contention between the Kalinga and Andhra powers.[25] All mandalika powers of the Andhra country always struggled hard with the Eastern Gangas and their successors, the Suryavamsa Gajapatis of Orissa.[26] That affinity of those Kalinga powers with this area seems to have continued until beginning of the zamindari period. Some of the mandalika chiefs at places like Nandapura and Oddadi (Oddhradi) in course of time stated to have transformed as zamindars at those places. The well-known emperor of the Vijayanagara Kingdom Srikrishna Devaraya came over here, stayed here for a certain period and declared war against the Gajapati rulers of Orissa. His Simhachalam inscriptions refer to his grant of villages like Aganampudi, Pinagadi and Narava (which are now merged with the city of Visakhapatnam) to the Lord Varaha Lakshmi Narasimhanatha of Simhachalam.[27] Thus, the province of Visakhapatnam witnessed all the political changes that have taken place in the historical periods.

Similarly, the areas in and around Visakhapatnam experienced the various changes and developments of the different religions. Begin with Gopalapatnam near Payakaraopeta, up to Salihundam near Srikakulam, the area consists of a number of Buddhist sites that dates back to the first and second centuries B.C, Gopalapatnam (Kuntipuram), Lingarajupalem, Rakasimetta (Pedappalam), Kotturu, Chintalapalem, Shek-Ali-Palem, Sankaram (Bojjanna Kondalu), Bavikonda, Thotla Konda (Mangamaripeta), Pavurala Konda, Jodugullapalem, Ramatirtham and Salihundam (which was described by Hiuen-Tsang as *Mahodaka-parvatha*), etc., are some of the important Buddhist sites of that area.[28] In course of time the growth of Buddhism in that province led to the missionary undertaking of the propagation and expansion of that religion in the countries over the sea.

The lead coins of the Andhra Satavahanas, the unique gold coin of the Gupta emperor Samudra Gupta, copper coins of Khubja Vishnu Vardhana, the founder of Vengi Chalukyan dynasty, and the coins of the Kakatiyas all found in that area indicate the ancestry of that province. Some of the famous Buddhist quotations like "He damma Hetuprabhaya" that were written in Kalinga script of fifth Century A.D., Chalukyan script of seventh Century A.D., Proto-Nagari script of eighth Century A.D., Oriya and Bengali scripts of eighth and ninth Centuries A.D., indicate the continuous flourishment of those Buddhist sites in different centuries.[29] The numismatic evidences at those Buddhist centers attested to the overseas - trade of that province. The availability of Roman coins at the Buddhist sites adjacent to Visakhapatnam indicates the trade activity of that province with Rome.[30] The availability of the Chalukyan coin with the title "Rajachandra" in Burma indicates the trade activity of that coast with Burma during the Vengi Chalukyan period. The names of villages like Dimili or Divvela (means light-house), Teruvupalli (route showing village into the sea), the ruins of the temple of Ratnakara Swami (sea-God) which exists in between the above two villages on the sea-coast of that province, indicates the navigation spirit of the people of this area.[31] The existence of the Visakhesvara temple which is stated to have been submerged into the sea; and which is stated to have given its name to the city of Visakhapatnam, was the traditional account that was not supported by any of the historical evidences. But with the advent of the Tamil and Ceyloneese merchants to Visakhapatnam, a number of temples of different religions like Karumannikkalwar and Perumballi jinalaya were constructed there.[32] The inscription found in the Appesvara, Chillesvara and Somesvara temples excavated from the sand dunes at Ajjikonda near the coast of the Visakhapatnam indicates the conquests of the Western Chalukyas to annex that area into their province.[33] The very famous temple of Sri Lakshmi Varaha Narasimhanatha at Simhachalam which consists of roughly 600 inscriptions,[34] and was praised by a number of poets in their literary works gave more historical information of that area.[35]

Manchana, the court poet of the Velanati Chiefs who has composed *Keyurabahu Charitra* is stated to have constructed 32 Vaishnava temples in Kaling Andhra, in which the present province under study is a part.[36] Venugopala swami temple at Elamanchili, Kesavaswami temple at Chodavaram, Vaibhogaraya temples at Juttada and Arjuna giri, and a number of the Jagannadha swami temples at places like Madugula etc., were the popular temples that belong to Vaishnavism. Nukalamma temple at Anakapalli, Sattemma temple at Melipaka, Ramachandramma temple at Elamanchili, Modakondamma temple at Paderu, Talupulamma temple at Lova, were the popular temples of the village goddesses in the province.

The rule of the Mandalika chiefs like the Matsyas of Oddadi, Chalukyas of Elamanchili, Gangas of Jantarnadu, Silas of Nandapura, who exercised their authority in the medieval centuries in this province is well-attested to in the inscriptions of the province.[37] The Eastern Ganga rulers who held sway over the province for centuries together gradually shifted their attention towards Orissa. As a buffer state in between major powers the area under study always became a bone of contention between enemical powers. The mandalika chiefs and Viramahapatras always played a crucial role in maintaining the political equilibrium of this area. For centuries together, this province acted as a link between two cultural zones, Andhra and Orissa. A number of forts were constructed for administrative and strategical purposes in this province. But none of those forts existed to the light of the day due to the nature of the soil as well as climatic conditions. In due course, along with other provinces in the Northern Coastal districts, this province of Visakhapatnam also went into the occupation of Qutb-Shahis of Golkonda. Golugonda, Kasimkota, Shermuhammadpuram, etc., became the strongholds of Qutb-Shahis in this province, and a number of their coins were found in the present agency areas around Narsipatnam in the Visakhapatnam district, some of which were collected and preserved in the Department Museum of History and Archaeology, Andhra University.[38] Thus, for centuries together Visakhapatnam province has a continuous significant history.

During the Muslim period Colonial agencies entered into this part of the country also, and simultaneously it is in that period a number of zamindari families originated in this province.

The politico-economic study of Andhra would remain incomplete without reference to the zamindaris which technically formed political units within the overall framework of the British paramountacy. The zamindaris cover a total area of 26.3 million acres, or 29 per cent of the Presidency area, with a population of 75, 54,000, exclusive of those in the agency tracts.

The Zamindari or Permanent Settled Estates are either the remains of ancient principalities, which the holder cannot sell or encumber beyond his own life interest, the succession being hereditary in the eldest son; or they are creations of British rule, dating from 1802 – 03, and subject to the usual Hindu rule of partition. The former have a political status which may be said to be quite wanting in the case of the latter. They were required to pay an annual fixed assessment of Peshkash. In A.D.1941, few years before the abolition of Zamindari Act the total number of Zamindari villages, in the then Visakhapatnam district were four thousand four hundred eighty-three (4,483) covering an area of 39,01,629 acres of land.

Except in abnormal circumstances, normally the zamindar leads a luxurious life. His fabulous amounts were wasted on uneconomic personal expenditure of pomp and splendour, foreign travel, horse racing or gambling, building palaces, sports, and politics. Thus, some of the zamindars ruin themselves out of ostentation, borrow in order to meet their expenses, and finally leave their lands in the hands of money-lenders. Both the English Company and the English Government encouraged the luxury consumption of the Zamindars or Princes for they were regularly decorated for extending lavish hospitality to British officials or royal personages, and for giving away money for a benefit or amusement of British civil and military officers (in the form of benefactions for hospitals or clubs or other institutions, primarily or solely meant for the use of the Europeans).[39] We can see the same in the case of the Gode family and some other zamindars like Sangamavalasa and Bobbili.

In no other period of Indian history we can find so large, so well-established, and so secure a group of wealthy landholders as that which grew up and flourished in between 1790 and 1940.[40] There were a considerable number of minor zamindaris, i.e, fifty-two, in the Ganjam and Visakhapatnam province. The law relating to zamindaris is principally that contained in the two Madras Regulations XXV and XXVI of 1802 Sections 2 and 3 of the former vest a proprietary right as against government in zamindars, their heirs and lawful successors forever, an assessment being imposed; the government and the zamindari exchanging, agreements. This does not bar the sale law, where government sell for arrears of assessment, when whole or part of a zamindari of the second class is alienated, the alienation must be registered in the office of the Collector of the District; otherwise the government will not recognise it.[41] All these type of instances were experienced by the zamindaris of this area.

In the Madras Presidency there are some rich landed estates managed most carefully by zamindarinis, free from all encumbrance. This in itself is sufficient to prove that Southern India, more especially the Madras Presidency, is not devoid of women who can manage large estates, and to show to the outside world that their intelligence and statesman-like qualities are not inferior to those of women in other parts of India. Some of the zamindarinis set out on tour whenever they find it convenient to do so, and hear the complaints and grievances of the ryots.[42] Majority of the zamindarinis are very kind enough to the poor of all classes and many people depend on their bounty. Among the zamindaris of the province under study, in some of the families, particularly in the Gode family of Visakhapatnam and Bhupati family of Madugula, we come across the significant administration of the zamindarinis.

The main sources of information for the reconstruction of the history and contribution of zamindars, in the Visakhapatnam Province, are the records. *District Records, Revenue Consultations,* District Gazetteers, District Manuals, besides a number of Letters of Correspondence are highly useful for the study on the subject. *The Fifth Report* edited by Firminger, Walter *F. Records of Fort St. George, Proceedings of the Committee of Circuit, in the Vizagapatam and Chicacole Districts,* B.S. Bliga's Studiens in Madras Administration etc., offer more valuable information on the subject. A number of writers brought to light through their works very relevant material on this subject. *The Aristocracy of Southern India by,* A. Vadivelu; *The Ruling Chiefs and Nobles* by the same writer; *Treaties, Engagements and Sanads* by C. W. Aitchison, etc., are some useful books for the study on this aspect.

Nicholas Dirks in his work the *Hallow Crown*, dealt with the poligars of Tamil Nadu in general *the ethnohistory of Indian Kingdom,* and of the little kingdom Pudukkottai in particular. In it he has studied the nature and authority in the old regime and the later contradictions with the colonisation of the political power, with the example of Pudukkottai. Extending the type of interdisciplinary approach to Kalinga, Georg Berkemer has made an outstanding attempt in his work of German language, Little Kingdoms in Kalinga. *Ideologie Ligitimation und Politik regionaler Elten*. Though, Berkemer published it in German, the subject that he discussed is made available in some English articles as well as in book reviews.

A number of scholars rendered several efforts to bring new light on this subject, by their valuable contributions. *Civil Disturbances During British Rule in India* by S.B.Chaudhuri; *Note on the Permanent Settlement* by Mudaliar, Gnana Sundara, P.K. *Nizam-British Relations 1754-1857* by Sarojini Regani; *Vizagapatam District, 1769-1834* by M.S.R. Anjaneyulu; *Andhra Between the Empires* by Y. Sudershan Rao; *British Beginning in the Andhra Desa*; and *The Revenue Administration of the Northern Sarkars* by Lanka Sundaram; *Economic Development of Andhra Pradesh* by A.V. Ramana Rao and some important research papers published by G.R. Varma, V. Ramakrishna and T.S.N. Murti are very useful for the study.

Telugu literary works like *Rangaraya Charitram* by Dittakavi Narayana Kavi; *Padmanabha Yuddham* by Chatrati Lakshmi Narasimham and a number of other works either written or patronised by these zamindari families are of highly useful for the re-construction of the history and contribution of those families. *Srikrishna Bhupati Taravali* written by Adidam Balabhaskara Kavi describes the achievements of Krishna Bhupati, the famous zamindar of Madugula. A number of chatus, slokas and stanzas composed by scholars like Sistu Krishna Sastri, Mantripragada Suryaprakasa Kavi and Adidam Sura Kavi gave much information about majority of the zamindars of this province.[43] *Satyavati Parinayam* by Kakarparti Buchchipatra Kavi describes various achievements of Gode Pedda Jagga Rao. *Oghavati Parinayam* by Akkinepalli Nrisimha Kavi describes the family history of the Gode zamindars. More than two hundred stanzas in that work described the history and achievements of the Gode family.[44] *Mallari Charitra* a Telugu dvipada kavya written by Marringanti Venkata Charyulu is actually the purana of Malhareswara Swami, the tutelary deity of the Gode family. The Gode zamindars considered that *Malhari Charitra* as their family history.[45] Being not satisfied with the information given in that work, Gode Janakamma encouraged Erramilli Perraju to write it elaborately with the same title. Though it is unpublished, its manuscript copy is available in the oriental manuscript library at Chennai. *Pusapati Rajula Purvottaram* the traditional account of the Pusapati zamindari focuses much light on the history and other details of the zamindaris here. Besides all these, the stanzas written by Tirupati Venkata Kavulu in their *Nana Raja Sandarsanamu* give some more information on this aspect. A number of village Kaifiyats relates to some important villages in the Visakhapatnam district are also thoroughly utilised in this work. Annual Reports of Epigraphy Volumes of South Indian Inscriptions (particularly Vols. IV, V, VI and X) and similar other works on empigraphy, regarded to the antecedents of this province also. In such hundreds of inscriptions issued at places like Simhachalam and Srikurman, only four inscriptions belonged to zamindars. Gode Chegava Rao issued a grant and Krishna Chandhra Dev, offered grants to the temple of Srikurmam. Except those four records, none of the inscriptions either at Simhachalam or at other places are useful for the study, as those zamindari malimies were in no way connected with the princely families of the medieval Centuries. All those medieval ruling families disappeared in the Muslim attacks (1599 A.D) and those later date zamindars were no related to them.[46]

The four inscriptions that were issued by the members of those families are also utilised in this study. Besides the above sources, the old structures and ruins at places like Madugula, Anakapalli, Sher Muhammadpuram, Visakhapatnam, Melipaka, etc., still remain in a state of decay.

Thus, the available source material offers ample information for the reconstruction of the history and contribution of the zamindars in the Visakhapatnam region. The material has been discussed and presented in different sections of the present work. An attempt is made to shift and interpret the material in a cautious manner so as to draw fairly reasonable conclusions.

References

1. *Manual of the Administration of the Madras Presidency*, Vol. I, p. 139.
2. Carmichael, D.F., *Manual of the District of Vizagapatam,* p. 3.
3. *A Statistical Atlas of the Madras Presidency,* p. 6.
4. Russell, G.E., *Reports on the Disturbances in Parlakimedy, Vizagapatam and Goomsoor, in 1832-36* Vol. I, pp. 6-7.
5. Mangamma, J., *Alluri Sita Ramaraju,* Hyderabad, 1983.
6. Carmichael, D.F., *Op. Cit.,* p. 40.
7. Suryanarayana, Kolluru, *History of the Minor Chalukya Families in Medieval Andhra Desa,* p. 118.
8. Anjaneyulu, M.S.R., *Vizagapatam District, 1769-1834,* p. 68.
9. Carmichael, D.F., Op. Cit. p. 226.
10. *Ibid.*
11. The explorations conducted by the Departments of Anthropology and History and Archaeology have brought to light a number of stonage sites in the Visakhapatnam District.
12. Some specimens of the stonage tools and excavation reports of Urn – burials and megalithic burials are preserved in the Department museum of Anthropology of Andhra University.
13. Hanumantha Rao, B.S.L., *Religion in Andhra,* p. 21.

14. Allahabad Pillar Inscription of Samudra Gupta, published in C.II, Vol. II.
15. Venkataramanayya, N., *Vishnukundinulu*, Plate No. 6.
16. Krishna Rao, B.V., *History of Eastern Chalukyas of Vengi*, p. 45.
17. Venkataramanayya, N., *Eastern Calukyas of Vengi*, p. 18.
18. Dandi, *Dasakumara Charitra, Asvasa I*, p. 3.
19. *S.I.I.* Volume VI, No.731.
20. Krishna Kumari, M., *Rule of the Chalukya Cholas in Andhra Desa,* p. 30.
21. *S.I.I.* Vol. IV, No. 749.
22. *A.R.E.* 1909 Part II, Para 45 and *S.I.I.*, Vol. X, No. 651 and No. 251.
23. Suryanarayana, Kolluru, Op. Cit., p. 137.
24. Suryanarayana, Kolluru, *Madhyandhra Yuga Charitraka Vyasamulu,* p. 139.
25. Suryanarayana, Kolluru, "Maritime History of the Ancient Kalinga Rulers", published in *Power to Punch*, Visakhapatnam, 2010, p. 3.
26. Rama Chandra Rao, C.V., *Administration and Society in Medieval Andhra (A.D. 1038 – A.D.1538) under the later Eastern Gangas and the Surya Vamsi Gajapatis*, p. 139.
27. *S.I.I.* Vol. VI, Nos. 694, 695, 696.
28. Subba Rao, R (Ed.,) *Kalinga Desa Charitra,* p. 48
29. *Proceedings of A.P.H.C.*, Vol. XII, 1988, p. 217.
30. Subrahmanyam, *B., Bavikonda, A Buddhist site in North Coastal Andhra Pradesh*, Hyderabad, 1994.
31. Suryanarayana, Kolluru, *Puratana Saiva Kshetram Panchadharla,* p. 3.
32. Suryanarayana, Kolluru, "Uttarandhralo Bouddha Kshetralu", paper presented at Lumbini Festival, Visakhapatnam, 1998.
33. *A.R.E.*, No.1 of 1941 – 1942, Part B, No.80.
34. *S.I.I.* Volume, VI, Simhachalam Inscriptions, No. 692 – 1215.
35. *Nrisimhapuranam* of Errapreggada and *Chatus* written by Srinadha etc.
36. Manchena, *KeyurabahuCharitra, Asvasa I*, Verse, 26.
37. Yasodadevi, V., "History of the Andhra Country: Subsidiary Dynasties (12th Century to 16th Century)", *J.A.H.R.S.* Vols; XVIII to XXVIII.
38. A number of Qutb-Shahi coins were discovered at places like Satyavaram, Golugonda and in some other places in the agency of present Visakhapatnam District. Some were kept under the custody of individual Coin – Collectors at Tuni and Rajahmundry; and some coins of silver and copper collected by Professor Kolluru Suryanarayana at Golugonda were kept in the Dept. Museum of History and Archaeology, Andhra University.
39. Amiya Kumar, Bagchi, *Private Investment in India*, 1900 – 1938, p. 214.
40. Dainel Thorner, *Land and Labour in India,* p. 109.
41. *Encyclopedia of the Madras Presidency*, pp. 58-59.

42. Vadivelu, A., *Aristocracy of Southern India*, Vol. II, p. 194
43. Dorappa, T., *Andhra Samasthanamulu – Sahitya Poshanamu*, pp. 135-321.
44. Arudra, *Samagra Andhra Sahityamu* – Vol. III, p. 334.
45. Varma, G.R., *Gudi – Gumpha*, p. 88.
46. Suryanarayana, Kolluru, History of the Minor Chalukya families in Medieval Andhra Desa, p. 140 (also see A.R.E.No.1312 of 1896).

Chapter - 2

History of Zamindars

Kakarlapudi Chiefs
(Early Zamindars of Anakapalli and Satyavaram)

One of the significant zamindari families that held their estates at different parts in South of Visakhapatnam with their centres at Anakapalli (on the banks of river Sarada), and Satyavaram (on the banks of river Tandava), is the Kakarlapudi family. It seems that it played a very important role in the politics of this province. The ancestor of that family is stated to have originally belongs to Kakarlapudi in the present Warangal district of Andhra Pradesh. The earliest known ruler of that family came to Chandanada, near by Nakkapalli and established a small kingdom and settled there.[1] Being disturbed by the local chieftains like Bahubalendras[2], the successors of Kasava Raju, like Devana Raju went to the court of Muhammad Quli Qutb Shah of Golconda, pleased him with their services and gradually settled in his court.

Appala Raju and Venkata Raju, the sons of Devana Raju played a key role in the Kalinga campaign of Muhammad Quli Qutb Shah and demolished the forts like Raparti and Kuntipuram, near Tuni. In return to those victorious military services rendered by them, Quli Qutb Shah honoured Kakarlapudi Appala Raju with the title 'Payak Rao'; and placed him as the incharge over the entire area situated in between the rivers Tandava and Sarada in A.D – 1611.[3]

'Payak' is the name of the military personal in the special contingent maintained by the Sultans.[4] As Appala Raju became the incharge of such special contingent under the Qutb Shahis, he was entitled as such; and his successors also borne the same title and hence popularly known as Payak Raos. First he made Sabbavaram as his headquarters, but in a short period he shifted it to the nearby place Anakapalli as it is 'pleasant in all seasons.'[5] To control the Southern provinces of his kingdom he made Satyavaram, which is situated on the banks of river Tandava as his provincial capital.

Another son of Devana Raju, Venkata Raju (Venkatapati Payak Rao) also came to Kalinga - Andhra, i.e., the present Northern Coastal Andhra Province, made Potnuru as his centre and obtained some villages from the Pusapati rulers of Vizianagaram.

His family held respectable position in the Court of the Pusapatis.[6] Venkatapati Raju's son Bapi Raju has nine sons and one daughter. That daughter was given in marriage to Tirumala Raju Gopa Raju of Alamanda, and the seven sons married the girls of the popular Kshatriya families of that period which closely support the Pusapatis of Vizianagaram. But due to some differences with Pusapati Vijaya Rama Gajapati, the family of Bapi Raju left the Vizianagaram estate and migrated to the Peddapuram estate of the Vatsavai family in the East Godavari District.[7] But later, realised the importance of the support of those Kakarlapudi rulers, Vijaya Rama Gajapati welcomed and requested the family of Kakarlapudi Bapi Raju to come and help in their battles with the Fouzdar of Chicacole, Badullakhan.[8]

Thus, the Kakarlapudi family entered into the areas of Visakhapatnam and established firmly in the politics of that area. Their political status gradually increased during the period of Ramabhadra Payak Rao. He occupied Satyavaram estate and acquired much political status and became the co-son-in-law of Pusapati Sita Rama Raju. During that period Anakapalli and Satyavaram became the strongholds of the Kakarlapudi family. Appala Raju, who was honoured with the title 'Payak Rao' by the Sultans of Golconda, ruled Anakapalli, and his brother Venkata Raju's family made Satyavaram as their centre of administration.[9] Thus, with Anakapalli and Satyavaram as centres, Kakarlapudi family held sway in the politics of this province during that period.[10]

The history of Anakapalli is closely knitted with the history of the Kakarlapudi family.

Though Anakapalli area had a continuous history from the Satavahana period, the name of Anakapalli is known from the Eastern Ganga period. In one of the inscriptions issued by Parvati Devi, the chief queen of Narasimha Deva IV dated in A.D. 1400 at Simhachalam, referred to Anakapalli.[11] It is surmised that it was constructed during the period of Aniyanka Bhima III, who ruled in the middle of thirteenth century. At the end of sixteenth century, another inscription at Simhachalam refers to Anakapalli, as an important centre in *Kalinga Dandapata*. When the Anakapalli area was under the control of Bahu-Balendra dynasty, the inroads of the Sultans of Golconda began. The army of Muhammad Quli Qutub Shah conquered Mukunda Deva II, drove him upto Bengal and annexed all those Kalinga areas into the Golconda kingdom, as attested to in the records at places like Srikurmam[12] and Simhachalam.[13] In all those battles Kakarlapudi Appala Raju and his brother Venkata Raju strongly supported and assisted the Golconda army, for which in turn they were designated as the rulers over Anakapalli areas.

As stated earlier, in the middle of seventeenth century that Kakarlapudi family supported the interests of Pusapati family in upkeeping the autonomy of this province, in the political turmoil that has taken place after the downfall of the Sultans of Golconda. Kakarlapudi Appala Payak Rao happens to be the co-son-in-law of Pusapati Ananda Raju I, and that relation between those two families united them in achieving their political goal. They declared war on the Fouzdar at Chicacole, acquired the military headquarters of Nizam that located at Kasimkota; and attacked the factory of British East India Company at Visakhapatnam.[14] Pusapati Vijaya Rama Gajapati, the son of Ananda Raju who founded the fort of Vizianagaram extended his authority from Rajahmundry to Berhampur only because of the willful support and co-operation of the Kakarlapudi rulers.

In a decisive battle that has taken place in A.D.1734 at Chebrolu in the East Godavari District, between the armies of Vijaya Rama Raju and his allies with the forces of Nooruddin, the Fouzdar of Rajahmundry, Kakarlapudi Gopala Payak Rao, played a very significant role.[15]

His 'Boya Fouz', without careing for their lives, cut the ropes of the seat (ambari) on the elephant on which the Fouzdar Nooruddin sat, dragged him from the elephant and killed.[16] Similarly in the battle of Vijaya Rama Gajapati with the joint armies of Jafur Ali, the Fouzdar of Chicacole, and the Marathas, that took place at Tummapala (which is adjacent to Anakapalli) in A.D. 1753, Gopala Payak Rao fought heroically and acquired the title 'Ranaranga Bhairava'. Thus, the courage and valour of Gopala Payak Rao is well attested to in the literature of the period.[17]

In the struggle for supremacy between the French and the English East India Companies, Salabat Zung, the Sultan of Hyderabad has given Sircars to Mr. Bussy. On that occasion for strengthening themselves, Pusapati Vijaya Rama Gajapati and Kakarlapudi Ramabhadra Payak Rao met Mr. Bussy at Rajahmundry.[18] As a faithful supporter to the French, Ramabhadra Payak Rao who succeeded to the estates of Anakapalli and Satyavaram assisted the French and Vijayarama Gajapati in the battle of Bobbili that has taken place in A.D. 1757.[19] Immediately after the battle, within days Vijaya Rama Gajapati was assassinated.

Pusapati Ananda Raju II, the son and successor of Vijaya Rama Gajapati understood that the French also had their hand in the muder of his father.[20] As a revengeful tact he decided to dislodge the French from the Sircars; and for that cause requested for the English help. Ramabhadra Payak Rao also, as per the decision of the Pusapati Chief changed the loyalties and turned towards the English. On September 2, A.D. 1758, he brought down the flag of the France on the towers of the French headquarters at Visakhapatnam, and raised the British flag in that place.[21] Later, as per the alliance between those local chiefs and the English, their united armies fought a number of battles with the French at places like Chandurti, Rajahmundry and Machilipatnam.[22] In all such battles Ramabhadra Payak Rao played a very significant role. He was succeeded by Appala Payak Rao III.

Pusapati Ananda Raju II suddenly died in A.D. 1760, and his adopted brother succeeded the throne of Vizianagaram. During his regnal period the entire administration is looked after by his step-brother Sitarama Raju, who acted as the diwan of Vizianagaram.[23]

Sitarama Raju colluded with the English armies to suppress all the local chiefs and bring all those provinces into the hands of the Pusupatis and thus to strengthen his authority over the Northern Sircars. With that selfish object he has not spared even the Kakarlapudi family which assisted the Vizianagaram interests throughout those years very efficiently and loyally. Pusapati Sitarama Raju, with the help of Captain Richard Mathews and the English army, attacked Anakapalli kingdom and killed Appala Payak Rao and his son Ramabhadra Payak Rao in A.D. 1776.[24] The rule of the Kakarlapudis at Anakapalli ended with that attack. All the provinces in the Anakapalli kingdom were declared as haveli lands by the English Company. In this context the company prepared to pay an annual amount of rupees ten thousand for the maintenance of Sitayamma and Rajayamma, the queens of Appala Payak Rao and Ramabhadra Payak Rao.[25]

Diwan Pusapati Sitarama Raju, who is very eager to occupy the Anakapalli province, was responsible for the attacks of the British on the Kakarlapudi family. With the decline of the Kakarlapudi power at Anakapalli, and when all those lands in that province were declared as haveli lands, Sitarama Raju taken them on lease for ten years and also agreed to pay the annual maintenance to the Kakarlapudi Queens, Sitayamma and Rajayamma.

But under his regime Anakapalli kingdom suffered a lot.[26] All his attempts for the proper utilisation of Sarada river waters for agriculture, and to bring the lands under submergence of Kondakarla Ava into cultivation ends in failure. He troubled the Kakarlapudi queens also by not paying the promised amount for their annual maintenance.[27] Owing to the various troubles under his rule, a number of people left Anakapalli and migrated to other areas. Realised the impact of all such steps taken under the rule of Pusapati Sitarama Raju in those provinces, the British company cancelled the agreement of lease with Sitarama Raju, and merged it in A.D. 1875, with the Vizianagaram kingdom which was under the direct control of Vijaya Rama Gajapati II.[28] By this annexation Vijaya Rama Gajapati had to pay an additional peshkash to the company besides the payment of rupees ten thousand for the maintenance of the Kakarlapudi queens Sitayamma and Rajayamma. Later, the Anakapalli estate was resold to the Gode Zamindars by the Pusapati chiefs in A.D. 1810.[29]

The later course of events and the changed relations between the English East India Company and the Pusapati family led them to the battle of Padmanabham in A.D. 1794, in which Vijayarama Raju was mercilessly killed.[30] The lands in the Anakapalli province were again declared as haveli lands and taken into the direct administration of the Company. But in the changing circumstances, the company also refused to pay the amount for the maintenance of Sitayamma and Rajayamma. Those two ladies, due to the lack of grants suffered with debts, and lived under Ireat poverty. Sitayamma died in A.D. 1804 and Rajayamma died in A.D. 1814. The adopted son of Rajayamma was not recognised as her heir apparent by the East India Company.[31]

Kakarlapudi Jagannadha Raju, also known as Sitarama Raju, one of the cousins of the adopted son, of Rajayamma, championed the cause of the adoptee, made a number of representations on that matter to the company which ends with failure. As all alternatives were closed to an end, in A.D. 1832, he started an armed struggle against the British company.[32] Towards the close of the year A.D. 1832, the disturbances reached to the climax and the government deployed a large force. George Russell, the first member of the Board of Revenue, was appointed as special Commissioner in December A.D. 1832, to ascertain the causes of insurrection, devise and carryout measures for their suppression and to recommend some measures.[33]

In January A.D. 1832, Jagannadha Raju, the champion of the Kakarlapudi adoptee abided with armed followers, assumed the title of 'Payak Rao', proceded to commit depredation and exacted contributions. The Collector in-charge Mr. Smith in his report attributed all those disturbances to the unconciliatory spirit and unpopularity of Gode Suryaprakasa Rao and his brother Narayana Rao, the then recognised zamindars of the estate[34] (who purchased it from the Pusapati's).

But Mr. Russell, the Special Commissioner who was appointed with extraordinary powers to settle that issue disagreed with the Acting Collector, Smith.[35] He specified that rebellion was not an insurrection of the people, arising from personal dislike or attachment to any estate holder, viz. Gode zamindar. He has stated that the inhabitants generally had no connection with the rebel faction, and though compelled to purchase safety for themselves and for their families by contributing to their demands, and deterred from giving information through fear of their resentment, were yet not interested in their success. Even then, by his extraordinary powers, he declared 'martial law' to suppress the rebellion of the Kakarlapudi family.[36] But Payak Rao and his troop still activated their armed struggle and continued it for more than two years. In this context, scholars like M.S.R. Anjaneyulu opined that the rebellious Jagannadha Raju had no influence and completely depended upon Naganna Dora,[37] the diwan of Golconda zamindari, which is in the agency of Visakhapatnam district. But Jagannadha Payak Rao is not that much weak. The *chatu* verses of the period clearly states the strength of that rebellion and how Visakhapatnam and Golconda areas shook with the sounds of the birangis (Figangis) used by the army of Payak Rao.[38] Acting Collector influenced Naganna Dora, the diwan who had much influence in the Golconda zamindari, and promised the authority over the entire area to him. Naganna Dora, by preventing open rebellion, could confirm the Acting Collector's belief in his fidelity while secretly thwarting him. Closely associated with the rebellious group of Jagannadha Payak Rao, he leaked the important information as well as war strategy, regularly to the British company.[39] It resulted in the capture and assassination of Kakarlapudi Venkatapati Raju, the close associate of Jagannadha Raju. Owing to this synical role played by Naganna Dora, Jagannadha Payak Rao correctly estimated the situation, changed the strategy, and retreated his forces to the forests adjacent to Telangana and sheltered there for sometime and again returned back to the Golugonda forest in A.D.1834.[40] Any how, with an intention to achieve his object, he continued his armed struggle. The betray of Naganna Dora costs his life, and in counter to it, the supporters of Payak Rao rushed into the house of Naganna Dora at one mid night, cut his head and affixed it to the very gibbet from which Venkatapati's body was hanged.[41] In protesting the enimical troops, as stated earlier, as a part of his strategy he fled to Rampa in the Godavari district, where again he was betrayed by the muttadar of Rampa. The army of the British Company captured him and hanged him at a place called Payaka Rao peta which on the banks of river Tandava.[42] His body, as per the fashion of those times, was suspended in an iron cage on a gibbet there, and left to moulder away. For decades together, his skull and few bones remained there;[43] but the masonry foundation was now left of the gibbet. Among the villagers the spot goes by the suggestive name of 'Payak Rao's slip-knot post'.[44] As correctly noticed by T.S.N. Murthy, probably in no instance in the armed struggles that took place in the then times the British Company exhibited that much of vengeance.[45] It itself indicates the significance of the armed revolt of Jagannadha Payak Rao that declared against the British to safeguard the interests of Kakarlapudi family on Anakapalli and Satyavaram zamindaries. In the light of the details reffered to in the traditional account of the Kakarlapudis, i.e., Kakarlapudi Vaṃsottaram, and in the other evidences the genealogy of this family is stated.

Later the successors of the Kakarlapudi family migrated to the estate of Kumili in the Bhogapuram area in the present Vizianagaram district and settled there under the subordination of the Pusapatis of Vizianagaram.[46]

Besides such significant revolts and political achievements, the Kakarlapudi Payak Raos contributed much to history by their construction activity and literacy patronage which will be discussed elsewhere.

Pusapati Chiefs of Vizianagaram

One of the most prominent zamindari that closely connected with the region under study was that of the Pusapaties of Vizianagaram.[46A] Unlike the other zamindars in the plains, they established themselves with their military prowess in that province. Due to their strength in those areas, almost all the ruling chiefs, Zamindars and the Europen Companies tried to maintain good relations with those chiefs. As stated already most of the information of this family, has already came to the light by the researches of a number of scholars.[46B] As the family history and contributions of this important zamindari family has already covered in the researches of different scholars, and because there is no additional information on the history of that family, in this study their relations with the other zamindars and with the Europen Companies only will be discussed.

The zamindari family of this premier estate boasted of themselves as they belonged to solar race and claimed its ancestry from Madhavavarma, a Rajput Chief who is stated to have led the Rajput tribes of Vasishtha, Dhanunjaya, Koundinyasa and Kasyapsa to the Southern region in 591 A.D. This might be one the reasons why the other zamindars had much respect for the chiefs of Vizianagaram and considered them as their overloards.[46C]

In their family histories, they claimed that they had their orgin at a village 'pusapadi' in the Krishna district, and hence it became their surname. In the Visakhapatnam province, prior to the estabnlishment of their capital at Vizianagaram, they made Kumili and later Potnuru as their headquarters.[46D]

As known earlier, during the rule of the Qutb-Shahis of Golkonda, Sher Mohammad-Khan was appointed as Foujdar of Chicacole in A.D.1652. Pusapati Madhava Varma, one of his trusted lieutenants, who followed him to Chicocole, had later settled down at Vizianagaram. Since then, the family had won many titles and was granted inams by the Qutb-Shahi rulers by the recommendations of the Foujdar of Chicocole. Later, they hold a predominant position in the Sircars, and at the time of the transfer of Northern Sircars to the English, they occupied the whole of the Sircars by subduing the other powerful zamindars.[46E]

The number of literary works like *Kshatriya Gotra sisa Malika, Rachiraju sisa Malika, Markaendeya purvothara khandam, Vishnu Bhakti Sudhakaram, Uskabhayudayam, Kurmapuranam, Narasa Bhupala Rajiyam* etc., elaborately referred to the ancestry and early history of the Pusapaties.[46F] As stated already, in all such works they claimed that they have migrated from North India to South India and gradually came and settled in this province.

In some of the traditional accounts they tried to connect themselves with Madhavavarma of Vishnukundin family, which ruled Andhradesa in the fifth-sixth centuries. But no connected history of this family from the earlist centuries is available. One Pusapti Rachiraju who was claimed as one of their ancestors served in the military service of Proudha Devaraya of Hampi Vijanagara.

Pusapati Rachi Raju seems to be a prominent personality of this family. He is credited with a number of honours and titles like "Chalukya Virarajya-Sthapanacharya" and "Nanne Sultan". His son

Tammmiraju conquered the Gajapatis. It is stated that the Mughal emperor Aurangazeb, presented ne Julfikar (two edged knife) of Ananda Gajapati -I. Peda Vijayaramaraju, the son of Ananda Raju I was the contemporary of Mr. Busy, during whose period the Battle of Bobbili has taken place. The keen role that played by this Pusapati family during the period under study, their relations with other zamindars as well as with the East India Companies will be discussed elsewhere.

The Battle of Padmanabham which has taken place in July 1794 put an end to the prestige and honour of this princely family. Narayana Gajapati, a boy of 8 years, the son and successor of Vijayarama Raju ran into the agencies and protected by the Mukhi Chiefs of Kasipuram. Later he came into an agreement with the English Company in 1825, for the annual payment of rupees five lakhs as the peshkash to the zamindari. But, being vexed with troubles created by the company, he left the zamindari to the company and settled at Benaras, and died there in 1845.

Thus, the important princely family which extended its authority over the entire Kalinga-Andhra, in course of time degraded to the postion of other zamindars of this province. After 1852, the administration of their zamindari went into the supervision of the English Company.

Vijayarama Gajapati (1826-1879), the son of Narayana Gajapati was honoured by the company, with a number of titles like 'Maharaja', K.C.S.I, 'His Highness', and also an honourary speculation of thirteen Figangi rounds. For more than thrice he served as the member of Imperial Legislative Council. His son Ananda Gajapati was also honoured with the titles like 'Maharaja', K.C.I.E, and 'Prince Charming', and for more than twice he served as the member of Inperial Legislative Council.

Due to the disputes on succession to the zamindari between A.D 1879 to 1904, the estate has gone to the Cout-of-Wards.

One of the members of this family, Vijayananda Gajapati, who became popular as 'Sir Vijaya' played a significant role in the stuggle for the formation of the Andhra State. He presided over the 'Andhra Mahasabha' held at Visakhapatnam in November, 1941.[46-G]

The other contributions of the family such as literary patronage will be discussed in the relevant chapters.

Bhupati family of Madugula

Madugula, which is situated in the hill tracts in between Andhra and Orissa, in the present Visakhapatnam district, is the headquarters of important and significant zamindars, who maintained close relations with the zamindars of Orissa. Like a number of other prestigious ruling families they climbed their ancestry from the rulers of Matsya Desa of the epic period. It is stated that, earlier they were installed at Paderu, which is their earlier seat in the agency.[47] They used to sit on a stone throne shaped like a fish, display a fish on their banners, use a figure of fish as their signature and zealously protect from harm the mahseer in the Matsya Gundam (fish pond), which is nearby Paderu in the agency of Visakhapatnam district. That pond and also the fish therein are considered sacred by the residents of the Madugula zamindari.[48] Some records from places like Dibbida, Muddurti and Simhachalam; and from the earlier traditions of the Matsya rulers, who ruled that country for centuries together, claimed that they awarded rulership over this country by the rulers of Orissa.[49] Other accounts say that they came to the Madugula province along with the founder of the Jeypore family, whose cousins they were, who gave them the Madugula country as a fief, along with the title of *Bhupati* (lord of the earth).[50] The *Matsya Gundam* is the place of origin of the river Muchikunda, the modern Machkand.[51]

The hill tribes in that vicinity narrate a traditional story connecting the rulers of Jeypore in Orissa with those hilly tracts in between Madugula and Golugonda. One of the ancestors of Jeypore kingdom, it is stated, had two of his cousins for umbrella bearers and was pleased to promote them to the dignity of feudal chiefs, placing one at Golugonda and the other at Madugula and honouring both with the title of *Bhupati* (lord of earth).[52] Later this Bhupati families, expanded to the other hill-estates like Gudem. Just few kilometers away from Madugula in the Visakhapatnam district, there is a village by name Oddadi, which means the beginning of the *Oddhra* Country (Oddhra+adi).[53]

The earliest known member of the family was Sri Cholabhupati Deva who is stated to have reigned from A.D. 721-771.[54] From A.D. 771-1770, twenty-one generations of rulers ruled, that Madugula Province, which is known in those days as Matsyadesa. Medieval history sources like Pitta-gedda inscriptions,[55] Dibbida copper plate inscription,[56] and a number of inscriptions at places like Maddurti,[57] Simhachalam,[58] Chodavaram[59] and Juttada,[60] focus light on the early rulers of the Matsya dynasty. Famous rulers of this family like Arjuna Deva and Prataparjuna ruled all these provinces. Though ruled as subordinates under different political powers like the Vengi Chalukyas, the Chalukya Cholas, the Eastern Gangas, the Kakatiyas, the Reddis and the Suryavamsa Gajapatis of Orissa, practically for all purposes they were independent.[61] Their military achievements and cultural contributions are well-documented in the records at places like Simhachalam.[62] But their linkage with the later zamindari family is not clearly known. Name of the inscriptions either at Simhachalam or ther places give scope to connect those later date zamindari families like the Bhupatis of Madugula, with the medieval mandalika chiefs like matsyas. Because this zamindari family claims the antiquity of more than thousand years, and as they themselves claim as they also belonged to *Matsya Vamsa*,_there is a scope to suspect their distant connections with the early rulers of Matsya dynasty.[63]

Sri Chola Bhupati is the earliest known ruler of this family.[64] His succession upto eighteenth Century A.D. is not known. But as noticed earlier, a number of rulers claimed Matsya descent in this part of the country as known from a number of inscriptions of the medieval centuries. The Kaifiat of Madugula records that Linga Bhupati, Visva Bhupati, Samba Bhupati etc., were the later date successors in this family.[65] Samba Bhupati had two sons, viz., Linga Bhupati Dev and Krishna Bhupati Dev.

Linga Bhupati Dev II had a son by name Appala Bhupati; and Krishna Bhupati Dev I had a son by name Jagannadha Bhupati Dev. It is a tradition among the zamindars that had their affiliation with the Orissa to bear the name Jagannadha and to construct the temples of Jagannadha Swami in their respective areas of jurisdiction. The temple of Jagannadha at Madugula was probably the construction of this Jagannadha Dev.[66] By his wife Ramayamma he begot three sons, viz.,

Linga Bhupati III (1817-1831), Harihara Bhupati (1832-53) and Krishna Bhupati Dev II (1853-1875). Besides these three, the literary evidences traced one Gopala Bhupati Dev, as another son of Jagannadha Bhupati Dev.[67]

Linga Bhupati III (1817-1831) had a daughter by name Jogimani Devi, by his wife Ramayamma. That Jogimani Devi was given in marriage to one Jeypore prince Mukunda Dev by whom she begot a son by name Krishna Dev, who later became the estatedar of Kalyana Sing upuram near Jeypore. As he has no sons, he adopted Mukunda Dev (1905) who married Chandramani Maha Devi.[68]

No details of Harihara Bhupati (1832-53), the second son of Jagannadha Dev are known. How long he continued in reign is not clearly known; but is surmised that he ruled for nineteen years. He was succeeded by his brother Krishna Bhupati Dev II, who ruled in between 1853-75. He had two wives Sitapatta Maha Devi and Nila Mani Patta Maha Devi. Sitapatta Maha Devi had no sons, and hence adopted one son Vikrama Dev who belongs to the family of Jeypore. Nila Mani Patta Maha Devi had a daughter by name Ammi Maha Devi who married Visvambhara Dev, the younger brother of Rama Chandra Dev of Jeypore. Her only daughter Rajendra Mani Devi is the last known succession to the Madugula zamindari.[69]

Though not known through other evidences, the Telugu literary works like *Jagannadha Bhupatiyam* that was written by one Jagannadha Bhupati of this family gives scope to suspect one Gopala Bhupati Dev, as the son of the above stated Jagannadha Bhupati I.[70] That Gopala Bhupati Dev's son Jagannadha Bhupati II is a great scholar both in Sanskrit and Telugu. He has written a work on the science of horses by name *Jagannadha Bhupatiyam* and another book on physical exercises of body by name *Vyayama Sastramu.* His daughter, Prabhavati Devi is also known as a famous poetess. But the details of Gopala Bhupati, Jagannadha Bhupati and Prabhavati Devi were not known otherwise.

Though the climate in the province of Madugula is not that much good, the soil in the plain areas is very fertile. Being irrigated by rivers like Sarpa and Varaha, and rivulets like Bodderu, Palagedda, Tabberu, etc., the agricultural production is upto the mark.[71] A number of varieties of forest products enhance the richness of the zamandari. The revenue of the estate of Madugula by the time of Zamindari Report is above 2.25 lakhs and the peshkash at the time of Permanent Settlement is rupees 80,000.[72]

The zamindari of Madugula is situated to the South of Srungavarapukota. Vizianagaram Estate formed its North boundary, Vaddadi bounded its East, the Kottakota Estate and Golugonda zamindari on the South and the wild tracts of the Jeypore zamindari runs behind it to the West.

On A.D. 1770, Sri Linga Bhupati II succeeded to the Matsya zamindari at Madugula. It is said that he joined hands along with other hill - zamindars against the Vizianagaram zamindari, which was assisted by the English East India Company.[73] He joined in alliance with the rebellious estatedars against the East India Company and the Pusapatis of Vizianagaram. For that support to rebellious hill - zamindars, Linga Bhupati became the target of the Pusapati Sitarama Raju, the diwan of Vizianagaram. Before the strategy and war-craft adopted by Sitarama Raju and his allies, all the efforts of Linga Bhupati and his supporters like Kakarlapudi Payak Rao of Anakapalli, the estatedars of Golugonda, Vaddadi, Uratla, Kottakota, etc., became a failure.[74] Sagi Narayana Raju, the military general of the Vizianagaram estate came over the revolting hill - zamindars along with the Company troops. As that revolt was severely suppressed, in a helpless stage, Linga Bhupati II ran away into Orissa and took shelter with the zamindars of Jeypore. It seems that he spent his life as a refugee at Jeypore.[75] His family also settled down there till the death of Sitarama Raju of the Pusapati family.

Sitarama Raju is stated to have made the oblong brick fort with five bastions at Madugula within which the later zamindars resided. The Circuit Committee, stated in 1784, that it had been constructed of their European model and was garrisoned with a battalion about thousand strong dressed and armed in the European manner.[76]

The conflict of the Pusapatis of Vizianagaram with the hill - zamindars like Madugula and Golugonda is referred to in some of the Mackenzie Records also. Oddadi Kaifiat states how Madugula Linga Bhupati mortgaged some of the villages like Govada near Chodavaram to the Pusapati Zamindars; which were later occupied and developed by creating irrigation facilities by the Pusapatis.[77] To execute their command, Pusapati Sitarama Raju has constructed a fort at Chodavaram. Linga Bhupati's brother continued the depredations and rejected the offer of an allowance of rupees 6,000 was expelled, and died soon after.[78]

After the extinction of the Pusapati family at Madugula, the Government of Madras recalled the Bhupati family and granted a sanad for the enjoyment of the zamindari to Jagannadha Bhupati Dev I, the son of Krishna Bhupati Dev I. The claim of Sri Jagannadha Bhupati Dev I was contested by one Appala Bhupati, his illegitimate cousin, who troubled him for fifteen years by remaining in hill tracts.[79]

In A.D. 1787, this family persuaded by Jogi Raju an elder relation to the family, occupied Madugula zamindari and created disturbances to the Company. Amidst these transactions, the Company came to an agreement with them by which the hill and the four Lovas and some adjacent districts valued at ten or twelve thousand rupees, were promised to rent to them, it having been further stipulated that the countries formerly possessed by the family should be fully restored to them.[80]

This is a very troublesome period in the history of Madugula zamindari. Strengthening himself in the agency areas, Appala Bhupati was troubling Jagannadha Bhupati Dev I to share authority. As he was not a legal heir, his claim was not considered by the company till his death. After that trouble, the then Collector of Visakhapatnam Mr. Alexander made Permanent Settlement in A.D. 1802-03 with Jagannadha Bhupati Dev I who came from exile.[81] It is known by then that there were 103 villages in the Madugula zamindari out of which 77 were jeroity and 26 agraharas. Owing to lack of regular rains and other difficulties, the revenue resources of the zamindari were deteriorated which put Jagannadha Bhupati I into financial troubles. He was obliged to incur heavy debts to discharge the public demands.[82]

In A.D. 1813, the estate was sold for arrears and bought for five thousand rupees by Chintalapati Raju who transferred it in A.D. 1814 to Chinchilada Venkata Raju and in A.D. 1817 it was again handed over to Linga Bhupati III, the eldest son of Jagannadha Bhupati I.[83]

As already stated Jagannadha Bhupati I had three sons, Linga Bhupati III Harihara Bhupati and Krishna Bhupati II, by his wife

Ramayamma. Jagannadha Bhupati I ruled for 14 years and was succeeded by his elder son Linga Bhupati III who ruled for 12 years. Linga Bhupati III had only one daughter Jogimani Devi who was given in marriage to Mukunda Dev of Kalyana Singupuram in the Jeypore zamindari of Orissa. The Bhupatis of Madugula had their matrimonial relations with the Jeypore family even earlier.[84]

Linga Bhupati III was succeeded by his brothers – Harihara Bhupati and Krishna Bhupati II successively.

Krishna Bhupati II succeeded to some of the provinces in the Madugula zamindari in A.D. 1833 and ruled for 43 years, i.e., upto, 1875. He had two wives – Sitapatta Maha Devi and Nilamani Patta Maha Devi.[85] In 1833 the Madugula zamindari was sold for arrears and was bought by the government for rupees one thousand. But few years later it was handed over back to Krishna Bhupati on his tendering the amount outstanding.[86]

A Sub-division in the Madugula zaminadari by name Chidikada was sold in 1821; and in A.D. 1833 Krishna Bhupati alienated it and sold it to one Mandapaka Jagannayukulu.[87] In A.D. 1835, The Raja of Bobbili taken it and later gave it to his brother –in-law, Inuganti Rajagopala Rao. After the death of Rajagopala Rao that division was retransferred to the Raja of Bobbili in 1856; and in A.D. 1862 Chidikada was given to one Sitarama Swamy, the son of another sister of the Raja of Bobbili. The later Raja of Bobbili went to the Court with a claim over Chidikada sub-division of the Madugula zamindar but was unsuccessful.[88]

In A.D. 1870, Krishna Bhupati II mortgaged the whole zamindari to the Maharaja of Jeypore for 16 years in consideration of a loan of Rupees five Lakhs.[89] In 1875, after the death of Krishna Bhupati II as per a 'will' which is stated to have been executed by him, his first wife Sitapatta Maha Devi adopted Vikram Dev, son of Krishna Chandra Dev the Maha Raja of Jeypore as son and heir apparent to the Madugula estate.[90] In A.D 1876 as Vikram Dev was minor, the Court of Wards interfered and looked after the affairs of the estate till 1889.[91]

Neelamani Patta Maha Devi, the second wife of Krishna Bhupati II had a daughter by name Ammi Maha Devi who was given in marriage to Visvambhara Dev Maha Raja, the younger brother of Ramachandra Dev Maharaja of Jeypore.[92]

The adoption of Vikram Dev by Sita Patta Maha Devi was challenged by Neelamani Patta Maha Devi. But it was set aside by the Privy Council. Neelamani Patta Maha Devi died in 1895. The management of the zamindari was handed over by the Court-of-Wards to Sita Patta Maha Devi, who ruled the zamindari of Madugula till May 24, 1901, the date of her death.[93]

The litigations, mortgaging and changing of management, naturally show the worst possible effect on the administration of the Madugula estate, which became a byword for inefficiency. The hold over the hill muttadars maintained by Sita Patta Maha Devi who died in 1901 was not that much effective; and they quarrelled among one another bullied their tenants and defied their suzerain until the district officers were forced to interfere and remove some, and punish others.[94] Matters have improved but little since, and it has been necessary to warn the holders of the estate that they will be held responsible for any trouble that may arise in the hills owing to their unsuitable methods of managing that country.

As there is no other heir - apparent, the daughter of Linga Bhupati III, Jogi Mani Devi who was given in marriage to Mukunda Dev of the estate of Kalyanas singupuram in Jeypore zamindari, succeeded to the estate. As her only son Krishna Dev passed away, his widow Neela Devi adopted one Mukunda Dev, which act was objectionable to the Maharaja of Jeypore. The Maharaja of Jeypore was unwilling to allow an outsider in the name of adoption to succeed the Kalyana Singupuram estate, a portion of the Jeypore zamindari.[95] But as a great grandson of Linga Bhupati III Mukunda Dev became a claimant to Madugula.

Mean while, in A.D. 1882 the transaction of mortgage running between the zamindar of Madugula and the Maharaja of Jeypore had been balanced by a Committee appointed by the Collector, and showed that the former owed the later some five lakh seven thousand rupees.[96] In A.D. 1890, it is agreed that the Maharaja should accept three lakh fifty – three thousand rupees in settlement of all his claims and that the repayments of this sum with interest at – 4 ½ per cent, should be secured by the mortgage with possession to the Maharaja of 68 villages of the estate.[97] This mortgage continued and the estate is divided into two parts, of which one under the administration of the Maharaja of Jeypore and the other, which includes the hill villages, by the Madugula family.[98]

The Government of Madras involved in the affairs of Madugula and recognised Mukunda Dev as well as Sri Rajendra Mani Devi, the grand-daughter of Krishna Bhupati Dev II, as the Joint heirs.[99]

Hence the Madugula zamindari was divided between them. But on February 25, 1905, Mukunda Dev died without issue and hence his queen Chandramani Maha Devi became the zamindarini to his share in the Madugula zamindari.[100] The remaining share in the Estate came under the authority of Rajendra Mani Devi.

Rajendra Mani Devi seems to be a very significant personality in the later zamindars of that estate. She has done all possible efforts to raise the prestige of Madugula among the other zamindaris of the period.[101] In protecting the rights of her subjects, in establishing and maintaining the endowment and charitable institutions, she has taken utmost care. She was highly religious and kind towards ryots. Her sympathy for the poor, her large heartedness and her nobility of conduct were described in eulogistic terms among the people in the province.[102]

As discussed earlier in the genealogy, some more zamindars of this family were referred to in the literature that was produced by the family members of the Madugula zamindari. Jagannadha Bhupati Dev I seemed to have one more son by name Gopala Bhupati Dev, who again was blessed by a son named Jagannadha Bhupati II who is glorified as a great scholar both in Sanskrit and Telugu. *Jagannadha Bhupatiyam*, a work on horses and *Vyayama Sasthramu*, a work on physical exercises were composed by him.[103] His daughter Prabhavathi Devi is also known as a famous poetess. She is stated to be the disciple of Puranam Suryanarayana Tirtha, a great scholar who was honoured with titles like *Kavya Smrithi Thirtha.*[104] Except literary appreciation no details of those members are referred to anywhere.

In A.D. 1931, Madugula zamindari merged in the Jeypore estate; and with the formation of the separate Orissa State, again became a part and parcel of Andhra Pradesh.

The zamindari of Madugula, though a small hill zamindari comprised of 77 Jeroity villages and 26 agraharas, situated in the hilly-boarders of Andhra and Orissa,[105] played a significant role in the contemporary politics. Its zamindars had their close relations with the other zamindars and estatedars of contemporary period like the zamindars of Jeypore, Anakapalli, Uratla, Kotthakota, Oddadi, Golugonda, etc. They had their hostile relations with the powerful Pusapati zamindars of Vizianagaram which supported the issues of the Company at that period.

Madugula zamindari falily is very popular for its religious endowments and literary patronage. It is strange to notice that out of the one hundred and three villages under their position, 26 villages are *agraharas*. Their endowments to scholarly Brahmins were described in eulogistic terms in literary works like *Pusapati Rajula Purvotramu.*[106] Vaishnava temples particularly those of Jagannatha were constructed by those zamindars at places like Madugula and Medicherla.

Some of the zamindars are scholars and patterns of letters and their literary patronage will be discussed else where.

Thus the zamindari of Madugula, though situated in the present Visakhapatnam District of Andhra Pradesh, from centuries back closely knitted with the affairs of Jeypore Estate.[107] That zamindari, though had its intimate relations with the zamindars of Jeypore and of the Kakarlapudi family of Anakapalli and Satyavaram, it had hostile relations with the zamindars of Bobbili, with the Pusapati zamindars of Vizianagaram and also with the British Company respectively, in different periods of their rule. Inspite of various unstable conditions and political fluctuations, this family tried hard to restore their authority over the hilly regions and on the adjacent plains of Madugula-Oddadi areas in the Visakhapatnam province. The alliances and struggles that they come across in their regime will be discussed later.

Bhupati Family of Golugonda

Another important seat of Chieftains in the hilly tracts in between the forest region bordering Andhra and Orissa, situated 15 Kilometres to Narsipatnam in the present Visakhapatnam District, is Golugonda. The name is supposed to be a corruption of Gollakonda, 'the hill of the Gollas', a race of shepherd-kings of whom misty traditions survive in that area.[108]

Golugonda, was an inaccessible 'country' and of "so pernicious a climate, that natives not particularly inured to it as well as Europeans have been even suffered very severely when duty has obliged them to reside there."[109]

It was bounded by the Jeypore and Rampa 'countires' to the West, the Madugula zamindari to the North, the Kotthakota and Vemulapudi 'districts' to the East and the 'peddapore' (Peddapuram) zamindari to the South. It consists of the low country and the hills. Unlike many hills - zamindaris, it had no plain in the East; and hence, 'its cultivation was scanty and circumscribed its climate unhealthy and its inhabitants poor and greatly in want of civilisation, circumstances that must of course ever tender its resources precarious.[110] Such geographical features influenced its history.

As in the case of the Madugula family, the chiefs of Golugonda also connected themselves with Jeypore estate. It is stated that an earlier Raja of Jeypore had two of his cousins for umbrella-barriers and was pleased to promote them to the dignity of the chiefs placing one Nilakanta at Golugonda and honouring him with the title of 'Bhupati', i.e., 'Lord of the earth.[111]

Nilakanta Bhupati obtained this country in the Visakhapatnam province from the Jeypore family.[112] Later, they became tributaries to the Pusapati Rajas of Vizianagaram. When the English were established at Visakhapatnam they required the Pusapati Rajas to resign this supremacy. In A.D. 1776, however, Bhairava Bhupati, the chief of Golugonda sheltered the chiefs of Parlakimidi and Madugula, the refractory subjects of the Company; and he was again subordindated to the Pusupatis.[113]

When John Andrews became the Chief of Visakhapatnam (July, 1769 – August, 1772), Vira Bhupati was the zamindar of Golugonda for an annual payment of rupees 5,000. As he became a defaulter and began to ravage the country, the Company shirked coercion because of the nature of that region; and also in consideration of their relations with the Pusapati family, expelled him from the zamindari of Golugonda.

But soon he submitted and was restored with a settlement of Rs 19,000.[114]

He became a defaulter again in A.D. 1776, and his country was again placed under the control of the Pusapatis. Vira Bhupati occupied the zamindari of Golugonda without acquainting either the English Company or Vijayarama Raju of Vizianagaram.[115] In 1779, the Chief and Council, on the request of Sitarama Raju despatched two companies and a 'field piece' and it again came under Vizianagaram.[116] The Golugonda zamindars continued their disturbances even after then, and the Vizianagaram chiefs, could not control it and extract the payment fully. To establish peace in that hilly region of the Visakhapatnam District, the Company restored the Golugonda zamindari to Bhairava Bhupati.[117]

In 1784, the Circuit Committee proposed to continue him as a feudatory to Vizianagaram zamindari many of whose troops alone were competent to deal with his recalcitrance.[118]

Bhairava Bhupati was assassinated by Mallabhupati in A.D. 1785,[119] and disturbances recurred persistently.[120] To restore peace Malla Bhupati and his group were imprisoned and Chinna Bhupati was made the zamindar. But Chinna Bhupati was irregular in his payments and as a result Pusapati Sitarama Raju deputed troops under Sagi Rama Chandra Raju to collect the money.[121] Ramachandra Raju treacherously circumvented Chinna Bhupati and his team and killed them. In the retort to that the allies and relatives and Chinna Bhupati attacked and killed Ramachandra Raju and his forces. Under such circumstances, to establish peace, Malla Bhupati was released from the prison and restored at Golugonda.[122] Thus, roughly for more than two decades Golugonda zamindari became a tough problem to Pusapati zamindari as well as the English Company. To keep Golugonda areas under their control became a bigger task to Vizianagaram and often it had to apply for military assistances of the Company which was always forthcoming.

Amidst such circumstances that troubled Vizianagaram zamindari, its Southern division continued "if not in a state of perfect and uniform tranquility at least not altogether improvident in regard to the state of its cultivation."[123] Even though Malla Bhupati did not revolt, his payments were not upto the mark, and his conduct was also not 'satisfactory'. In 1795, despite the indifferene of his conduct and total insufficiency, as he was in a state of quiet; Mr. Webb allowed him to continue.[124] Finding his receipts from the country extremely limited, he in 1796 at the time of the settlement with the hill zamindars, fixed the peshkash at Rs 11,000.[125] In that year a partial disturbance occurred as one Ramanapatrudu wanted to replace him with Krishna Bhupati of fourteen years. But the plot was discovered in time by the Collector and the Zamindar, and the conspirators were dispersed and that Ramana Patrudu was imprisoned.[126] At the time of the Permanent Settlement, the peshkash was fixed at Rs 10,000 in perpetuity. Even after 1804, Malla Bhupati defaulted.[127]

As the local circustnaces did not so easily admit of carrying into effect the Acts of the Regulation and as the country was impervious to troops the Collector could not extract the peshkash.[128]

Krishna Bhupati succeeded as the Golugonda zamindar, after the death of Malla Bhupati, in A.D. 1805. But even under him, there was no improvement in the payment of peshkash, and the zamindari did not yield the average net collection on which the Permanent Settlement was fixed.[129] He also suffered as the zamindari was decreed to Anantha Bhupati a man of 15 years. Krishna Bhupati applied to the provincial court and in 1811 Anantha Bhupati was declared as the heir of Golugonda, by provincial court. In A.D. 1812, the District Collector restored the zamindari to Anantha Bhupati.[130] As he was not strong enough, the estate management was completely looked after by his diwan Punnapotula Naganna Dora. Naganna Dora, who was very influential, restrained the zamidar with a monthly allowance, also did not allow him to interfere in the administration; and also not permitted the hill sirdars and muttadars to communicate with him.[131] Still the zamindari was in arrears, and the Collector had no option except to favour Naganna Dora without whose acquiescence no Amin can collect even one rupee. It is also due to the "difficulty of access to these mountain regions, the unhealthiness of the climate and the inviterated devotion of the inhabitants to the will of their feudal chiefs."[132] In 1833, Naganna Dora was killed by some "unknown assassins.'[133] Internal feuds, domination of hill sirdars and physical features figured prominently in the history of Golugonda and scenes of confusion and bloodshed prevailed throughout this zamindari for more than thirty years.

After the death of Naganna Dora, Jamma Devamma the grandmother of Anantha Bhupati, occupied and began to manage the zamindari. As the zamindari was in arrears and advertised for sale, she came to Visakhapatnam to prevent it by all means. As the weakness and imbecility of the zamindar were notorious, she could not procure loans in his name, but she was told that money could be procured if the zamindari was transferred to her. She applied for transfer and on consent of the zamindar it was transferred. During her absence, his mind was poisoned and her life was threatened.[134]

The District administration persuaded Anantha Bhupati to resign in favour of Jamma Devamma. But the hill sirdars or muttadars objected that they had not been consulted on this issue. It is not acceptable to those tribal leaders as no women had ever ruled them before.[135] When that dispute was going on that unfortunate lady Jamma Devamma was murdered. Being provoked by this act, Mr. Freese, the Collector moved up troops and confiscated the Golugonda estate.[136] Anantha Bhupati was convicted of complicity in murder, and was confined in the fort at Gutty in the Anantapur District, where he died.[137] This zamindari was sold in auction for arrears and bought in by the government in A.D. 1837, for Rs 100. The hill sirdars and muttadars, the strong supporters of the Bhupati family were not at all disturbed and *pattas* were also given for their muttas by the government.

But those tribal sirdars, who are interested in enjoying freedom by nature, found that their status was seriously affected by their being subordinated to an ordinary Amin. This developed a type of discontentment and finally all those tribal leaders united and decided to restore the authority of the Bhupati family over the Golugonda estate.[138] They have implemented their plan of auction, held their rents, barricaded the hills, and made consistent excursions with fire and sword against the villages in the plain areas. They anointed one Chinna Bhupati, a boy of nineteen years as their 'Raja', and for roughly three years, i.e., from A.D. 1845 to 1848 they successfully held their jungle against the government troops.[139] But later, China Bhupati gave up himself and was granted villages worth of Rs 4,000 annually as maintenance.

It is co-incidental that- in A.D.1857-58, i.e., during the time of the Sepoy Mutiny, another insurrection with a similar object broke out in those forests under the leadership of Chinna Bhupati's nephew, Sanyasi Bhupati. But Captain Owen, with the support of some other hill sirdars suppressed that revolt. Sanyasi Bhupati and his followers were tried[140]; but later the government kept them as State detenues under surveillance and allowed them to enjoy their share in the maintenance of villages. Probably, as a consequence of this revolt in the Golugonda region in A.D.1864-65, police stations were established in the hilly regions and for some time the province was quiet. But in A.D. 1879-80, the Rampa rebellion brokeout in the neighbouring Godavari agency created some unrest in these areas also.[141] Captain Blaxland who came with Company police and Jeypore Raja's, sepoys, tried to restore law and order in that area. They were attacked by a group of insurgeant and were driven back on June 3, 1879. Tagi Virayya Dora, the muttadar of Gudem Pathaveedi continued the revolt for some more years by attacking the sepoys.[142] His message to his pursuars was that he would never surrender unless his Raja Chinna Bhupati asked him to do so. But on October 7 in the same year Virayya Dora was shot-dead. With this disturbance and frequent revolts, the government draws its attention on the affairs of the Golugonda area. Some of the muttas like Dutsarti and Guditeru of Golugonda Zamindari were transferred to Godavari region in 1881.[143]

The remaining muttadars in the Golugonda Zamindari were given sanads stating that their muttas on service tenure, subject to the payment of an annual payment (Kattubadi) and had to the conditions that the muttadar has to capture and handover to the authorities, offenders who were in the mutta or came into it, and to give immediate information of 'fituris' or other offences.[144] Those muttas were declared inalienable by sale, gift, or otherwise. It is specified that as long as those conditions were fulfilled the muttadar and such of his heirs as government might appoint, was to enjoy the mutta under the protection of the government. The non-fulfilment of such conditions was penalised with the forfeiture of the mutta.[145]

Few years later, it is around A.D.1886, inspired by the preachings of some Konda Dora priests who toured round the hills in that area propagating that the hill-gods had directed a fituri, a group of about

30 men, burnt and looted the police stations and rest houses at places like Gudem, Chintapalli and Lambrasingi Pataveedhi.[146]

Another 'fituri' has taken place at Golugonda in 1891. Discontended with the allowance granted to him by the government, Santa Bhupati, son of Chinna Bhupati rebelled against the British. Assisted by a team of 200 men he has looted the house of a constable, who shot Taggi Virayya Dora some years before. Then they rushed to Krishnadevi--Peta police station and killed five constables caring of all the arms and ammunition and setting fire to it.[147] But with in a short period those fituridars dispersed due to the sudden death of their leader Santa Bhupati. Some of his followers were arrested and Santa Bhupati's family was granted a compassionate allowance by the government. As none of the muttadars gave any prior information or any other assistance to the government either before or during this 'fituri', serious action was taken by the government on a number of muttadars as they violated the orders in the sanad the details of which were mentioned earlier.[148] The muttadars of Lambasingi, Kottaveedhi and Lotugadda were deposed. The muttadar of Gudem Kottaveedhi was arrested and the muttas of Koyyur and Chithampadu, Bandavalasa was resumed by the government. In some cases the heirs of the old muttadars were appointed in their places.[149]

With the resumption of Koyyur, Chittampadu and Bandavalasa, only ten muttas left with Golugonda estate. Gradually the government resumed Lambasingi Pataveedhi and Lotugadda in 1886 and Antadamutta, in 1895. A few years later, the original estatedars of Golugonda, i.e., the Bhupati family was granted a compensate allowance;[150] a number of muttas of that estate was resumed and the remaining five muttas, Lambasingi Kotta Veedhi, Makaram, Gudem Pataveedhi., Gudem Kotta Veedhi and Darlakonda were allowed to continue under muttadars.[151] Lands of the resumed muttas were managed under the Ryotwari system by village establishment under revenue officers.[152]

The areas under the control of the Bhupatis, both plain and hilly regions consist of a number of religious shrines. Temples at places like Balighattam and Lotugadda belong to Saivite where as the Goddess Sambari at Gudem is of tribal affiliation. At Balighattam, a small village 3 km. south-west of the present Narsipatnam on the banks of river

Varaha at the foot of small hill, there is a Brahmalingesvara Temple.[153]

There is another important Saivite shrine at a place called Lotugadda which is roughly 40 km to the north-west of Narsipatnam in the Golugonda hills. It contains the ruins of three or four old granite temples dedicated to Siva.[154]

In the same Golugonda hills, 17 km. north-west of Narsipatnam at Gudem, one of the chief places of the Golugonda Bhupatis, very nearer to the remains of a fort, there was a tribal Goddess Sambari. Animal sacrifices and blood offerings were so common and no native is stated to have ventured to go to that place at restricted periods. There were a number of stories and legends on the miracles of that Goddess, and she is stated to have punished a team of Europeans who laughed at her miracles as the superstitions of the people.[155]

The Bhupati family at Golugonda is stated to have constructed a mud fort at Narsipatnam which had its remains until few decades back.

All those areas came into the possession of the Pusapatis of Vizianagaram from A.D. 1865.[156] Along with those hill and forest provinces, some of the adjacent estates on the plains like Uratla, Vajragada, Tangedu, Kondala Agraharam, etc., went into the hands of the Pusapatis.

Uratla, a village, at a distance of 15 km. south-east of Narsipatnam is the chief place of the estate of the same name. It was one of the estates formed out of the haveli lands and sold by auction at a fixed peshkash in 1802 to the Pusapati family of Vizianagaram.[157] That Pusapati family sold that estate in 1810 to Sagi Sriramachandra Raju, whose family is very significant in that area till now.[158] That estate was sold for arrears in 1832 and bought by a lady named Dantuluri Achchiyya, who gave it to her daughter Sagi Subhadrayya in 1843.[159] After the death of Sagi Subhadrayya in 1867, that estate came to the possession of her adopted son Sagi Venkata Suryanarayana Jagannadha Raju. But due to his mismanagement of the estate, the peshkash fell into arrears and the estate was taken over by the government for a period. Subsequently the estate has been divided into a number of portions, and registered separately to different persons.

Chouduvada, near Chodavaram, was given in return to the services rendered by Jagannadha Raju's uncle Kakarlapudi Narasa Raju in 1875.[160] Similarly in the same year he has granted Ponduru and Mallavaram to his other uncle Kakarlapudi Chinna Narasa Raju. After the death of Chinna Narasa Raju in 1876, as his son was minor, the estate was taken under the court of Wards. The estate of Bayyavaram was sold to Datla Ranachandra Raju in 1877. He disposed of it to J. Rangachari who after a decade sold it to a dancing girl named K. Simhachalam. After the death of Simhachalam in 1896, her two adopted daughters Kannamma and Ramayamma became the estate holders.[161]

Tangedu and Gotivada, the strongholds of the Sagi family, which laid south-east of Narsipatnam were transferred to Sagi Sitarama Raju in 1877.

Kondala Agraharam, 10 km. nearby Narsipatnam was disposed of to Pusapati Suryanarayana Raju in 1879, which was later succeeded by his daughter-in-law, and grand daughter Buchchi Bangarayya and Chitti Ammanna alias Venkata Narasayya.[162]

Timmapuram, Tadaparti and Jaggampeta estates were sold to Lola Sanyasi Raju in 1884; who in turn transferred after few years to a dancing girl named as Pilla Gangu alias Chamanti. This lady Chamanti had already obtained one sub-division of the estate by name Peddapalem in 1884.[163]

After the alienation of the seven different portions in the Uratla zamindari, as stated above, the rest of the estate was taken by the zamindar of Tuni either under mortgage or through the process of the Civil Court in 1898.[164]

Ten kilometres away from Narsipatnan at a place between two hills, there found the ruins of a very large fortress known as Vajragada. The literary works of the medieval period refers to this Vajragada, as one of the conquered forts of the Reddi ruler that played significant role in the history of the then times.[165] Adjacent to the hilly tracts between Andhra and Odhra countries, the fort of Vajragada seems to have played a significant role in the medieval period. The local tradition narrate that it was constructed by Golla Kings just like that at Gollakonda, i.e., Golugonda. Actually it is referred to as 'Diamond

Fort' as it is called as Vajragada. But originally it seems to be Vajragada (Vrajagada) which means the fort of the Gollas. Local traditions and ballads like *'Katama Raju Kathalu'* otherwise known as *Yadavapuranam* refers to some forts of Yadavas, i.e., Gollas of this province.[166] Some illegible Telugu inscriptions of fourteenth-fifteenth centuries and some sculptural pieces and temple reminiscencesat Vrajagada attest to its past glory. Whatever may be its historicity, the local histories on that fort at Vajragada referred to the hostility of the chiefs of Vajragada with the rulers of Madugula, which occurred due to the kidnap of the daughter of the ruler of Madugula by the Chief of Vajragada.[167]

The Revenue Policy of the English Company towards the Tribal Areas of the Province

The forest and hill ranges of the province in which the hill zamindars like the Gudem, Golugonda, and Madugula exercised their power, have undergone a number of administrative changes during this period.

As a part of the northern Sircars, that area posed on Aurangzeb from the rulers of Bedar in 1687 and to the Subaship of the Nizam in 1724. At the time of Karnataka wars, that province was granted to the French in 1752 and it eventually came under the British in 1765. This is the changing history of this province in the eighteenth century.

The Mughal emperor issued a Firmana to the English Company to this effect:[168]

"...the English Company did expel the French therefrom: we, therefore in consideration of the fidelity and good wishes of the above high mighty...English Company have from our throne, the basis of the world, given them the aforementioned Circars by way of Inam or free gift from...April, 1762...Looking upon this high firman as an absolute and positive order, obey it implicitly."

By then, the entire area was under the control of the Nizam of Hyderabad and he obeyed the Firmana and issued a Sanad to the English Company on November 12, 1766 indicating the transfer of authority to them as stated below:[169]

"Be it known...from the...12th November, 1766, the whole of the said circurs...are now given to, and conferred upon forever and ever agreeable to their petition signed by us. In return for which, they the English Company, are to pay the annual sum of nine lakhs of rupees and to stand to all sebbendy charges, and whatever earthly or heavenly mischances may happen. You therefore our above mentioned Desh-mohees etc. are hereby required with contented minds, to live in obedience to the above Company's Deputies and to pay the proper revenues at the fixed and stated times."

Like in the other parts of the country, in this province also land was mostly under the zamindars with the hereditary tenures. When they came under the Muslim rule all their assigned duties like apprehending of thieves, murderers and other violators of laws and assisting the overlords in invasions and suppressing the rebelions etc., their expenses could be reimbursed by them from their rents they collected.

Fort St. George in its letter dated March 8, 1769 defined zamindaris as "lands held by certain rajas or chiefs as their hereditary estates, paying a certain tribute to the government and being subjects to suit and service, in manner very similar to the ancient feudal tenures."[170]

When the lands in that granted province went into the hands of the English, immediately they have taken initiation to get command over the administration.[171] A Committee was constituted with five members to circuit those provinces and to ascertain the fact which would be issued regular income to the Company.[172] They should ascertain with all possible exactness the produce of the country, the number of inhabitants, the state of the manufacturers, the fortified places, the gross amount of the revenues, the articles from which they arise, the mode by which they are collected, the charges of collection, the specific proportion usually received by the raja or zamindar, and that allotted to the cultivator as the reward of his labour. Their intention was not to deprive the hereditary rajas of zamindars of their annual income.

The Committee toured the area in 1775 and the zamindars were called to Madras in 1778. For a period of five years, the amount fixed for them to pay to the government was raised by 12½ per cent; and the settlement extended upto 1789, i.e., for a period of ten years.

Assessment of the zamindaris was raised to 3/4th of their gross revenue. But due to famine, the collection of revenue became very difficult which resulted in pushing the zamindars into arrears. The government appointed District Collectors in 1787 with a recommendation to rent out villages, which caused some disturbances in the oldest zamindaris that were suppressed with the military interference.

The District Collectors came to a settlement with the chiefs, head, and inhabitants of the villages, who in turn sub-rented the lands and come to an agreement on the rent each cultivator has to pay. Thus, they became jointly and severely responsible for the aggregate demand upon the village. But the interests of the peasants or ryots were not protected either from the zamindars or chiefs that were nominated by the government or by the Collector.

As the lands in the province belong to both plain and hilly regions, the English Company has given importance for survey of the hilly regions also. Until then no regular measures were undertaken to survey those areas. The Collectors were ordered to constitute the villages in those tribal areas into muttas. Arrangements were done to survey the agency that extends throughout the Northern Sircars from A.D.1792, which became materialised in 1815. On the problems that they have faced in the survey and on the wilderness of the country of the Visakhapatnam agency the survey officer reported thus.[173]

"The tract of the country among the hills...constituting a part of the northern boundary is wild and uncultivated with here and there a few huts hurdled together, not deserving the name of villages, and thinly inhabited by a race of people as wild as the country...The difficulty of procuring supplies, the wild and inaccessible nature of the country, with the want of road and its...noxious climate, have rendered the survey hazardous and laborious..., Vizagapatam...different from all other territories dependent of Fort St. George, chiefly because, bounded to the westward by a wide tract of hill and jungle, inhabited by civilised and indeed unconquered barbarians, many of them not ever nominally dependent on any government: their climate and their poverty have secured them from conquest...nobody seems even to know the boundary...this tract has never been explored...there is a blank here left in the maps.

After the survey of the hilly tracts, the haveli lands were apportioned into muttas and sold at public auction subject to the terms of permanent zamindari tenure. The muttadar stood between the government and the peasant. Because of the muttadar, the burden of the revenue officers as also the collection charges lessened for the government. Sir Thomas Munro condones the ignorance of the European officers when he said thus:[174]

"We proceed in a country of which we know little or nothing, as if we know everything and as if everything must be done now and nothing could be done hereafter...We endeavour to get rid of the difficulty by precipitately making Permanent Settlements which relieve us from the troubled task of minute or accurate investigations and which are better adapted to perpetuate out ignorance than to protect the people." At the times of difficulties in collecting the land revenue, basing on the demand, troops were also called in. Whites, a member of Board of Revenue in his minute dated March 25, 1793 described that was very difficult to maintain troops in those areas.[175]

He felt that it was proper to restrict the zamindars to the internal duties of their lands and not to trust them in any incidence the large body of military for the purpose of defence, but who in fact were oftener employed in resisting the orders of the government. Eighty seven villages in the Visakhapatnam district were rented out and most of them were villages in the hilly region neither surveyed nor touched by the settlement department.

The revenue fixed for payment by the zamindars and muttadars, was more than what they could pay. Whenever the ryots of even the zamindars found it difficult to collect money it was inevitable for them to borrow from the money-lenders against their own lands. When the debtors failed to repay the amounts they were dragged to the Courts on the plains. The tribals interpreted this as injustice done by the government. To clear their loans or debts yet times those zamindars had either to mortgage or to sell away a part of his estate or propriety to nominal rate.

In this context, it is essential to discuss in brief on the muttas and on the muttadar system, in the Visakhapatnam agency. The groups of villages located in the inaccessible and backward hill tracts which became revenue units after settlement were called muttas. The intermediatary who collected the revenue in that mutta and paid a certain amount of it to the government was called a muttadar.[176]

The muttadar of Golugonda received a sanad in 1802 and agreed to pay Rs 10,000 as peshkash to the English Company. To collect such a huge amount year after year was not possible, and the mutta fell into arrears and offering it for sale, the Company purchased it for a nominal amount of Rs 100 in 1837. In the Golugonda hills there were ten muttas which were leased out to hereditary mokhasdars: Dutcherti (Rs 1200); Makavaram (Rs 500); Koyyur (Rs 400); Gudem with Dharakonda (Rs 357); Antada Kottapalli (Rs 130); Guditur (Rs 80); Lotugadda (Rs 30); Chittempadu - (Rs 30); Bandivalasa (Rs 20). There were as many as 253 villages in those muttas and when they came under the British, the Governor of Madras wrote as follows: "a system which is adapted to districts where the authority of government is peramount cannot fail to be applicable to those mountainous tracts where upto the present period, after a lapse of more than thirty years, we in truth possess no police and no power."[177]

A muttadar was to assist, authorities in the upkeep of roads and traveller's bungalows and in keeping the principal forest, and to clear forest paths so as to enable the elephants to move up and down with loads. When the government wanted labour to carry loads it was for the muttadar to supply it. He had no right to the revenue from duties, abkari or taxes on the sale of spirits and liquors or from fairs. A muttadar has to maintain the register of births and deaths in the villages and was responsible for discipline in the area. He kept a watch on the arrival of strangers or suspicious characters and also on the activities of the agency people. No hereditary right to the office of muttadar was recognised and on the death, resignation, dismissal or removal of a muttadar, the Agent to the Governor has to personally investigate all claims and submit his report, where upon the government select the successor.

Being attached with revenue, the muttadar had neither time to cultivate, nor supervise the cultivation of his own-land. The muttadar collected revenues as determined by the government and retained one-third of the rents collected from the pettandars in the mutta for him, subject to a minimum, but was not entitled to enhance the rents payable by the *Pettandars*. A muttadar had powers to suspend any munsiff for not more than twelve months and could even dismiss him but could not impose any fine on the munsiff. Though a muttadar had no right on the forests, he had to render every support to preserve the forests from destruction by felling or fire. This implied the prevention of 'podu' cultivation and encouragement of settlers to take up permanent cultivation. He has to act as an informer and give timely information of any disturbance or offence against law. A muttadar was responsible for the law and order situation and was expected to apprehend robbers, rebels, and other bad characters and deliver them upto the authorities. When called upon, the muttadar has to present himself at the camp of the Agent or his assistants. Whenever there was a disturbance or uprising, the mutta involved was resumed by the government and handed over to someone else while such muttadars were often deported under agency warrants.[178]

Some of the villages were transferred from mutta to mutta and some of the muttas were transferred from agency to agency for administrative convenience. Gudem hills which were a part of the Visakhapatnam agency were attached to Rampa agency in the Godavari district. The five muttas of Gudem, Lotugadda, Lambasingi, Peddavalasa and Makavaram were kept in the Golugonda agency. The zamindaris and estates of hilly areas were taken over with the Act of 1839 and the Collector of Ganjam and Visakhapatnam became Agent to Governor.[179]

The muttadars and their attendants were quite merciless when they went out for revenue collection. A series of rebellions broke out in the agency on that issue. The 1879 Rebellion was the cumulative effect of the all discontent in the Rampa agency.[180] The mansabdar of the area created a general impression that his collecting excess rents and cesses were supported by the government where in the tribals were harrassed. His servants and the police exacted as they liked while the sub-renters raised a heavy tax. The mansabdar wants to collect more for him. All these resulted in the outbreak of a revolt at Rampa; and at the cost of a number of lives of police people and the tribals it was suppressed by the government. As a result of that revolt, the mansabdar was deposed and the muttadars began to deal with the government directly. Lands were distributed to muttadars with some important conditions such as a stipulated annual rent is to be paid to the government and the muttadar must be loyal and to assist the government in the maintenance of law and order. This rebellion at Rampa inspired a number of muttadars in the agency areas of Visakhapatnam.

In 1891, a rebellion broke-out at Golugonda. Its muttadar was assisted by the persons that actually participated in the Rampa rebellion on May 22 of that year.[181] About 200 revolutionaries looted the house of a policeman and moved over to Krishnadevipeta police station, killed five constables and carried-off all arms and ammunition. The police station was set to fire and the rebels ran into the forests and not traceable to the police. As their leader suddenly died, they dispersed; but not a single muttadar gave any assistance to the authorities.

In the prevailing revenue system it was not difficult for the government to resume the two muttas of Chittampad Bandivalasa and Koyyur. The muttadars of Lambasingi, Kotthaveedhi and Lotugadda were removed from power and instead their heirs were appointed.[182] The muttadar of Gudem Kothaveedhi, Sobilan Dora was arrested and deported under an agency warrant. Lambasingi Pathaveedhi mutta was resumed in 1886, Lotugadda in 1895 and Antada in 1907. Thus, five out of the ten muttas in Golugonda agency came under the government while the remaining five, viz., Lambasingi, Kothaveedhi, Makavaram, Gudem Pathaveedhi, Gudem Kotthaveedhi and Dharakonda continued under the muttadars.[183]

After Rampa rebellion, China Veera Bhupati, the muttadar of Gudem, left Gudem and reached Golugonda. In course of time, Gudem mutta was divided into two parts, the first one Gudem Pathaveedhi under the orders of the Agent to the Governor changed to Peddavalasa; and the second one Gudem Kotthaveedhi retained as Gudem mutta. China Veera Bhupati nominated Mottadam Sanyasi Dora as muttadar of Gudem Kotthaveedhi and Taggi Gantam Dora as the muttadar of Gudem Pathaveedhi which was changed as Peddavalasa. Sanyasi Dora was succeeded by his son Sobilan Dora who challenged the British authority in the rebellion of 1891 and was imprisoned at Visakhapatnam.[184]

Mottadam Veerayya Dora, son of Sobilan Dora was given charge of the mutta of Gudem Kotthaveedhi in 1912. During the Lagarai movement in 1916 the rebels encamped at Yaragonda for months together, which information was not given by Veerayya Dora to the Agent of the Governor. By this act, he was interned at Narsipatnam in 1917 and when he escaped, he was interned at Vizianagaram.[185] He was caught when he escaped from Vizianagaram also, and under IPC section 176 he was kept under police lock-up at Rajavommangi. Thus, with such experiences, the life of Veerayya Dora ends in prison.

Another important mutta which was originally separated from Gudem in 1879 was the mutta of Peddavalasa. Kankipati Nadipi Padal its muttadar, who used to pay half of the collected rent resigned to his position in 1919.[186] Yendu Padal, a claimant to the mutta failed to get it, as the right to appoint the muttadar is vested in the hands of the Agent. The Agent nominated Gadapala Veeranna Padal of Rinthada as the muttadar of the Peddavalasa in 1920, and in the immediate next year it was given to Kankipati Sarabhanna Padal. The mansabdar of Peddavalasa, Antada, Ebulu and Jerli opposed the act of the Agent and a rebellion broke out in 1922 under the leadership of Yendu Padal.[187]

Another important mutta in the hill region of this province was the Lotuggadda mutta. This mutta was under Chinna Veera Bhupati of Gudem, till he shifted his headquarters to Golugonda in 1879.[188] Later when its muttadar joined the Santha Bhupati Fituri of Rampa, he was sentenced to rigorous imprisonment for 1½ years. From then, until 1916, i.e., the period of Sagina Ramanna Padal, a number of persons succeeded to the post of mutta munsiff of Lotugadda on a monthly pay of Rs 20.

In 1922, in the rebellion under the leadership of Alluri Sitarama Raju, Ramanna Padal strongly supported the rebels by supplying food and giving them protection.[189] For such an action he was dismissed and Taggi Nadipi Dora was appointed muttadar of Lotugadda. Ramanna Padal lost his life in the rebellion and his son continued as a munsiff of Bailu Kunchangi. In due course, Sagina Yerra Padal, the son-in-law of Taggi Nadipi Dora became the muttadar of Lotugadda.

Another important mutta in this region was Lambasingi (or) Lamma Singi, 15 kilometres to Downuru. Bonangi Karri Padal and his brother Ganganna Padal, the two diwans served under the Bhupati of Gudem, received this mutta in 1836 as a gift. After their death,

Narasanna Padal, the son of the former became the muttadar. As stated earlier in the rebellion of Golugonda in 1886 when the police station and rest house were looted, Narasanna Padal had shown some sympathy to the rebels and not helped the police, for which his mutta was forfeited.[190] But later during the period of his grandson in A.D. 1914, his family regained their mutta. In the rebellion of 1922 led by Alluri Sitarama Raju, Lambasingi played a significant role.[191] The muttadar supported the government while the village munsiffs supported the rebels. Saramanda Borra Dora (Borrayya), Dopuru Balanna and Chintala Pedda Ramanna were interned at Krishna Devipeta for one month under agency warrant as they were suspected of supplying rations to the rebels, collecting money in the village for the rebels and sending false reports to the police station, proclaiming their ignorance about the whereabouts of the rebels.[192]

Minor (Small) Zamindaris / Estates: In the province:

Kasimkota

Kasimkota became very familiar as the chief centre of political activity during the Muslim, the Company and the Zamindari periods. It is a very ancient city and is referred to in the Eastern Ganga inscriptions located at Simhachalam.[193] In Sanskrit 'Kasimi' means mud or greenery. That is located 5 kms, to the south-west of Anakapalli. During the Muslim rule, it was the chiefest fort in the country and the headquarters of a command in the Chicacole Sircar. It continued to be the chief town of a division for sometime after the British acquired the district in A.D. 1768. The troops of the English Company joined the army of the Pusapati Chiefs of Vizianagaram at this Kasimkota to attack the French at Rajahmundry and Machilipatnam in 1758.[194]

As stated above, though Kasimkota was referred[195] to in the stone inscriptions of Varaha Lakshmi Narasimha Swami temple at Simhachalam, in the later medieval centuries it became a centre of power under the Velamas. When the prestigious Velama zamindari at Bobbili was under seize, those Velamas supported the cause of the Bobbili chiefs.[196] Later, to protect themselves from the wrath of the Pusapatis and the French, the then zamindar of the Kasimkota, Chlikani Rama Rayanimgaru, ran away to the shelter of Pithapur chiefs and spent the rest of his life there at a place called Chitrada.[197]

Mallama Devi, the queen of Gopala Krishna Ranga Rao who was killed in the Battle of Bobbili; and Jaggamamba, the queen of Peda Niladrirayanimgaru of Pithapur were the daughters of the Kasimkota Chief. As the Kasimkota estate has gone into the hands of the Pusapatis, the successors of Chelikani family settled in the Godavari tract.

In A.D. 1803, the estates of Kasimkota and Melupaka which was under a Brahmin owner were put to auction under Permanent Settlement. They were bought by the Pusapatis of Vizianagaram. Kasimkota was taken for Rs 4,343 and Melupaka was taken over for Rs 5,265 respectively. After a short period the Pusapatis gave them to Karumunchi Venkatachalam, after whom those two estates succeeded to his maternal grandson, Mantripragada Venkata Rao.[198] After his demise in A.D. 1845, as his successors Chiranjeva Rao and Venkatachalm being minors, Kasimkota and Melupaka estates were put under the Court-of-Wards. Later in A.D. 1865, a widow of that Mantripragada family by name Ramayamma and an infant daughter Maha Lakshmamma succeeded to the estate. In A.D. 1883, she has purchased out of her 'Stridhana' property, the estate of Mamidivada in the Sarvasiddhi Taluk. After her death, her estates have gone to the possession of her daughter, Mahalakshmamma.[199] Later, she assigned the estate of Mamidivada to her two minor daughters, Nedunuri Ramalakshmamma and Valluri Chinnammayi. Their brother was appointed as guardian, who later became the proprietor of those two estates.

Panchadharla

The esate of Panchadharla was framed out of the haveli lands and put to auction at a fixed assessment in A.D. 1802. After few years, some more villages were added and the estate was named as Chipurupalli estate. That estate comprised of 24 villages and was bought in by the government at sales for arrears and the remaining nine were formed as proprietary estates. Bharanikam, Chipurupalli, Indulapaka – Bonangi, Ravada, Mamidivada, Appikonda, Kurada, Kondayavalasa and Siddesvaram, was bought by Gode Suryaprakasa Rao in A.D. 1822.[200] Later in partition of the esates, Bharanikam went to the possession of Maharani Lady Gajapati Rao. As stated earlier, except Mamidivada, rest of the areas were under the possession of Kasimkota estatedars and later they were bought by Ganga Battulu Samayya. Chipurupalli (adjacent to Appkonda) was bought by Garuda Sanyasi Chetti in A.D. 1825.[201] He sold it to Gode China Venkata Jagga Rao in A.D. 1844, on whose death it passed to his son Venkatanarayana Rao. Venkatanarayana Rao died without male issue in 1882, and the estate came under the Court of Wards, in A.D. 1895, when his widow adopted her daughter's son, Venkatanarayana Rao who became proprietor of the estate of Chipurupalli later.

The above stated Ganga Bhattula Samayya either sold or transferred the remaining villages also at about A.D. 1820. Indulapaka and Bonangi were sold to Vasantha Rao Lakshmi - Narayana Rao; Ravada was sold to Datla Venkatapati Raju; Appikonda was given as gift to Gangabattula Rajanna; Purada Kondayyavalasa was sold to N. Venaktaramana and D. Venkataramana who later diposed it to others. Siddhesvaram, the last in the eight estates, was sold to the above said V.R. Lakshmi Narayana Rao.[202]

Thus, all those small estates in this province of Visakhapatnam frequently changed hands in the first quarter of nineteenth century.

In the same province at a place called Pudimadaka, there was formerly a port, which was described as one of the safest ports. It was closed to regular trade in 1881, for the curious reason that it was too far from Visakhapatnam and Kakinada, for the European merchants to be able personally to supervise exportation, which resulted in the native contractors so adulterating the exports that the shippers incurred heavy losses.[203]

Rayavaram

Another important estate, which was formed in 1802-03 out of *haveli* land put upto auction as permanently settled estate, was Rayavaram, a historical village, stated to have its antiquity, with the famous Krishnadeva Raya.[204] In 1802 A.D., it was bought by the Pusapatis of Vizianagaram, who in 1810 A.D. sold it to Sagi Ramachandra Raju, his maternal aunt's husband. When it was attached for the arrears in 1815 it was purchased by Gode Suryanarayana Rao for Rs 40,500.[205] But dissatisfied with the constant irrigation dispute between the ryots of Rayavaram, with the neighbouring Saravasiddhi ryots, Gode Suryanarayana Rao became unhappy and as a result he resold it to the government in A.D. 1844.[206]

Similarly, Sarvasiddhi, one of the ancient and historical place[207] in this area, which was originally constructed in Seventh Century A.D. by the Vengi Chalukyas, was formed as an estate in 1802. As in the case of Rayavaram estate, Sarvasiddhi was also purchased by Pusapatis who resold it in 1810 to Sagi Ramachandra Raju. As it fell into arrears, it was auctioned by the government and the Pusapatis purchased it in 1831.[208]

Gode Family

(Visakhapatnam and Anakapalli Province)

In the wake of the decline of the Mughals, the European trading companies stepped –up not only their activities of trade and commerce; but the companies such as the English East India Company, making clever use of the internal rivalries and dissentions among the local rulers and also through the advantage of their developed technology and methods of warfare, put an end to the power of regional states. Thus, the establishment of British Colonial rule took place in India. In larger parts of the country, by the end of Eighteenth Centuary and by 1857, they firmly settled in power.

The English activities on the Coromandel can be traced back to 1611 A.D, when their ship "Globe" captained by Hippon, touched the shore of Nizampatnam (Patapalli) first, and then Machilipatnam.[209] The factories were established simultaneously in the year 1621. But, due to some pressures from the local officials of the Sultan of Golkonda, the factory was shifted from Machilipatnam to Armoogam.[210]

As a result of numerous representations made to the Sultan of Golkonda, the Enlgish succeeded in procuring a 'firman' from the Sultan in 1632.[211] Accoridng to that firman, the English were permitted not only to trade at the port of Machilipatnam, but also to trade at other ports in the kingdom of Golkonda. But, the English were required to import Persian horses and 'rareties' from Europe. It was also made obligatory that the Sultan of Golkonda was to enjoy the first preferential selection of all their imports. The 'firman' is considered to be the first written sanction from a ruler in India allowing the English the right to trade on the Coromandel Coast. So, it is known as 'Golden Firman'.

The 'Golden Firman' for trade in the Sultanate of Golkonda, dated February 26, 1634 mentions Visakhapatnam along with Machilipatnam, Nizampatnam and Bimilipatnam.[212] Sultan Abdulla Qutb Shah granted his 'favour and protection' to Captain Thomas Joyce to carry on trade 'freely and plentifully' for mutual advantage. Thus, the English were familiar with Visakhapatnam and established commercial relations with the native mercantile community there from the fourth decade of the Seventeenth Century.

Thus, the English procured Visakhapatnam from the Sultan of Golkonda as a free gift, and they built a factory and a fort there in 1683.[213]

But, Golkonda was captured by Aurangzeb in 1689 and Visakhapatnam factory was captured under the orders of Aurangzeb in 1690. The English who were staying in the fort were brutally killed.[214]

However, Aurangzeb granted a fresh kowle for Visakhapatnam permitting the English to re-establish their factory and also to fortify the town in 1690.[215]

During this period, the English at Visakhapatnam were only merchants, interested in concessions. They were neutral and tried to improve their trade upto 1694. By 1753, Visakhapatnam had to emerge as a power because of the worsening conditions in the Sircar from 1694.

The year 1753 marked a turning point in the history of Northern Sircars. The French obtained the Chicacole, Rajahmundry, Ellore and Mustafanagar Sircars by the Treaty of Aurangabad (November 23, 1753). The possession of these extensive coastal tracts provided them increased opportunities for trade and enormous prestige. This significant event caused a change of attitude in the policy of Fort St. George authorities by obliging them to counteract.

The Aurangabad Treaty disappointed Saunders, the Governor of Fort St. George, who coveted the Sircars.[216] He cautioned the Council at Visakhapatnam: "we are more concerned than surprised at this event when we consider what influence they have at Aurangabad by means of their troops. The possession of these countries will put it in their power greatly to hurt the Company's investment and we imagine they will lose no opportunity of doing it."[217] But the English had to bide their time.

The French acquisition of the Northern Sircars displeased the local chiefs also; prominent among them were Jaffar Ali, the Faujdars of Rajahmundry, and Pusapati Vijayarama Raju, the ruler of Vizianagaram. The latter was ambitious to become the master of the Sircars with the English help. But the French military supremacy obliged him to put up with the French regime and manage the Chicacole Sircar on favourable terms biding his time.[218]

Jaffar Ali and Vijayarama Raju sought the English assistance in vain. The English Governor wrote to the Company at Visakhapatnam thus:

"The Nawab and the Rajah have both applied to us for assistance, it is not prudent to refuse them though we can gratify neither and yet we would willingly appear a friend to both without making any direct promise.[219]

These subtle English machinations and recalcitrance of the zamindars threw the Sircars into turmoil.

The most remarkable feature was the steadfast friendship of Vijayarama Raju towards the English against all odds. Even though the English confined themselves to affectionate advice and promises he assured them of his royal friendship[220] his nephew and successor Ananda Gajapati Raju followed suit. Further, as Mr. Bussy rebuked his late uncle, Ananda Raju was alienated.[221] Determined to dislodge the French, he urged strongly the English to Co-operate. But he received only evasive replies. Visakhapatnam itself surrendered to Mr Bussy on June 27, 1757.

Dissatisfied with the negative attitude of Fort St. George, Ananda Raju directly corresponded with Lord Clive in Bengal. Bussy was suspicious of him since the Battle of Bobbili and apprehending his correspondence with the English, he punished him by enhancing the peshkash.

When Mr. Bussy proceeded to Pondicherry to lead to attack on Madras[222], Pusapati Ananda Raju seized Visakhapatnam and hoisted the English flag on the factory (September 2, 1758).[223]

Pusapatis initiative was highly potential with their characteristic vision, Clive utilised this; Moreover, Nizam Ali Khan, the younger brother of Salabat Jang, asked for his help. He dispatched Col. Forde to the Sircars to help the Pusapati chiefs and wrote to Madras.

"If this expedition only threw the country into such confusion as to prevent our enemies from collecting any revenues, it will answer in a great measure, the design and the expense."[224]

The Madras Government deputed John Andrews, the chief of Machilipatnam, to co-operate with Col. Forde. The *dubashi* of Lord John Andrews, the Chief-in-Council, and Gode Jagga Rao played a very significant role in the Company affairs of the times. That Gode family in course of time migrated to Visakhapatnam – Anakapalli areas, established as zamindars and showed their impact on the socio-economic as well as religio-cultural systems for more than two centuries.

In the following pages, an attempt is made to reconstruct the history and contribution of the Gode family, with the help of available material, and fill-up a gap in the annals of Visakhapatnam district.

No connected work has been done till now to assess contribution of this family. G.R. Varma,[225] Arudra,[226] M.S.R. Anjaneyulu,[227] T. Donappa,[228] T.S.N. Murthi,[229] Y. Sudarshana Rao,[230] V. Rama Krishna,[231] K. Suryanarayana[232] and Angara Surya Rao,[233] attempted to bring to light the various aspects on the history and contribution of the Gode family. But the objectives of their research papers are different and only a sketch is found in them, rather than a detailed discussion on the subject.

Early History of the Gode Family

The English rule witnessed a number of changes in revenue, educational and administrative spheres. More significant of these were the revenue policies, and in particular, the Permanent Settlement in Bengal and Madras Presidencies. As a consequence of the introduction of Permanent Settlement in the Northern Sircars of the Andhra region, a number of zamindaris were created. Those zamindars – the aristocracy became the staunch pillars of support to the Enlgish. Among those innumerable zamindars, the prominent were Vizianagaram, Pithapuram, Visakhapatnam, Anakapalli, Nuzvid and Venkatagiri.[234]

The Gode zamindari family played a notable role, in the development of Visakhapatnam – Anakapalli areas during the period. Their ancestor, Gode Pedda Jagga Rao served as a 'dubasi' under John Andrews in the second half of eighteenth century and migrated from Machilipatnam to Visakhapatnam.

Though the early history of Godes is not clearly known, it is surmised that their ancestors served as 'Sardars' under Mughal and Nizam Governments and became rich. Like a number of native significant personalities of the period who served as 'dubasis' under East India Companies, Gode Jagga Rao acquired name and fame. Just as dubasi Kandregula Jogi Pantulu[235] under Lord John Faibus, dubasi Gode Jagga Rao played a significant role in almost all the political activities of Lord John Andrews. By some of the literary works like *Oghavati Parinayam* of Akkinepalli Narasimha Kavi, *Mallari Charitra* (also known as *Karna Kulinula Charitra*) of Maringanti Venkatacharyulu, which were composed at a later date under their patronage, give some clues about their early history.

They belong to 'Perike' community, a conmunity of business people moving with ganny bags on the backs of oxen.[236] They claimed themselves as *Puragiri Kshatriyas*. Basing on the availability of the same community in Telangana portion of Andhra Pradesh and in some portions of Karnataka, writers like G.R.Varma, opined that they were *Vira Kshatriyas* that came from Karnataka. They were known as communal chiefs in different capacities as *Kulapatulu, Dasailu* and *Dongari Varu.*[237] It is stated that they were referred to in the capacity of village – head or communal head from the period of the rulers of Vijayanagaram, as is referred to in a document at Somela village in the Chittoor district.

In Maratha language the meaning of the word Gode is sweetness. Saiman I.S.P. Nadhan considered Godes as basically Tamilians. He studied how Gode Mangapati, who played a significant role in the

Anglo-French rivalries and in the business affairs of the Company, was made as the zamindar of Chintadripeta in Tamil Nadu.[238]

The Godes traced their origin from one Vira Mallu whose details were not known. As observed by Chilukuri Virabhadra Rao, this may be connected with the story of Alla Viramallu, who became a *Virakallu* (Hero stone) in the temple of Tripurantakam. He suspected those perekis as Kapus of Munnur. Gode family claims ancestry from Janya Malla, the brother of Vira Palla. They belong to Chatrasirimalla *Gotra*. Their tutelary deity is *Mallari* or *Mailara Deva.*[239]

Gode family seems to be one of the most ancient and highly respected families in the aristocracy of Southern India. They traced their origin from Giriraju, a king stated to have belonged to the well-known Ikshvaku dynasty of the Solar race and stated to be the founder of the city of Bhogavati. It is traditionally believed that Giriraju being childless, offered to do penance in return for offspring, and the God Siva, blessed him with a son, named Siddhiraju, the father of five sons, who afterwards waged war with Parasu Rama. The second of them, Janyaraju, was the progenitor of the Gode family.[240]

Gode Surya Prakasa Rao (1788-1841) encouraged Akkinepalli Narasimham to write *Oghavati Parinayam* in dedication to him. In the opinion of scholars like Arudra *Oghavati Parinayam* is a small *Kula Puranam,*[241] the family history of the Godes. *Mallari Charitra* of Mariganti Venkatacharyulu, written under the patronage of Gode Janakamma is also giving more details of this family.[242] Gode Janakamma herself appreciated that work as a description of their family customs (*matkulacharam*). She wants to enrich the subject with more additions in detailed and entrusted that work to Erramilli Perraju. Thus, the family members of the Gode Zamindari encouraged the poets under their patronage, to write their family history. Their earlier life under the Gode Pedda Jagga Rao continued under the services of the Nizam and in the English Company at Machilipatam.

Kakaraparti Buchchipatra Kavi in his *Satyavati Parinayam* described the early history of this family. He has stated that these Godes belong to the 'Solar dynasty'. To protect themselves from the wrath of Parasa Rama, they refused to wear *Yagnopavitha*. They claimed descent from Channamalla. In the lineage of Channamalla, Akkama Bhupati born and he gave birth to a son by name Bhupati. Bhupati is said to have rendered distinguished services to the Nizam's government, in recognition of which he received large grants of land at Rajahmundry, where he immortalised his name by building two temples and dedicating them to Siva and Kesava respectively.[243] That Bhupati begot two sons – Suranna and Ramachandra. That elder son Suranna also known as Pedda Surya Rao is stated to have served as 'Sardar' under the Mughals.[244] He was a great builder and erected shrines to Hari Hara at Vakatippa. He married Gumpamma and begot five sons - Uppana, Sarvesa, Jagga Rao, Bhupati and Gopala. The third son Jagga Rao is the famous Jagga Rao, the dubasi of Lord John Andrews at Machilipatam.

Gode Pedda Jagga Rao who served as dubasi under Lord John Andrews established himself in the contemporary political and economic activities of the English Company. When a number of Zamindars and Izardars in Northern Sircars revolted against the English Company with all loyalty and sincerity Gode Jagga Rao assisted the English Company, in suppressing all those revolts and to bring all those areas under the control of the English. Particularly in suppressing the revolt at Mylavaram, Gode Jagga Rao had shown extraordinary courage, brought the areas under control, captured the revolutionaries and got appreciation from the English Company. Having acquired Mylavaram to the Company and also by pacifying the rebellious populace of the region, he was taken into confidence of the Company administration.

It was not long before, it was found out that the East India Company under great obligation to Gode Jagga Rao, for the timely help he gave them, not only through his personal influence but also in monetary transactions by placing his resources at their disposal in times of emergency. The capture of the fort of Mylavaram by the Company was due to his help, and they showed their appreciation and regard by presenting him with a 'Shaiban Palkee', an umbrella, and other *insignia* of royalty.[245] The Court of Directors from England was impressed and appreciated the timely assistance rendered by Jagga Rao in their letters dated May 25, 1798 and April 17, 1799.[246] *Satyavati Parinayam* elaborately described the various privileges and honours that they bestowed by the East India Company upon this zamindar for his valuable timely support in consolidating the power of the Company.

It is customary for the English to honour such people who rendered great services for the benefit of the Company. Kandregula Jogi Pantulu received Divi Sima area, and Gode family got some provinces in the present Coastal Districts of Northern Andhra in return to their faithful services to the Company.[247]

After acquiring the Sircars in November A.D.1706, the Company preferred to administer the government through the existing system. So, Rajahmundry, Ellore and Kondapalli Sircars were leased out for three years to Hussain Ali Khan as 'deputy'. The Sircars of Chicacole was entrusted to the Pusapati family as the 'delegate.'[248]

In June A. D.1769, the native agency discontinued and the Sircars were placed under the charge of 'Provincial Chiefs and Councils.'[249] The Chief and the Council of Machilipatam was in-charge of the Sircars of Kondapalli, Rajahmundry and Ellore. The southern part of Chicacole Sircar was placed under the control of the Chief and Council of Visakhapatnam. Edward Cotsford was appointed a 'Resident' to the defunct Ganjam Factory to revive it, and manage the Itchapur division.[250] 'This internal government' continued upto November 20, 1794.[251] The Provincial Boards had the revenue jurisdiction.

The primary object of the direct management was to transact revenue affairs systematically. The English realised that the country has suffered anarchy since a decade. So, they aimed at cultivating the Sircars as regular revenue yielding areas, to enable them to meet the new burden of their acquisition which became inevitable.

When a new province was established in Visakhapatnam and Lord John Andrews was deputed as Chief of the Council there, Gode Jagga Rao also followed him to Visakhapatam from Machilipatnam. The family of the Godes thus entered to that province of Visakhapatnam, the area that identified with them and showed their impact in that area for more than two centuries.

During that period the Company introduced Permanent Settlement during the years 1802-04 to remove "all the generated evils of unsettled principles of revenue administration" to "reform and establish it on a firm and efficient footing not less to the advantage of the people than to the security of the revenue"; suppressing "rebellion and insubordination" which was conspicuous, by 'annihating' the troops of the zamindars and bringing them to subjection, and 'acknowledge' and submit to the principle, that as they must be indebted to the beneficience and wisdom of the English Government for every advantage they were to receive so in like manner, they must feel indebted solely to its protection, for the continuance and enjoyment of them.[252]

Sir Thomas Munro, the Governor of Madras in a Minute of January 7, A.D.1823 written after a tour of the Sircars, summed-up the then position as under.[253]

"The affairs of the Sircars can never be well-administered, not the great body of the people protected against oppression, nor the country be secured from disturbance and the incursion of plunderers, until our government becomes more respected in those provinces than it is at present..."

Throughout this period, the zamindars, chafing at their reduction as mere landholders and, aided by wild and unhealthy country, kept the district in continual ferment with their recalcitrance and feuds. The disturbances, which entirely resulted from their own feuds, impoverished them and made them defaulters. Such estates of the zamindars were auctioned by the English and the estate of Sher Muhammadpuram was purchased at the Permanent Settlement by Gode Jagga Rao.[254] That estate comprises sixteen *jirayati* villages, six *srotriyam* villages and five *mokhasa* villages. He has purchased that zamindari for Rs 18,445 subject to an assessment of Rs 19,343.

Thus, started zamindari career of the Gode family, extended its authority to the majority provinces in the area, raised to the position of calling them as 'Maharajas' in the succeeding decades.

The modernisation process that was commenced during the Nineteenth Century, coupled with the introduction of English language and education and compulsions of the administrative needs of the Colonical rulers, posed a serious threat to the traditional learning and indigenous professions based on that. The impact of this could be seen in the slow but steady shift of interest of these sections of society towards learning of English language and education in order to secure jobs in the government.[255] Gode Jagga Rao, like other enlightened zamindars of the period encouraged and patronised education and literary activity. Three generations of Kakaraparti poets have received the patronage of the Gode family. The first one Kakaraparti Tirupati Patra Kavi dedicated his work, *Satyabhama Krishna Samvadhamu* to Gode Pedda Jagga Rao. In his estate, he has given agraharas--Suryanarayanapuram and Subhadrapuram in the name of his father and mother Suryanarayana and Subhadramma. He made endowments to a choultry at Banaras, and also constructed temples. It is described in *Satyabhama Krishna Samvadamu* that Pedda Jagga Rao spent his leisure time amidst of scholars and poets as "*hridyana vidya gadya pathana sravana lasita vadana.*"

Gode Jagga Rao was a great promoter of Telugu literature, and had secured the services of the well-known Pandit, Paravasthu Srinivasachari of the Nellore district. He was orthodox; and true to the precepts inculcated in the *Sastras* of old, he practised the *Sapta Santana*, i.e., seven good works of perpetuity, one proof of which is a still-living monument - the famous temple dedicated to Kodandaramaswami, which subsequently received an endowment from his friend, the *Maharaja* of Vizianagaram.[256] In those days, he was second to none in point of popularity.

Gode Pedda Jagga Rao begot a number of children by his two wives. So far it is known that he has three sons - Suryaprakasa Rao, Bhaskara Rao and Suryanarayana Rao; and three daughters - Subhadramma, Bangaramma and Lakshminarasamma. But at Simhachalam in an inscription dated S'1720 (i.e., A. D.1798) one Chengal Rao (Chengalvaraya), son of Gode Jagga Rao appears as the donar of a gold 'Satagopam' to Lord Sri Varaha Lakshmi Nrisimhaswami.[257] His other details or his relations with his brothers or sisters are not known. But in the *Vizagapatam Factory Records*, it is stated that Gode Chinna Venkata Jagga Rao was driven from his home by intrigues and disturbance and represented to the Chief that Chengal Rao was molesting his family and appealed to allow him to return to his estate.[258] By that it is understood that Chengal Rao (Chengalva Raya) seems to have troubled the succession of his brother to the estate. With the involvement of the Chief, Gode Chinna Venkata Jagga Rao is allowed to return and to occupy his zamindari of Anakapalli.

He married two wives, Chellamma and Krishnamma and blessed with four sons and three daughters. Though there was no female education, the three daughters of Gode Jagga Rao were not kept in complete ignorance, and a decent education was accorded to them.[259] The eldest daughter was named after his mother Subhadramma, who associated herself with the literary activity of her father from childhood. Her zeal and enthusiasm towards learning, made her as a great scholar and writer of the contemporary times. Poets of the age appreciated her as *Ayatavidya samagra* and *Andhra girvana bhasha parijnanaprasasta.*[260] She described that she got training under certain Ramesam and Parvatism. She has composed a number of works out of which more than a dozen was published by Gode Narayana Gajapati Rao. Her contribution to literature will be discussed elsewhere.

She was given in marriage to Madine Surayya, the son of her aunt. She seems to be the first and significant poetess among the ladies in the zamindari families. She was blessed with two sons and the eldest one was named after her father Jagga Rao, who was appointed as Principal Sadhar Amin. Queen Victoria honoured that Madene Jagga Rao as 'Companion of Star of India' (C.S.I).

The English rule witnessed a number of changes in revenue, educational and administrative spheres. More significant of these were the revenue policies and in particular, the Permanent Settlement in Bengal and Madras Presidencies. As a consequence of the introduction of Permanent Settlement in the Northern Sircars of the Andhra region, a number of new zamindaries were created.

Significant Personalities in the Gode Family

Zamindars of Gode family made a significant contribution for economy and culture in the Visakhapatnam-Anakapalli provinces. Their period is a landmark for the growth of arts and letters in Northern Coastal Andhra.

They held ownership of estates of Anakapalli, Embaram, Kuppili, Koruprolu, Gottipalli, Godicherla, Bharanikam, Munagapaka, Sri Ramapuram, Sher Mohammadapuram, all situated in the then Vizagapatam District.[261]

Sher Mohammadpuram was their first estate. As stated earlier Gode Pedda Jagga Rao bought Sher Mohammadpuram estate and few other villages from the English Company for Rs 18,445.[262] Pedda Jagga Rao was at that time a 'Dubasi' at the Chief Council of the Company in Machilipatnam.

As known already, the Gode family belonged to *Puragiri Kshatriya* caste popularly known as Perikivaru. They belonged to *Chatrasala gotra*. Begin with the purchase of the above estate, Gode family acquired few more estates such as Anakapalli in 1810, Godicharla in 1818, Nakkapalli in 1820, a few parts of Cheepurupalli in 1812, Munagapaka in 1830 and a few others later.[263] The total income from those estates was about 7 to 8 lakhs of rupees out of which the peshcush was about one and a half lakh of rupees.

Gode Suryaprakasa Rao

As stated earlier, Gode Pedda Jagga Rao had three daughters and four sons - Subhadramma, Bangaramma, Lakshmi Narasamma; Suryaprakasa Rao, Bhaskara Rao, Suryanarayana Rao and Chengal Rao. Among the sons, Suryaprakasa Rao, the elder one is a learned scholar in different languages. He studied Sanskrit and Telugu literatures, English, Parcy and sciences, like botany, architecture and the science of horses. He studied botonical science in Western methods and approach and by implementing those systems raised beautiful gardens in his Anakapalli estate. Very rare and important kinds of plants were collected and it is stated that those gardens were well-appreciated by the Governors and other important European officials like Dr Benza and Mr. Russell of the period. He was well-known for his enlightenment and culture as well as for his military prowess. As observed by A. Vadivelu, he was probably the first Hindu in Southern India who spoke and wrote English as well as an English man, which is to say without any foreign accent, and with idiomatic correctness. Although he had the benefit of Western civilisation to a remarkable extent and also the privilege of moving freely in European society, yet he maintained his orthodoxy unimpaired. He was a great sportsman and hence his company was very much sought by many Englishmen, in and around, the Visakhapatnam district, whenever they went on hunting excursions.[264]

He constructed a dam across the river Sarada and then diverted its water to Kondakarla Ava. He also tried to the maximum utilisation of that river waters for irrigation purposes, which still yields good results in the cultivation in Anakapalli areas. Until then, the varieties of sugarcane like *Rayagada* and *Dubbukeli* that were cultivated by the ryots of the area, were frequently get effected by diseases and hence in A.D.1839, Gode Suryaprakasa Rao introduced Maritious variety of sugarcane to get rid of the diseases and trained the ryots of the area in the preparation of jaggery in the most advanced method.[265]

During the period of Gode Suryaprakasa Rao, some un-warranted situations disturbed the relations between the zamindars and the English in Northern Sircars.[266]

Anakapalli zamindari was originally belongs to the Payak Rao of the Kakarlapudi family. After the death of Appala Payak Rao, (Nallamandu Payak Rao), English Company put Anakapalli zamindari to auction and the Pusapati family acquired it in 1802 and resold it to Gode Suryaprakasa Rao in 1810. But the heir apparants of the Kakarlapudi family revolted against this deal and disturbed the normal peace in the district. When the Permanent Settlement was formed in 1802-03, the estates of Satyavaram and Anakapalli were sold along with the other 'haveli lands' and purchased by the Pusapatis of Vizianagaram, who in 1810 transferred them by private agreement to Gode Suryaprakasa Rao. In January, 1832, Kakarlapudi Jagannadha Raju also known as Sitarama Raju, a cousin of the adoptee who died earlier, provided with armed followers, assumed the title of 'Payak Rao' preceded to commit depredations and exacted contributions.

As already stated the Acting Collector Smith, in his letter to the Board of Revenue dated July 24, 1832, attributed these disturbances to the "unconciliatory spirit" and unpopularity of the proprietors of the estate in that neighbourhood, and particularity of Gode Suryaprakasa Rao and his brother Suryanarayana Rao.[267] But Russell, after enquiry, concluded that the Acting Collector was mistaken and that "it was not an insurrection of the people", arising from personal dislike or attachment to an individual. The inhabitants generally had no connection with the rebel faction, and though compelled to purchase safety for themselves and families by contributing to their wants and deterred from giving information through fear of their resentment were yet not interested in their success."[268] Jagannadha Raju who led the insurrections, had no influence, but was a mere puppet of Naganna Dora, the diwan and 'the person possessing the entire influence of the Golugonda zamindari which is the hill country bordering on the disturbed parts"[269] in whom the Acting Collector confided and recalled the troops and committed the country to him. Naganna, by preventing open rebellion, could confirm the Acting Collector's belief in his fidelity while secretly thwarting him. The insurgents emboldened by success, resorted to the hills, the natural strongholds and rendered still 'more so by stockades' as the government could not subdue them. Otherwise, the whole district was placed under the martial law on December 11, 1832.[270] Jagannadha Raju and his followers soon after fled into the Nizam's country. But he reappeared at the beginning of May, 1834 leading adventurers collected in the Nizam's territories.[271] Now he was deprived of the main support as Naganna Dora died. Hard pressed by the troops, he escaped into the Rampa, a hill zamindari in the Rajahmundry district behind Golugonda. The Rampa chief betrayed him and he was executed near Payakraopeta, on the banks of river Tandava as described earlier. Thus, disturbances created by Jagannadha Payak Rao in safeguarding their interests continued for more than two years and came to an end with the assassination of Payak Rao.

Some of the *Chatu* verses eulogize the strength and spirit of this revolt of Jagannadha Payak Rao against the English. The main intention of the rebellion of Jagannadha Payak Rao was to retain his authority over the Anakapalli zamindari which was already purchased by Gode Suryaprakasa Rao.

In all the activities of the English Company in suppressing the revolts of Jagannadha Payak Rao, which the English called 'fituris', Gode Suryaprakasa Rao who already purchased Anakapalli zamindari supported the English and made serious efforts in putting an end to the revolt. In high terms, Kakaraparthi Buchchipatrayya described the heroic role made by Gode Suryaprakasa Rao in strengthening the English. He got appreciation of the English officers like Russell and Adam for the courage and valour executed in that fight against Jagannadha Payak Rao. Mr. Russell in his Report dated November 18, 1834 states thus: "General Rumley, General Taylor, Mr. Russell and a host of other English gentlemen speak in honourable terms of the assistance rendered by him from time to time. He used to march with English officials into the hills and trace the haunts of phituridars, and had to bear fire many a time."[272]

But in the estimation of some of the writers like T.S.N. Murti the revolt of Payak Rao which costs his life, was a fight of the native rulers, against the authority of the English Company.[273] The Company Records themselves admit that revolt got public sympathy. A tradition says that Gode Suryaprakasa Rao was cursed by the ladies of the Payak Rao for the cynical role played by him, in this contest. Whatever it be, from thence onwards, there was no uninterrupted male succession in the Gode lineage.[274]

But on the part of the Godes, to retain their zamindari of Anakapalli which was purchased earlier, they had no option except to serve and support the interests of the English during that period.

Referrring to Suryaprakasa Rao's keen interest on the promotion of land, and on his concern towards the ryots, Governor Sir Frederick Adam states that "Gode Suryaprakasa Rao met me on the border of his estate, and I frequently saw and conversed with him in my progress through the district. His landed property is extensive and I believe he has expended much money in its improvement, and treats his ryots with kindness and liberality. At Anakapalli, the chief town of his estates, he has formed, at considerable expense, an extensive garden which is stocked with valuable and rare trees and plants collected with much trouble from various distant quarters. He has another garden similarly stocked at Vizagapatam."[275]

Anakapalli-Visakhapatnam zamindari of the Godes comprised of 17 divisions, viz., Anakapalli, Kasimkota, Kondakarla, Munagapaka, Dimili, Sarvasiddhi, Melipaka, Rayavaram, Panchadharla, Sriramapuram, Nakkapalli, Godicharla, Uratla, Vemulapudi, Kottakota, Uppada and Waltair. That zamindari, as stated earlier, originally purchased in an auction by the Pusapatis of Vizianagaram and resold to Gode Suryaprakasa Rao.

Sher Mohammadpuram purchased by his father Gode Peda Jagga Rao went as a share to his younger brother Gode Suryanarayana Rao.

As another brother Gode Bhaskara Rao died with out issues, his property is also shared by the remaining two brothers.

Suryaprakasa Rao died in 1841 at the age of 53 years. He had two sons and one daughter by his wife Janakamma. The two sons died in childhood, and after Suryaprakasa Rao the affairs of the zamindari were looked after by his wife Janakamma.

Gode Janakamma, unlike the other orthodox zamindari ladies, thoroughly participated in public life and used to talk with the English officials on zamindari issues. On the advice of the English officers, she has constructed a girl's high school in Visakhapatnam. She has undertaken a number of public works and patronised a number of poets and scholars. The literary activity under her patronage will be discussed later.

As her two sons predeceased her, her daughter Ratnayamma who was givern in marriage to Lakshmi Narasimha Rayalu of Gudivada became the heir - apparent to the zamindari of the Gode family.

Ratnayamma is also not blessed with children and hence adopted a daughter by name China Janakamma, who was later married by Gode Naryana Gajapati Rao.

Gode Suryanarayana Rao

Gode Suryanarayana Rao, the third son of Peda Jagga Rao succeeded to the entire zamindari. He has purchased some more zamindaris like Nakkapalli and Kuppili, from the Kakarlapudi family and enhanced the prestige and glory of Gode family among the other zamindars of Northern Sircars. His achievements were described by Kola Seshachalam in his *Nilagiri Yatra.*[276] He has given land grants to a number of temples, made a number of endowments to Vanamamalai *Matha*, made provision to the worship of Pardhasaradhi temple at Madras, and constructed bathing-ghats at Sapta Godavari. Besides his zamindari, it is stated that he assisted the Pusapatis as minister, in their administrative matters.

He was chiefly distinguished for his skills and management in revenue affairs. He was also renowned for his large heartedness, for he extended his charities to all religious institutions. He donated a site near his house at Vizagapatam to the London Mission. For the victims of the famine of 1833, that extended from Nellore to Visakhapatnam, he opend a 'Poor house', in which thousands were fed twice a day. This institution was maintained for a long time after his death. He contributed liberally towards all institutions of public utility. He fully appreciated the benefits of liberal education, and sent his sons to Madras and Calcutta for higher education.[277]

Surayanarayana Rao had three wives – Nilayamma, Achchiyamma and Sitayamma.

Sitayamma has given birth to Gode Naryana Gajapati Rao and Achchiyamma has given birth to Gode Chinna Venkata Jagga Rao. Gode Narayana Gajapati Rao married Chinna Janakamma, daughter of Ratnayamma; and Chinna Venkata Jagga Rao married Bangaramma, daughter of Chavala Jaggarayudu. With those marriages, Suryanarayana Rao raised as a prominent zamindar in the Northern Sircars. He has construced magnificent palaces for their residence adjacent to Upputeru in Visakhapatnam by spending a lot of money in A.D. 1830.

Gode Chinna Venkata Jagga Rao (A.D. 1817 – 1856)

Gode Chinna Venakata Jagga Rao, the eldest son of Suryanarayana Rao born in A.D. 1817, studied until 16 years of age in Visakhapatnam, went to Madras for higher education, as there were no institutions to train Western education in this part of the country. At Madras, he was trained under T.G. Tylor, a great astronomist of the times.

Chinna Venkata Jagga Rao may be stated as the first and the foremost scientists among the Telugu people who studied and viewed various subjects like astronomy, geography and mathematics with both Hindu and Western perceptions.[278] He published the results of his researches like his study on planet Bruhaspati, on the position and purpose of zero, etc., in the popular English magazines like *Madras Journal of Literature and Science*. His paper on *'Heli'* the Comet in A.D.1836, was well-received by scholars and scientists of the period.[279] For a short period, he served the duties of T.G. Tylor, the Government Astronomist at Madras. Owing to that interest he established an astronomical laboratory and an observatory with all its modern equipment at Dabagardens in Visakhapatnam in A.D. 1838, to teach people the process of time.[280]

He equipped that observatory with all the necessary instruments and apparatus at an enormous expense, all of them being imported from England and the Continent. He was a friend of almost all the European officers throughout the district; and those belonging to the public works department always admired his mathematical talents. His valuable contributions to the Geographical Society of which he was also the member and his correspondence with the learned Dr Baist give abundant evidence of originality of thought as well as of his avidity for work.[281] Appreciating the observatory constructed by him at Visakhapatnam even after few decades, Lord Cannemara, the Governor of Madras praised it as it assists the shipping on the coast.

His deep interest on envionmental study and on modern crops is testified by the work *Nilagiriyatra* written by Kola Seshachalm, which was dedicated to him.[282] That work vividly describes the climate on Nilagiri hill range and explains how it is suitable to raise some western crops like radish, beetroot, noolkol, tamps, carrot, cauliflower, leaf maroya, rasberry, mulberry, strawberry, blackberry, hill gooseberry, peaches, pears, apple, etc.[283] The introduction of such crops at Nilagiri hill ranges is attested to in another work *Nilagiricharitramu* written by Betapudi Subbarayudu, who worked at that place at the time of C.P. Brown. Being a master in astronomy he served temporarily as Government Astronomist in the place of his teacher, T.G. Tylor at Madras. Owing to his keen interest on Sanskrit and Telugu literatures, he became patron member to Hindu Literary Society of Madras in A.D.1636. A number of poets and writers in Madras received encouragement by Chinna Venkata Jagga Rao; and Kola Seshachalam dedicated his work *Nilagiri Yatra* to him.

The National Indian Association, London appreciated the benevolent services of Jagga Rao on astronomical matters. It quotes his desire to communicate to the residents around "the state of my barometer or the approach of bad weather", and he enjoined upon his heirs, "in case I breathe my last before doing so, they should make the institutions permanent at the cost of any estate."[284]

Chinna Venkata Jagga Rao seems to be the first modern scientist among the Telugus. Unfortunately all his research works have not seen the light of the day.

By the Vizagapatam Factory Reports, it is noticed that once when Jagga Rao was driven from his home by intrigues in disturbance, represents to the chief how he was molesting by Chengal Rao and appealed to the Chief, to allow him to come back. As per his request he was allowed to return to his estate. Who is the Chengal Rao that disturbed Jagga Rao is not clearly known so far. Interestingly one Gode Chengal Rao (Changalvaraya), son of Gode Jagga Rao appears as the donor of a record dated A.D.1798 at Simhachalam.[285] By this it is understood that Chengal Rao that troubled Chinna Jagga Rao was no other than his uncle.

Chinna Venkata Jagga Rao got reputation as a great scientist, a great writer, Scholar, patron of letters and arts, and also as a great musician. He married Bangaramma, daughter of Chavala Jagga Rayudu and begot a daughter Achchayamma.

Chinna Jagga Rao purchased Chipurupalli village from Garuda Sanyasi Chetti in 1844. W. Francis states in the *Vizagapatam District Gazetteers* that after the death of Jagga Rao, his estate passed to his son Venkata Narayana Rao.[286] In the known history of the Gode family, Chinna Jagga Rao had only one daughter by name Achchayamma by his wife Bangaramma. Now it seems that China Venkata Jagga Rao had another son by name Venkatanarayana Rao who died without male issue in A.D.1882. Owing to lack of male succession, his estate came under the Court Of Wards. In 1895, his widow adopted his daughter's son Venkatanarayana Rao who became the proprietor to the estate of Chipurupalli later.

He lived for a short period and died in his thirty-ninth year i.e., in 1886. His daughter Achchayamma succeeded to the estate in A.D.1864. She married Ankitam Venkata Narasinga Rao, son of Sriramulu of Machilipatnam, who migrated to Visakhapatnam after that marriage. Even now, there is a street named after Achchiyamma in old town of Visakhapatnam.

Achchayamma, the daughter of China Venkata Jagga Rao looked after the affairs of the estate from 1864. After her death Ankitam Venkata Narasinga Rao became the zamindar of the estate.

In memory of his wife, he made a liberal donation of Rs 1,15,000 in her name, for the establishment of the Hindu College which is named as Mrs. Ankitam Venkata Narasinga Rao College in 1892. The establishment of that college, the first great seat of higher learning in the Northern Andhra, was a historical event which contributed to the spread of enlightenment in modern Andhra. He also developed and enriched the astronomical observatory, established by Chinna Venkata Jagga Rao. He is highly educated, served as Deputy Collector and was honoured as 'Rao Bahadur' by the English.

Gode Narayana Gajapati Rao (A. D. 1828-1903)

The most prominent of the Gode family whose name is immortalised in the annals of Andhra aristocracy for his contribution to modern education and fine arts, was 'Maharaja', 'Sir', 'K.C.I.E', Gode Narayana Gajapati Rao Bahadur (1828-1903).[287] He maintained cordial relations with several zamindars of his period. He was the disciple of Paravastu Srinivasacharyulu, a leading Sanskrit Scholar of Visakhapatnam. For about a decade (1840-1849), he was educated at Calcutta Hindu College. At Calcutta, his teachers included the well known scholars and reformers of the period, viz., Richardson, Dwarakanath Tagore, Kerr, Ramachandra Mitter, Knighton, Nash, Radhakantha Dev, Raja Satyacharan Ghosal and others. He was trained in English literature and modern science.[288]

The early maturity of his understanding was admired by all and his college course of study attended with brilliant success. It is said that as an English scholar, few equalled him. His own composition beared this out and the difference which the most eminent men of his time paid him 'puts' it beyond doubt. His career as a student foreshadowed his career as a man, and he distinguished himself in many branches of study. Poverty which has been generally the handmaid of success in the case of all our scholars, poets, and statesmen, could not act as an incentive to him as he was immensely wealthy; he became a scholar and Statesman by natural aptitude.[289]

After his stay in Calcutta, he returned to Visakhapantam in April, 1849, and joined his brother in the management of revenue affairs pertaining to their estates. After his arrival and until after his father's death in 1853, then the responsibility of the management of the estates devolved on him and on his brother, he was principally occupied in giving general information to those concerned on revenue and other matters. Continuing the noble example of loyalty, public spirit and philanthropy set by his ancestors, he invariably took a prominent part in all works of public utility and improvement, and identified himself with every good movement, whether intellectual, social or political that was started in the Presidency.

Narayana Gajapati assumed the zamindarship of Anakapalli-Visakhapatnam by virtue of his marriage with Chinna Janakamma, the adopted daughter of Ratnayamma. He represented the Constituency of Zamindars and landlords in the Legislative Council of Madras Presidency and held the office for sixteen years from 1863 to 1880. During this long period of uniterrupted labour, he proved himself a warm friend of liberalism and was greatly devoted to the rights and privileges of his countrymen. He possessed the firmness and decision requisite to a member of that august body, had great sagacity and foresight, and commanded much influence both personally and by his great zeal for the public good. He was conferred the title of 'Raja' in 1881 by Viceroy Rippon, and the award of the 'Honour of Service' from the Pope Leo XIII in 1891, the title of C.I.E., and 'Maharaja' in 1898 from the English and the prestigious title of 'Sir' (K.C.I.E) from the English Emperor Edward VII in Delhi Durbar held in 1902.[290]

As a high dignitary in the country he was specially invited on all important State functions. Lord Napier invited Gajapathi Rao on the occasion of the visit of the Duke of Edinburgh to Calcutta and arranged a special interview with him. Similarly, he was invited in 1875 to meet the Prince of Wales at Madras and in 1877 to Delhi to present at the Assemblage. He was granted in 1894 the right to wear freely and legally the robes characteristic of Knighthood in the aforesaid order together with its *insignia*.[291]

Apart from the honours recieved, Narayana Gajapati was active in various social services and educational activities such as establishing 'Victoria Ghosha Hospital' (originally Rani Lakshmi Narasayamma Zamana Hospital.) and 'Hindu Reading Room'. Narayana Gajapati's son-in-law, Raja Vairicherla Virabhadra Raju (1877-1918) the Zamindar of Kurupam, was also a member of the Madras Legislative Council and the Imperial Legislative Council. He spent one lakh of rupees to construct 'the Edward VII Coronation Market', opposite to the

Town Hall in Visakhapatnam, which came to be known later as "Kurupam Market."[292] He has presented a statue of Queen Victoria, 'a munificent gift to the town of Madras' on the occasion of the Golden Jubilee, and it was unveiled by the Governor of Madras, Lord Connemara.

In 1901, he has contributed a princely sum of rupees, one lakh, to the construction of a memorial to Queen Victoria at Calcutta.

As a member of the Central Committee Famine Charitable Fund at Calcutta, he subscribed rupees five thousand, and as a member of the Provincial Committee of the Famine Charitable Fund at Madras, he has contributed rupees four thousand.[293]

Narayana Gajapati was an admirer of Brahma Samaj as he imbibed the Brahmo ideas from Devendranath Tagore and Keshavchandra Sen, during his stay at Calcutta as a student. He was responsible for the starting of Anglo - Vernacular School at Visakhapatnam in A.D. 1860, which later developed into Hindu College and was finally christened as Mrs. A.V.N. College.

As a member of the Madras University Senate, Narayana Gajapati took active interest in the growth of education in Andhra region of the erstwhile Madras Presidency.[294] He generously contributed for the establishment of a 'Gold Medal' in Royal Asiatic Society in England, for an encouragement to oriental learning amongst the English speaking people throughout the world.

Narayana Gajapati is a good friend of the then British officers and Agents. Incidentally those that served as the Agents of the government at Visakhapatnam during his period, like Lord B. Smollet were very liberal and sympathetic towards the natives. In his Report to the government, he submitted that the salaries of the Indians who were in the service of the government have to be increased thrice. He advised his government to concentrate on the needs and welfare of the country people, than aiming to get more revenue. Similarly, due to their association with Narayana Gajapati, London Missionary Society established English Medium Schools at Visakhapatnam in 1855.

He was a significant estatedar and a number of zamindars of the period were his close associates. He made a visit with all splendour and glory to witness the Coronation Ceremony of the Raja of Venkatagiri.[295] Rama Varma, the Maharaja of Travancore, was his dearest friend. His relations with the other contemporary estate holders will be discussed elsewhere.

A number of poetical works were dedicated to him, of which mention should be made of *Satyavati Perinayam* written by Kakaraparti Buchchipatra Kavi. He financed the publication of a good number of literary works and dictionaries, and got translated the stories into Telugu from Persian, Urdu, Arabic languages as 'Char Darurish' stories.[296]

Anakapalli, the headquarters of the zamindari estate was elevated to the position of the municipality only due to the efforts of Narayana Gajapati. As a member of Madras Presidency Council, he tried hard to elevate a number of towns to the position of municipalities. Owing to his efforts, 'The Town Improvement Act of Madras' was passed in 1877, and 'the Madras District Municipality Act' was passed in 1884, and under those Acts towns like Anakapalli were changed into municipalies in the year 1878.

He continued the patronage of agriculture, particularly sugarcane, a fetching commercial crop to the agriculturists of Anakapalli area that situated in the Sarada river valley. Other allied industries like weaving, preparation of bronze utensils and preparation of bangles were also promoted under his patronage. He constructed a school, one hospital, market yard, a number of palaces and bungalows at Anakapalli.

The droughts during 1871-72, 1877-78, 1885-86, 1889, 1896-97 and the floods in 1870 and 1878 disturbed the normal life of people in his zamindari. To safeguard the people, he has undertaken a number of prospective measures. He distributed house-sites to a number of fishermen in Visakhapatnam. He passed away in May, 1903.

Narayana Gajapati Rao was one of the most honoured representatives of the aristocracy of South India. He displayed an enthusiastic warmth and uneffected sincerity. A. Vadivelu glorified good qualities of Narayana Gajapati in laudable terms thus:

"He was wedded to public life, he was active and enterprising; and possessed the rare talent of conciliating the minds of men and of infusing a spirit of unanimity into a heterogeneous mass of discordant parties. He hated all party feelings in movements of public good, and with a liberality becoming a nobleman would scorn all trifling distinctions. He was a truly greatman whom the world has agreed to praise after putting him to the severest test. His demeanour was pleasant, his conversation agreeable, and his manners affable and gracious. Even to those who were his inferiors he never exhibited the pride and hasteur which generally characterise the Indian Aristocracy, but was always calm and dignified. He belonged to that class of Indians who in every generation and in the most modest spirit discharge their duties and act their parts in life with devotion and efficiency and never 'play to the gallery'. He never made cheap bids for popularity by a compromise of his principles or by an extravagance of statement. He represented the best traditions of Indian Statesmanship, Indian thought and Indian personality. He had in his heart that love of truth, that rectitude of principle that wise benevolence, and above all that reverence for God."[297]

Narayana Gajapati married three wives. The first two predeceased him and the third wife Chinna Janakamma, the adopted daughter of Ratnayamma succeeded to the zamindari after him in A.D.1903. They had no sons and blessed with only two daughters - Sitayamma and Lakshmi Narasamma. Sitayamma married Thagore Saheb the prince of Wadwan; and Lakshmi Narasamma married Vairicherla Virabhadra Raju, son of Suryanarayana Raju the Zamindar of Kurupam and Chemudu.

Chinna Janakamma was also a good scholar in Sanskrit, Telugu and English. After the death of her husband she composed a work *Bhagavat Prardhana*. She looked after the estate affairs for some years after the death of her husband. She was very pious, charitable and generous. Soon after the retirement of Diwan Bahadur R. Dharma Rao Naidu, Diwan to the late Maharaja, this lady with the benefit of Western education of a high order and without the aid of a diwan, had the rare ability to manage for about nine months, an extensive estate in a statesman like marner. She assisted her husband in his last days in caring on the affairs of the vast and extensive estates in the zamindari. Though he had been in seclusion for many years, full effect was given by the China Janakamma to all his wishes, whether with regard to the charities he had instituted, or wanted to carry on the institutions he desired to maintain. As per the wishes of her husband she has constructed "The Victoria Diamond Jubilee Medical College", and a 'Poor house'.[298]

That poor house has a brief significant history to its credit. Originally it was an institution like choultry that aimed to feed the poor and shelterless, founded by Gode Suryanarayana Rao five decades back. In 1833, when a severe famine shook the entire coastal Andhra, a relief measure was taken-up to give food and shelter to the people. It was established near to his palace with arrangements to feed innumerable number, twice every day. Until his death, i.e. upto A.D.1853, he maintained it by feeding about a thousand poor every day. Narayana Gajapati Rao continued the same policy, maintained it for few years, and at the request of the Collector of Visakhapatnam shifted it outside the town. Gradually it was supported by public contributions and in 1899 it was abolished by the municipality. China Janakamma wanted to revive the charity again to that poor house and managed it with her own funds.[299]

Sitayamma, (Sitabai) the eldest daughter of China Janakamma lost her husband, Raja Thagore Saheb of Wadhwan and returned as widow to her maternal house, and settled at Suryabagh in Visakhapatnam. She had no children and spent rest of her life in literary activity, and in performing religious works. *Samvadatrayam*, a Sanskrit work which deals with the marriage ritual of Lord Venkateswara Swami of Upmaka, and another work *Upmaka Kshetramahatyam* was translated under her patronage.

Lakshmi Narasamma, the second daughter of Narayana Gajapati was given in marriage to Sri Raja Vairicherla Virabhadra Raju Bahadur, the zamindar of Kurupam and Chemudu on May 19, 1897. But unfortunately, after giving birth to three children, at the time of fourth delivery, i.e., on July 7, 1901, she passed away.

Lakshmi Narasamma received a good training under the careful guidance of several European ladies like M.S. Bolland, a lady of much wisdom.[300] This Rani Saheba of Kurupam was able to talk English with great ease and fluency. She was very fond of knowledge and used to read very useful and instructive books. During the brief span of her married life, she gave ample proof of the possession of remarkable qualities, which endeared her to the hearts of many poor and distressed persons. She had a musical talent, and had mastery over the piano. She was extremely good natured, and she would go about to the houses of the poor among her ryots, with her Raja Saheb, making kind enquiries of their welfare. Those afflicted with illness would find in her a great helper, and those with sorrow, a ready consoler. Her purse was always open to the poor, and she took a pride in succouring the needy and helping the deserving. To every one of her servants, she was extremely kind, and treated them like her own children.

A. Vadivelu glorifed this Lakshmi Narasamma as a "perfect angel remarkable alike for rare beauty of person, and great moral excellence."[301] Their eldest daughter Kamala Devi married the Zamindar of Gangapur, and younger daughter Rukmini Devi married the Zamindar of Dasapalla Estate. The details of her son, Suryanarayana Raju were not known. In course of time, as there was no heir apparent, the Zamindari of Anakapalli-Visakhapatnam went into the hands of those estatedars of Dasapalla, Kurupam and Chemudu, who held matrimonial relations with the Gode family.

Contribution of the Gode Family to Agriculture, Economy Literature and Culture

The contributions of Gode family in the socio-economic as well as religio-cultural spheres were in no way lesser than the services rendered by any of the significant zamindars of the times in the Madras Presidency. In the Northern Sircars, next to the Pusapati Zamindars of Vizianagaram, they stood second in the acquisition of big estates.

The English rule witnessed a number of changes in revenue, educational and administrative spheres. More significant of these were the revenue policies and in particular, the Permanent Settlement in Bengal and Madras Presidencies. As a consequence of the introduction of Permanent Settlement in the Northern Sircars of the Andhra region, a number of new zamindaris were created. Those zamindars became the staunch pillars of support to the English.[302]

Among those zamindars, a prominent family was that of the Godes. They continued the earlier tradition of royal patronage to art and literature. It suited to boost-up their image and also to the royal style of living in 'durbars' of the monarchical tradition of earlier years.

Normally it is stated that the life of the people under zamindars was oppressive and subject to exploitation.[303] The truth of this statement can be noticed when the people supported Jagannadha Payak Rao, who revolted against the English that supported the zamindari of the Godes.[304] The then Collector of Visakhapatnam division, Smith made it clear in his letter dated July 24, 1832 A.D. to the Board of Directors that the real cause of the revolt was the non-cordial relations of the Godes with the people in the zamindari.[305] But in the succeeding periods the Gode zamindars maintained very cordial relations with all sections of the people.

Pedda Jagga Rao, the first known significant zamindar became very popular as *Sapta Santana Nirmata*, founder of Sapta Santanas (seven meritorious deeds). Suryaprakasa Rao, who is highly educated in different subjects and different sciences in Western methods and approach, introduced all such systems for the benefit of the ryots in his zamindari. With his outstanding knowledge in botanical science he raised beautiful gardens like Poolbagh (also known as *Ranigari Thota*) at Anakapalli.[306] Very rare and important varieties of plants were raised in those gardens which were well-appreciated by the English officials like Dr Benza.[307] Being realised the importance of river waters like that of Sarada and Langulya for the irrigation in his zamindari estates, he constructed a dam across the river Sarada and diverted the Sarada waters to *Kondakarla Ava*, and thus utilised them for irrigation and agriculture development. When the popular sugarcane varieties like *Rayagada* and *Dubbukeli* normally adopted by the ryots of the area, were subject to diseases, and Suryaprakasa Rao introduced in 1839 A.D., Maritious variety in their place, which yielded successful results.[308] Owing to this initiation, Parry Company established its branch at Anakapalli to train the peasants in the advanced methods of preparation of jaggery; and also to give loans to ryots for its equipment.

Dr Benza in his notes of his journey to the Northern sircars with Sir Fredirick Adam in A.D.1835 observed thus: "he is very partial to European manners and adopted them (not for affection sake). He speaks and writes the English language uncommonly well, and his pronounciation evinces hardly and foreign accent. He disregards the show and glitter, the suite of attendants, the umbrella-carriers, and other indispensible appendages of his countrymen, of rank corresponding to his own, and wears none of their ornaments. He came to visit the Governor on a superb Arabian horse, without a single attendant. We accompanied him on his return to Anakapalli, and he conducted us to his garden, which was laid out in a most beautiful style, rich with indigenous and exotic plants and trees."[309]

Gode China Venkata Jagga Rao, who was considered as a great scientist of their period, had deep interest on environmental study and on modern crops. He closely studied the relation between the environment and crops. *Nilagiri Charitramu*, a work that was written in dedication to him by Kola Seshachalam thoroughly described how some of the hil ranges were suitable to raise Western crops like radish and beetroot.[310] Thus, for the improvement of agriculture and thus to promote the life standards of the peasants, the zamindars of the Gode family spared no efforts.

Gode zamindars were great builders. They constructed religious shrines, royal palaces, bungalows, choultries and buildings for hospitals and educational institutions.[311]

Pedda Jagga Rao was a devotee of Sri Rama and constructed a temple to Kodandaramaswami at Visakhapatam.[312] His daughter Subhadramma in praise of that Lord, written "*Kodanda Rama Satakam* with a maukuta *Charu Vaisakhapuradhama – Jaggrayahridayabdhisoma Kodandarama.*"[313] That temple was the present Sitaramaswami temple, near Ghosha Hospital in Visakhapatnam.[314]

Gode Suryaprakasa Rao, as described earlier, constructed magnificent palaces which were appreciated by English officials. He constructed a dam across the river Sarada.

Gode Janakamma, the wife of Suryaprakasa Rao, with an intention to promote female education constructed one school for girls in Visakhapatnam with the help of the missionaries and the District Collector William Reid, which was later developed into St. Joseph's College. That school was perhaps the first school established for women in Andhra.[315]

Gode Suryanarayana Rao constructed bathing ghats at Sapta Godavari and liberally donated lands to temples. He made endowments to the Vanamamalai *Matha* and Pardhasaradhi temple at Madras.[316]

Gode Suryanarayana Rao acquired great knowledge in the science of architecture (*vastu*) and constructed some palaces in 1830 A.D., for their residence at Visakhapatnam near Upputeru. Nadiminti Sarvamangala Sastri, his court-poet, in one of the verses, expressed his shock and astonishment for the lavish expenditure done on construction activity during the period of Suryanarayana Rao, thus:

Karunamadhadharunam silpakanam tadhaivacha
Gode narayana dravya mayyo ayyo vrudha vrudha[317]

Gode China Venkata Jagga Rao, as he happened to be a great scientist, constructed an astronomical laboratory and an observatory at Dabagardens, in Visakhapatnam with an intention to teach people the process of time.[318] That observatory is called the local people *Chukkalameda*, whose traces existed upto 1956.[319]

Gode Narayana Gajapati Rao may be stated as the chief architect of modern Visakhapatnam and Anakapalli. He has constructed a magnificent building for residence, buildings for school, hospital and travellers' bungalow at Anakapalli. Foundations were laid during his period for Anakapalli market.[320] He was responsible for the establishment of Anglo-Vernacular School in Visakhapatnam in 1860, which later developed into Hindu College and was finally christened as Mrs A.V.N. College, during the time of Ankitam Venkata Narasinga Rao, the son-in-law of China Venkata Jagaa Rao, in memory of his wife, Achchayamma.

During his regime East India Company's power was dismissed and Queen Victoria's rule began. As stated already, in appreciation to his services, British Government honoured Narayana Gajapati with a number of titles like 'Sir', 'K.C.I.E.', and 'Maharaja'. Though liberal in his outlook, and though influenced by Brahma Samaj[321], he patronised Hindu religion. Being rulers, the missionaries converted a number of Hindus into Christianity. In 1836, missionaries established 'London Mission Memorial Church' on the main road of Visakhapatnam and deliberately made conversions in huge number. To safeguard the interests of Hinduism, at the request of the elders of the town, to put a check to the religious conversions, he opened a 'Hindu Reading Room' on the main road just opposite to London Church. The Hindu Reading Room flourished as a centre of Hindu religious activities, and as a magnificent library of Hindu works.

He joined hands along with other zamindars like Pusapatis for the establishment of a civil hospital at Visakhapatnam which latter transformed as King George Hospital.

His son-in-law, the Raja of Kurupam, Vairicherla Virabhadra Raju purchased a Dutch Bungalow and established a hospital named after his wife, Lakshmi Narasamma, which hospital later changed as the Ghosha Hospital.

He has established a hospital at Kurupam, the chief town of his estate and has named it after his late lamented wife, Sri Rani Lakshmi Narasamma. This institution was a great blessing to the inhabitants of villages belonging to his zamindari as also to the neighbouring zamindaris.

He established Kurupam Market in Visakhapatnam as a gift to King Edward, and later to Queen Victoria.[322] In those days, it was the only market in Visakhapatnam.

It was during the last days of Narayana Gajapati Rao, in A.D. 1887, the 'Golden Jubilee Year' of Queen Victoria's reign was celebrated in all important cities in India; and to commemorate that occasion, a "Statue of Victoria" was installed in the four-road junction of the old city of Visakhapatnam.[323]

One important memorial, Kurupam tomb very nearer to beach in eastern side of Visakhapatnam was constructed by the Kurupam Zamindar, Vairicherla Virabhadra Raju as a symbol of love, to ensure that his story of love was not lost in some obscure pages of history. That beautiful monument, which still exists in Visakhapatnam as a heritage site, incorporates the architectural styles of different cultures including the Mughal, the European, the Dravidian and the North Indian.[324]

The Gode zamindari family made a significant contribution for the flourishment and promotion of literature, which will be discussed in another chapter.

They were great patron of poets, and some were themselves good writers. Madine Subhadramma, daughter of Pedda Jagga Rao, China Janakarmma, the wife of Narayana Gajapati Rao, composed a number of works. Under their patronage flourished a number of poets like Kakarparti Tirupati Patra Kavi, Krishna Kavi, Buchchipatra Kavi, Akkinepalli Narasimha Kavi, Yaramilli Perraja Kavi, Nadiminti Sarvamangalesvara Sastri, Ranimahagni Chinna Nrisimha Kavi, Paravastu Srinivasa Jagannadha Swami, Paravasthu Venkata Ranganadha Swami, Gorty Venkata Sastri and Kakarparti Sitarama Swami.

As discussed earlier, there was no male succession to the Gode family. Ankitam, Vairicherla, Jeypore, and Dasapalla families succeded to the Gode zamindari and followed the footprints of the Gode family in patronising literature.

Rani Sitabai and Rani Lakshmi Narasamma, the daughters of Gode Narayana Gajapati Rao, seemed to be the last successors of the Gode family.

But, one Gode Jagannadha Rao, whose relation with the main Gode family is not known, appeared to in some of the stanzas with a suffix (*makuta*), *Jnanabhogi Gode Jagannadha Yogi*. Nimisha Kavi Venkatesam composed a *Sataka* in the *Sisa* metre on the subject of Vedanta addressing to Gode Jagannadha Yogi.[325]

In the known history of the Gode family, the position of Gode Jagannadha Yogi, who was called as 'Jnana Bhogi' is not known. Nidadavolu Venkata Rao identified this Jagannadha Yogi as a brother of Narayana Gajapathi Rao.[326] No doubt, Narayana Gajapati Rao had a stepbrother, Gode China Venkata Jagga Rao, the greatest scientist in this family. Though chronologically he belongs to the same decades, without concrete grounds, it is very difficult to identify that great scientist as this Jagannadha Yogi. His relation with the main family is not known.

Thus, next to the Kakarlapudi and Pusapati zamindars, the Gode zamindars played a significant role in the annals of Anakapalli – Visakhapatnam areas, for more than two hundred years.

The details of the early members of the family were not clearly known, from the period of Gode Jagga Rao, who accompanied Mr John Andrews, chief of the Council of East India Company from Machilipatnam to Visakhapatnam. From then onwards, Gode family held sway over the Visakhapatnam province for more than five generations and showed their impact, on the economy and culture of the land.

They held ownership of estates of Anakapalli, Embaram, Kuppili, Koruprlu, Gottipalli, Godicherla, Bharanikam, Mungapaka, Sriramapuram, Sher Mohammadpuram – all situated in Visakhapatnam District. They supported the English Company against the rebellious estatedars and were taken into confidence by the Company administration, and held significant position as well as reputed honours among the other zamindars.

Almost all the zamindars and their ladies were learned scholars and patronaged literature in their durbars. Surya Prakasa Rao acquired considerable knowledge in botany and other sciences. Venkata Jagga Rao promoted the cause of learning and the development of sciences; and also established an astronomical laboratory at Visakhapatnam. As discussed earlier a number of works of different poets were encouraged and patronaged during this period. It is due to their effort, the first standard dictionary of Sanskrit to Telugu *Sarvasabda Sambodhini* was compiled. It is also stated that first Telugu Newspaper *Vrittanti* was founded by them.[327] Not only mere patronage, a number of books got published with their financial assistance. They welcomed and honoured the renounced poets and scholars of the times.

The Gode family and their descendants undoubtedly laid the foundation for the growth of modern Visakhapatnam. There was no field, no public cause, that they did not donate to most of the existing institutions in Anakapalli – Visakhapatnam areas, which anybody proudly boast of all shining examples of their philanthropy and magnanimity. The Victoria Gosha Hospital, Vizagapatnam Medical School (the forerunner of the Andhra Medical College), the Civic Hospital which later developed into King George Hospital, the Gajapati Rao Orphanage and Poor House, Mrs. A.V.N. College, Kurupam Market, Turner's Choultry, Hindu Reading Room, Rani Chandramani Devi Hospital - all those and many more institutions were established in Visakhapatnam by the Gode family and their descendants. The road connecting Maharanipeta area with the beach was laid by them. They also helped in the development of many temples in the town, including the Sitaramaswami temple, of which the Ankitam family continues to be the trustees. All those stand testimony to the munificence and magnificent liberality of the zamindari family. At Anakapalli, Poolbagh, Travellers Bungalow, Godavari Palace, Market yard and the very establishment of Anakapalli Municipality was done under the regime of the Gode family.

Ankitam Family

As discussed earlier in the history of the Gode family, the Ankitam family came to Visakhapatnam areas during the period of Ankitam Sriramulu who was the Diwan to the Nawab of Machilipatnam. Their ancestors held respectable and important positions under the Qutb Shahis of Golkonda.[328]

Gode China Venkata Jagga Rao's daughter Achchayamma was given in marriage to Rao Bahadur Ankitam Venkata Narasinga Rao, the son of Diwan Ankitam Sriramulu of Machilipatnam. During his childhood when he lost his father Sriramulu, he was taken to Visakhapatnam and brought up under the care of his maternal grandfather.[329] He completed his education under Mr Porter and then under Rev. J. Hay, D.D., the father of moder education in Northern Sircars. By sheer didn't of energy, good character and perseverance, at the very young age he entered the service in the English Company and rose to the position of Deputy Collector. His marriage with Achchayamma of the Gode family closely connected the Ankitam family with the history of Visakhapatnam.[330]

As stated earlier in the history of the Godes, Gode Venkata Jagga Rao had no sons; and his only daughter Achchayamma inherited to the zamindari. As she happens to be the wife of Ankitam Venkata Narasinga Rao, in order to manage the estate, he has resigned to his post of Deputy Collector. Mrs Achchayamma Narasinga Rao is a lady of fine character, elevated thoughts and noble disposition. In recognition to her noted qualities, the Government of Madras conferred on her the personal distinction of 'Rani'.

An educated and a cultured man himself Ankitam Venkata Narasinga Rao enlarged the Observatory founded by Gode China Venkata Jagga Rao, his father-in-law. He enriched that Observatory by spending lakhs of rupees. He added with modern equiment and furnished the government daily with Meteorological Reports. He was appointed as "Honorary Meteorological Reporter to Government of India" for Visakhapatnam. In recognition of his services, the Government of India conferred on him, the title of 'Rao Bahadur'. He was elected Fellow of the Royal Astronomical Society in 1871 and of the Royal Geographical Society in 1872. The National Indian Association, London, compliments A.V. Narasinga Rao for maintaining the Observatory, and for the conduct of his careful and regular observation on temperature, rainfall, and wind direction etc.[331]

A.V. Narasinga Rao has erected an expensive and durable Flag Staff on the Dolphin's Nose, and the time signals were hoisted on it every day morning to indicate time. That signal tower was an old observatory and it was placed at the disposal of the English for the exhibition of a lantern for the benefit of the shipping. But during October 1876, on the occasion of a cyclone, the light and the position of the house were destroyed.

In memory of his beloved wife Achiyamma, Venkata Narasinga Rao made a liberal donation of rupees 1,15,000 for the establishment of the Hindu College which was renamed as Mrs Ankitam Venkata Narsinga Rao College in 1892.[332] It is the first great seat of higher education in Northern Andhra which contributed to the spread of enlightenment in modern Andhra.

He was succeeded by Ankitam China Venkata Jagga Rao, who was also a learned scholar. He also spared no efforts for the promotion of the Observatory and Library founded by his grand father at Visakhapatnam. He established a hospital for the public service. He has shown much interest in the collection of antiquarian remains of historical importance of different countries. He is a member of various prestigious associations, and with that connection, he visited England. He has interested in technology, particularly in techno-crafts. He was a brilliant intellect, with handsome personality and fascinating manners and was honoured with the titles like 'Sri Raja' and 'Rao Bahadur'.

He published a number of books like *Drigganita-panchangam* and *Deviastangahridayam.*[333] He married five wives of different communities and begot three daughters.

It is stated that he followed and practiced 'tantricism' which caused his death.[334]

References

1. *Kakarlapudi Vari Vamsavali*, p. 2.
2. Rajendra Prasad, H. (Ed.) *Visakhapatnam Zill Grama Kaifiyatulu*, p. 17.
3. *Proceedings of A.P.H.C.*, Vol.XII, p. 217.
4. *Ibid*, p. 220.
5. *Proceedings of A.P.H.C.*, Vol.XII, p. 217.
6. *Ibid*, pp. 3-4.
7. *Ibid*, p. 6.
8. *Ibid.*
9. *Ibid*, p. 4.
10. Rajendra Prasad, (Ed.) *Op .Cit*, p. 1.
11. *S.I.I.* Vol.VI, No. 731.
12. *Ibid*, Vol. V, No.1312.
13. *Ibid*, Vol. VI, No.1184.
14. *Proceedings of A.P.H.C.*, Vol. XII, 1988, p. 217.
15. *Ibid*, p. 5.
16. Satyanarayana Murty, T., *Padmanabha Yuddham*, p. 7.
17. *Somanadha Kavi*, Rekapalli, *Rukmavati Parinayam Asvasa I* Stanza-9.
18. Satyanarayana Murty, T., *Padmanabha Yuddham*, p. 14, also referred to in some stanzas in *Rangaraya Charitramu*, written by Dittakavi Narayana Kavi.
19. *Ibid.*
20. A letter dated 8-3-1758 sent by the Vizagapatam Chief to the Governor of Madras States this fact. *Rangaraya Charitramu* also states "Raju Chavukunanta parasura balamu santasam bande….."
21. Col. Malleson, *Decisive Battles of India*, p. 57.
22. Forde. L., *Lord Clives Right handman* pp. 71-72, and J.D.B.Gribble, *A History of the Deccan*, Vol.II, p. 59: cited by M.S.R. Anjaneyulu in *Vizagapatnam District, 1769 – 1834*.
23. Satyanarayana Murty, T., *Padmanabha Yuddham*, p. 30.
24. *Ibid*, p. 42, V.D.R., (3744 : 102 – 3).
25. Anjaneyulu, M.S.R., *Vizagapatam District, 1769 – 1834* p. 40; Collector to B.O.R, 12 April. 1814, V.D.R. (3752 : 87).

26. Satyanarayana Murty, T., Op. Cit., p. 42.
27. Revenue Consultation 6A; 654 cited T.Satyanarayana Murty in *Padmanabha Yuddham*, p. 87.
28. Anjaneyulu, M.S.R., *Op. Cit.*, p. 39.
29. Francis, W., *Vizagapatam District Gazetteer*, p. 327.
30. Satyanarayana Murty, T., Op. Cit., p. 66.
31. Smith's letter to the Board of Directors dated 24th July, 1832 A.D., V.D.R.
32. Acting Collector to B.O.R., 24th July 1832, V.D.R., (4744 : 309).
33. Anjaneyulu, M.S.R., *Op. Cit.*, p. 68.
34. 24th July 1832, V.D.R. (4744 : 305-14)
35. Russell, G.E., *Report on the Disturbances in Parlakimidy, Vizagapatam and Goomsoor, in 1832* – 36, p. 6-7.
36. *Ibid,* p. 6.
37. Anjaneyulu, M.S.R., *Op. Cit.*, p. 70.
38. "Payaka Rao Tupaki Gunduche Kalage Visakha Pattanamu Kampamu Nondenu Golugonda...."
39. Anjaneyulu, M.S.R., *Op. Cit.*, p. 70.
40. Francis, W., *Op. Cit.*, p. 249.
41. Russell, G.E., Op. Cit., Vol. I, p. 6.
42. Francis, W., *Op. Cit.*, p. 313.
43. General Burton, *An Indian Olio,* p. 323, cited by Francis, W., in p. 313.
44. Francis, W., Op. Cit., p. 312.
45. *Proceedings of A.P.H.C.,* Vol. XII, p. 271.
46. *Ibid,* p. 223.
46A. Nagamamba, E. *History of the Pusapati Family* (Unpublished theis submitted to Andhra University 1986).
46B. Besides the number of articles and books some of the scholars like E. Nagamamba, T. Balanagamani etc., worked on this subject for their Doctoral Degrees; and A.V.D. Sharma also published some monographs on this aspect.
46C. Sudershan Rao, Y., *Andhra between the Empires*, p. 29
46D. Nagamamba, E., Op. Cit. p. 167.
46E. Anjaneyulu, M.S.R., Op. Cit. pp. 202-203.
46F. Donappa, T. Op. Cit. p. 290.
46G. Rao P.R. *History of Modern Andhra*, p. 237.
47. Subba Rao, Rallabandi, (Ed.) *Kalinga Desa Charitra*, p. 298.
48. *Ibid.*
49. Carmichael, D.F., (Ed.) *Manual of the District of Vizagapatnam*, p. 320.
50. *Ibid.*

51. Tulasi Devi, M., *Matsyas of Oddadi* (Unpublished Thesis of Andhra University) p. 2.
52. Vadivelu, A., *Aristocracy of Southern India* Vol. II, p. 190.
53. Tulasidevi, M., *Op. Cit.,* p. 3.
54. *Visakhapatnam Zilla Grama Kaifiyatulu-Madugula,* pp. 13, 14.
55. Epi. Andhrica, Vol. VI, p. 77.
56. Epigraphia Indica, Vol. IV, p. 356.
57. Venkata Pradeep, L., *History of the Mandalika Families in Medieval Kalinga Andhra* (Unpublished Thesis of Andhra University), p. 365.
58. *S.I.I.,* Vol. VI, Nos.836, 950, 980, 1169 etc.,
59. *Ibid,* Vol. X, Nos. 741, 742.
60. Tulasi Devi, M., *Op. Cit.,* p. 367.
61. Yasoda Devi, V., *"History of the Andhra Country Subsidiary Dynasties". J.A.H.R.S. Vol. XVIII – XXVIII.*
62. *S.I.I.,* Vol.VI, Nos. 966, 950.
63. Anjani Kumari, B., *Madugula Zamindari – An offshoot of the Jeypore of Orissa – studies on Orissan History, Cultural Heritage of Orissa,* Vol.III, 2011, pp. 13-18.
64. Vadivelu, A., *Op. Cit.,* p. 190.
65. *Visakhapatnam Zilla Grama Kaifiyatulu – Madugula,* pp. 13-14.
66. Anjani Kumari, B., *Op. Cit.,* pp. 13-18.
67. *Ibid.*
68. Vadivelu, A., *Op. Cit.,* p. 190.
69. *Ibid.*
70. Donappa, T., *Andhra Samasthanamulu – Sahitya Poshanamu,* p. 321.
71. *Visakhapatnam Zilla Grama Kaifiyatulu – Madugula,* pp. 13-14.
72. Francis, W., *Op. Cit.,* p. 322.
73. Sudershan Rao, Y., *Andhra between the Empires,* p. 14.
74. Anjaneyulu, M.S.R., *Op. Cit.,* pp. 204-205.
75. Collector of B.O.R, 9 July 1794, V.D.R. (370 : 337).
76. Francis, W., *Op. Cit.,* p. 321.
77. *Visakhapatnam Zilla Grama Kaifiyatulu – Vaddadi,* pp. 31-33.
78. Anjaneyulu, M.S.R., *Op. Cit.,* p. 205.
79. *Ibid,* p. 206.
80. Representation of Jagannadha Bhupati to John Snow, April 5, 1794, V.D.R. (3699 : 329-333).
81. Anjaneyulu, M.S.R, *Op. Cit.,* pp. 206-207.

82. Letters of the Collector to B.O.R, 26th January 1808, 20 May 1813, V.D.R. (3745 : 22) and V.D.R. (3750 : 138-55).
83. *Ibid,* 29 August 1817, V.D.R. (3755 : 261, 270).
84. Sarma, A.V.D., *Integration of Andhra and Orissa Cultures*, Delhi, 1986. pp. 24-25.
85. Vadivelu, A., *Op. Cit.,* Vol. II, p. 192.
86. Letter of Sub-Collector to the Collector, 16 October 1834, V.D.R. (4746: 359 – 61).
87. Carmichael, D.F., *Op. Cit.,* pp. 320-322.
88. Francis, W., *Op. Cit.,* p. 321.
89. *Ibid.*
90. Vadivelu, A., *Op. Cit.,* p. 192.
91. *Ibid.*
92. *Ibid.*
93. Francis, W., *Op. Cit.,* p. 321.
94. *Ibid*, p. 322.
95. Vadivelu, A., *Op. Cit,* Vol. II, p. 192
96. Francis. W., Op. Cit., p. 322.
97. *Ibid.*
98. Vadivelu, A., Op. Cit., Vol. II, p. 193.
99. *Ibid.*
100. *Ibid.*
101. *Ibid.*
102. *Ibid.*
103. Arudra, Samagra Andhra Sahityam, Vol. III, p. 367.
104. *Ibid.*
105. Carmichael, D.F., *Op. Cit.,* p. 320.
106. Donappa, T., *Op. Cit.,* p. 321.
107. Sarma, A.V.D., *Op. Cit.,* pp. 24-25.
108. Suryanarayana, Kolluru, *Madhyandhra Yuga Charitraka Vyasamulu,* p. 51.
109. Correspondance Relative to the permanent settlement of zamindaris in the late second division of Vizagapatam, p. 17.
110. *Ibid.*
111. Carmicheal, D.F., *Op. Cit.,* p. 316.
112. Letter of Zamindar of Golugonda to the Collector, March 25, 1822, V.D.R., (4735 : 146).
113. Anjaneyulu, M.S.R., *Op. Cit.,* p. 182.

114. Chief of B.O.R, July 9, 1794, V.D.R. (3700 : 342).
115. Letter of Sita Ramaraju to the Chief, May 31, 1779.
116. Resolution of the Chief and Council, May 31, 1779, V.D.R. (3714 : 57).
117. Statement of the Gross Revenue of the Zamindari under the Vizianagaram Family, August 30, 1783, V.D.R. (3686 : 375).
118. Report of the Committee of Circuit p. 16.
119. July 28, 1785, V.D.R, (3688 : 195-196.
120. February 5, 1786, V.D.R. (3689 : 35).
121. Anjaneyulu, M.S.R., *Op. Cit.,* p. 182.
122. Letter of Collector to B.O.R, 27 June 1831, V.D.R., (4743 : 212).
123. Snow to B.O.R, March 11 and 12, 1794, V.D.R. (3699 : 146, 182, 191-92).
124. Snow's Minute, August 30, 1794, V.D.R. (3702 : 33-35).
125. Letter of Webb to B.O.R January 5, 1797 B.O.R (BORC, p. 93).
126. Letter of Brown to Webb, January 6 and 20, and February-2, 1797, V.D.R. (3709 : 27-28, 57-65, 95-96, 155-58).
127. Letter of Collector to B.O.R, September 2, 1804, V.D.R. (3741 : 216).
128. Letter of Collector to B.O.R, July 18, 1805, V.D.R. (3721 : 106).
129. Letter of Collector to B.O.R, July 11, 1807, V.D.R. (3744 : 119).
130. Letter of Collector to B.O.R, 8 August 1812, V.D.R. (3749 : 178).
131. Letter of Collector to B.O.R, December 22, 1829, V.D.R. (4741 : 448).
132. Anjaneyulu, M.S.R., *Op. Cit.,* p. 184.
133. Russell, G.E., *Op. Cit.,* Vol. I, p. 7.
134. Letter of Magistrate to the Chief Secretary to the Government, 30 May 1836, V.D.R. (6639:300-02).
135. Letter of Collector to B.O.R , 30 June 1837, V.D.R (6641:312-26).
136. Anjaneyulu, M.S.R., *Op. Cit.,* p. 186.
137. Letter Of Collector to B.O.R, 30 June 1837,V.D.R.(6641:312-26).
138. Francis, W., *Op. Cit.,* p. 249.
139. *Ibid.*
140. *Ibid*, p. 250.
141. Proceedings of *A.P.H.C*, Vol. XXVI, p. 110.
142. Francis, W., *Op. Cit.,* p. 250.
143. *Ibid.*
144. G.O. NO. 744, Judicial, dated 26th March 1888.
145. *Ibid.*
146. Francis, W., *Op. Cit.,* p. 251.
147. *Ibid.*
148. *Ibid.*

149. G.O. No. 1685, Judical, dated 12th August 1895.
150. Francis, W., *Op. Cit.,* p. 252.
151. *Ibid*, pp. 251-252.
152. *Ibid.*
153. Itihas, Vol. XXII, p. 71.
154. G.O. No.1941, judicial, dated 23rd November 1882.
155. Francis, W., *Op. Cit.,* pp. 252-253.
156. *Ibid*, p. 254.
157. *Ibid.*
158. *Ibid.*
159. *Ibiḍ*, p. 254.
160. *Ibid.*
161. *Ibid.*
162. *Ibid.*
163. *Ibid.*
164. *O.S. No.9 of 1894* on the file of the Vizagapatanam District Court.
165. Soma sekhara Sarma, M., *History of the Redid Kingdoms* p. 171.
166. Suryanarayana, Kolluru, *Op. Cit.,* p. 71.
167. Francis, W., *Op. Cit.,* p. 256.
168. Firman issused by the Mughal Emperor to the English Company, dated August 12, 1765.
169. Sanad under the seal of Nizam Ally Cawn for the Five Circars, November 12, 1776.
170. *Ibid.,* Appendix-II.
171. *Ibid.,* Appendix-V.
172. *Ibid.*
173. Phillimore, *Historical Records of the Survey of India,* (1815-1830) Dehradun p. 31.
174. 5 January 1824, General Reports of the B.O.R, paras 1236-1241, W. Francis, *Op. Cit.,* p. 57 and 5 January 1839, V.D.R., (6643:3-6).
175. Phillimore ; *Op. Cit.,* p. 31.
176. Letter of Collector to B.O.R, 21 October 1828 V.D.R.(4740:293).
177. B.O.R to the collector 20 February 1811, V.D.R.(3727:109-11).
178. G.O. No. 744, Judicial, dated 26th March 1888.
179. If by the regulation II of 1819 the governor-in-council had power to arrest and commit to jail by warrants, by the Act XXIV of 1839, the District Collector got power to deport men from the agency.
180. Francis, W., *Op. Cit.,* p. 251.
181. *Ibid.*

182. *G.O. No.1685,* Judicial dated 12th August 1895.
183. Francis, W., *Op. Cit.,* p. 252.
184. *Ibid,* p. 251.
185. *Ibid.*
186. *Proceedings of A.P.H.C.,* Vol. XXXIV, p. 244.
187. *Ibid,* p. 245.
188. *Proceedings of A.P.H.C.,* Vol. XXXIV, p. 244.
189. *Ibid,* p. 245.
190. *Ibid,* p. 244.
191. Narayanarao, G., *Vipalavagni – Alluri,* Visakhapatnam, p. 39.
192. *Proceedings of A.P.H.C.,* Vol. XXXIV, 2010, p. 243.
193. *S.I.I.,* Vol.VI, No.731.
194. *Proceedings of A.P.H.C.,* Vol. XII, 1998, p. 221, 1988.
195. *S.I.I.,* Vol. VI, No. 731.
196. Narayana Kavi, Dittakavi, *Ranga Raya Charitra,* Asvasa – III, Stanza 29.
197. Satyanarayana Murty, T., *Op. Cit.,* p. 22.
198. Carmichael, D.F., *Op. Cit.,* pp. 332-333.
199. Francis, W., *Op. Cit.,* p. 222.
200. Carmichael, D.F., *Op. Cit.,* p. 333.
201. *Ibid,* p. 339.
202. Francis. W., *Op. Cit.,* p. 221.
203. *Ibid,* p. 314.
204. Except tradition, there is no connection to this village with Krishna Deva Raya. After conquering Aratla Kota, near Penta Kota and Satyavaram, Krishna Raya came to Simhachalam via agency route and not touched Rayavaram. Basing on a damaged record which refers to one Raya the local people connect this village with Krishna Raya, which is not correct.
205. Carmichael, D.F., *Op. Cit.,* p. 349.
206. *Ibid.*
207. Suryanarayana, Kolluru, *Puratana Saiva Kshetram Panchadarla,* p. Introduction, p. 2.
208. Carmichael, D.F., Op. Cit., p. 347.
209. Henry Morris; "*A Descriptive and Historical Account of the Godavari District in the Madras Presidency*", p. 177.
210. Board of Revenue Records: Appendices to the Estates Land Act Committee Report, Appendix II, p. 8.
211. Henry Morris, *Op. Cit.,* p. 180.
212. In the India Office there are three independent translations of this important grant. In these translations Vizagapatam is spelled as Ishankpattanam,

Visiagapatam and Izapatam. William Foster; *The English Factories in India 1634 – 1636*, Oxford, 1911, p. 14.

213. Henry Morris, *Op. Cit*, p. 193.
214. *Ibid.*
215. *Ibid.*
216. Saunders to Richard Bouchier (Governor of Bombay) RFSG: Dairy, 24th September 1752, pp. 43-46.
217. RFSG: Letters from FSG, 12th January 1754, p. 3.
218. RFSG: Dairy, 7th January 1754, pp. 7-8.
219. RFSG: Dairy, 12th January 1754, p. 3.
220. RFSG: Country Correspondence (MRO, 1913), 1757, p. 28.
221. Gribble, J.D.B., A History of the Deccan, London, 1924, Vol.II, p. 48.
222. Mallerson, G.B., History of the French in India, Edinburgh, 1909, p. 505, see also H. Dodwell, Duplex and Clive, London, 1923, p. 100.
223. RFSG: CC, 1758, pp. 47-48.
224. Bengal to Madras, 14th September 1758, Select committee consultations, 18th October 1758, Vol. 52, pp. 416 – 417, quoted in Lanka Sundaram *"The Revenue Administration of the Northern Circars"*, JAHRS, Vol. VI, p. 90.
225. Varma, G.R., *Mailaradeva*, pp. 93-94.
226. Arudra, *Op. Cit.,* Vol. III, p. 334.
227. Anjaneyulu, M.S.R., Op. Cit., p. 70.
228. Donappa, T., *Op. Cit.,* p. 134.
229. Murty, T.S.N., *Proceedings of A.P.H.C.,* Vol. XII, p. 217.
230. Sudershan Rao, Y, *Op. Cit.,* p. 31.
231. Ramakrishna, V., *Proceedings of A.P.H.C.,* Vol. XII, p. 228.
232. Suryanarayana, K, "*Contribution of the Gode family to Agriculture*", Proceedings of A.P.H.C. Vol. XXXII, p. 83.
233. Surya Rao, Angara, *Op. Cit.,* p. 49.
234. Donappa, T., *Op. Cit.,* p. 11.
235. Anjaneyulu, M.S.R., *Op. Cit.,* p. 34.
236. Varma, G.R., *Op. Cit.,* p. 93.
237. Varma, G.R., *Gudi – Gumpha*, p. 87.
238. *Ibid.* p. 93.
239. *Ibid.*
240. Vadivelu, A., *Op. Cit.,* Vol. II, p. 1.
241. Arudra, *Op. Cit.,* Vol. III, p. 334.
242. Donappa, T., *Op. Cit.,* p. 134.

243. Vadivelu, A., *Op. Cit.,* Vol. II, p. 2.
244. Varma, G.R., *Op. Cit.,* p. 93.
245. Vadivelu, A., *Op. Cit.,* p. 3.
246. *Ibid,* pp. 3-4.
247. Sudershan Rao, Y., *Op. Cit.,* p. 73.
248. Firminger, Walter. F., (ed.), The Fifth Report from the Select committee on the affairs of the East India Company, Vol. II Madras Presidency (Madras, 1866). Appendix B: James Grant, '*Political Survey of the Northern Circars*', pp. 131-265.
249. *Ibid.*
250. 26th April 1768 as stated in Military Consultations (61: 540 – 48) cited by M.S.R. Anjaneyulu, p. 91.
251. Firminger, W.F., *Op. Cit.,* p. 3.
252. Revenue letter from the Court of Directors to Fort. St. George, 11th February 1801, W.F., Firminger, Op. Cit., p. 51.
253. 5th January 1824, *General Reports of the B.O.R.*, Paras 1236-1241; W. Francis, *Op. Cit.,* p. 57 and 5th January 1939, V.D.R., (6643 : 3-6).
254. Francis, W., *Op. Cit.,* p. 327.
255. Proceedings of *A.P.H.C.,* Vol. XII, p. 228.
256. Vadivelu, A., *Op. Cit.,* Vol. II, p. 4.
257. *S.I.I.,* Vol.VI
258. Francis, W., *Op. Cit.*
259. Vadivelu, A., *Op. Cit.,* p. 4.
260. Arudra, *Op. Cit.,* p. 137.
261. Francis, W., *Op. Cit.,* p. 221.
262. *Ibid.*
263. *Ibid.*
264. Vadivelu, A., *Op. Cit.,* Vol. II, p. 5.
265. *Proceedings of the A.P.H.C.,* Vol. XII, p. 271.
266. Anjaneyulu, M.S.R., *Op. Cit.,* p. 71.
267. Government to the Chief and Council, 24th July 1832, V.D.R, (4744 : 305 – 14).
268. Russell, G.E., *Reports on the Disturbances in Parlakimidy, Vizagapatnam and Goomsoor in 1832 – 36*, Madras 1856, Vol. I.
269. Letter of Acting Collector to B.O.R., 24th July 1832, V.D.R, (4744 : 309)
270. Russell, G.E., *Op. Cit.,* p. 6.
271. Letter of Collector to B.O.R., 26th May 1834, V.D.R. (4746 : 155).
272. Vadivelu, A., *Op. Cit.,* Vol. II, p. 7.
273. Proceedings of the *A.P.H.C.* Vol. XII, p. 222.
274. Varma, G.R., *Op. Cit.,* pp. 93-94.

275. Vadivelu, A., *Op. Cit.,* Vol. II, p. 7.
276. Arudra, *Op. Cit.,* Vol. III, p. 348.
277. Vadivelu, A., *Op. Cit.,* Vol. II, p. 8.
278. Arudra, *Op. Cit.,* Vol. III, p. 340.
279. *Madras Journal of Literature and Science*, Vol. III, No.1, January 1836.
280. "Kalagati Sighra Sphurti Bodhimpaga"
281. Vadivelu, A., *Op. Cit.,* Vol. II, pp. 9-10.
282. Arudra, *Op. Cit.,* Vol. III, p. 340.
283. *Ibid*, p. 253.
284. Vadivelu, A., *Op. Cit.,* p. 180.
285. *S.I.I.,* Vol. VI., No.1192.
286. Carmichael, D.F., *Op. Cit.,* p. 339.
287. Varma, G.R., *Op. Cit.,* p. 98.
288. T. Donappa's Reprint of the article 'Vitaranaseeli Gode Narayana Gajapati' Enadu, Telugu Daily, Visakhapatnam edition, dated 13-5-1975.
289. Vadivelu, A., Op. Cit., Vol. II, p. 13.
290. T. Donappa's Reprint of the article 'Vitaranaseeli Gode Narayana Gajapati' Eenadu, Telugu Daily, Visakhapatnam Edition, dated 13-5-1975.
291. Vadivelu, A., *Op. Cit.,* Vol. II, p. I.
292. *Ibid,* Vol. I, p. 126.
293. *Ibid,* p. 21.
294. The Madras Revenue Register, Vol. III, August 1869; The Gode family was a pioneer in the enlightenment of the Northern Sircars of Andhra is borne out by the fact that Gode Venkata Jagga Rao was the founder of the first Telugu news paper 'Vrittanti' and author of same essays in English on mathematical and astronomical subjects printed in the MJLS during 1835-36 V. Ramakrishna states that the above fact was referred to by C.P. Brown also.
295. Varma, G.R. , *Op. Cit.,* p. 94.
296. *Ibid.*
297. Vadivelu, A., *Op. Cit.,* Vol. II, pp. 14-15.
298. T. Donappa's reprinted article 'Vitaranaseeli Gode Narayana Gajapati' Enadu, Telugu Daily, Visakhapatanam edition, dated 13-5-1975.
299. Arudra, *Op. Cit.,* Vol. III, p. 151.
300. Anjani kumari, B., *Contribution of the Gode Zamindari in the fields of Agriculture, Economy and Culture in Vizagapatam District*, p. 52.
301. Vadivelu, A., *Op. Cit.,* Vol. II, p. 27
302. Sudershan Rao, Y., *Op. Cit.,* p. 167.
303. Anjaneyulu, M.S.R. , *Op. Cit.,* p. 67.
304. Vizag District Records (4744:305-14), 24th July 1832.

305. Russell, G.E., *Reports on the Disturbances in Parlakimidy, Vizagapatam and Goomsoor, in 1832-36,* Vol. I, pp. 6-7.
306. Govinda, G., (Ed.,), *Anakapalli Directory*, p. 35.
307. Carmichael, D.F., *Op. Cit.* p. 333.
308. *Proceedings of A.P.H.C;* Vol. XII, p. 222.
309. Carmichael, D.F., *Op. Cit.,* p. 334.
310. Suryanarayana, K., "Contribution of Gode Family to Economy and Agriculture", Proceedings of *A.P.H.C.,* Vol. XXXII, p. 83.
311. Satyabhama Krishna samvadamu, p. 10.
312. *Charitraka – Parisodana* Silver Jubilee Volume, Vol.II, No.1, 2010, p. 79.
313. Donappa, T., *Op. Cit.,* p. 150.
314. Surya Rao, Angara, *Op. Cit.,* p. 52.
315. *Proceedings of A.P.H.C.,* Vol. XII, p. 222.
316. Varma, G.R., *Op. Cit.,* p. 92.
317. Stanza cited in *Andhra Samasthanamulu – Sahitya Poshanamu,* p. 144, footnotes.
318. 'Kalagati Sighra Sphurti Bodhimpaga'.
319. Surya Rao, Angara, *Op. Cit.,* p. 53.
320. *Proceedings of A.P.H.C.,* Vol. XII, p. 222.
321. Varma, G.R., *Op. Cit.,* p. 93.
322. Surya Rao, Angara, *Op. Cit.,* p. 54.
323. *Ibid.*
324. In Lawsons Bay Colony i.e., just Opposite to New Vuda Park, that Monument still exists as a symbol of royal pride and eternal love. The local people call it as '*The Tajmahal of Visakhapatnam*'.
325. Anjani Kumari, B., *"Contribution of the Gode Zamindari in the Fields of Agriculture, Economy and Culture in Vizagapatam District,* p. 57.
326. Donappa, T., *Op. Cit.,* p. 153.
327. Though this is doubtful some of the scholars are of the opinion that this *Vritantini* is the first Telugu newspaper.
328. Anjani Kumari, B., *Op. Cit.,* p. 41.
329. Vadivelu, A., *Op. Cit.,* Vol.II, p. 180.
330. Surya Rao, Angara, *Op. Cit.,* p. 62.
331. Vadivelu, A., *Op. Cit.,* Vol.II, p. 181.
332. Ramakrishna, V., *Proceedings of A.P.H.C.,* Vol. XII, 1988, Anakapalli, p. 281.
333. Donappa, T., *Op. Cit.,* p. 145.
334. G.R. Varma, *Op. Cit.,* p. 88.

Chapter - 3

Relations of the Zamindars

(i) Relations of the Zamindars with the British Government

In the history of colonial Andhra, zamindars played a crucial and prominent role. As some of them were "feudal despots" one may criticise the nature and character of their role in the colonial era. Yet we cannot neither minimise nor ignore the part played by them during 'those' centuries of foreign rule. There was a radical transformation in the nature, attitude and thinking of the feudal lords from the second-half of the Nineteenth Century. Coming under the influence of English education, British administration and modern thought many of them began to cultivate a sense of responsibility towards the society and the people. They began to involve themselves in public activities. Their liberal policies and constructive role in the domain of social, educational, cultural and economic activities won the appreciation and approbation of the people. In some cases even the Britishers appreciated the spirit of those zamindars in promoting all such aspects, and honoured them.

Some of the zamindars were irresponsible and extravagant and lacked social responsibility. High land revenue demand, its rigid and punctual collection added to their troubles. Unable to manage the affairs of their estates, they persuaded the Madras Government to take over their zamindaris into their charge.[1]

As a result, some of the estates were under the control and administration of the Colonial Government for some years.

The government paid them certain allowances per annum, and those zamindars were asked to leave the estate and to stay somewhere. In certain cases, later they were asked to return to their native estates and to assume the charge of their noble inheritance.[2] In some other cases the zamindars themselves request the Company Government to restore their authority on their original estates. For example, in 1852, the government handed over the Pusapati zamindari to the soul charge of Vijayarama Gajapati III. We can see the similar instances in many cases like those of the successions that have taken place in the Madugula and Gode zamindaris.

The then government expected the zamindars to become strong supporters of the British rule and reforming benevolent landlords. The available records provide only glimpse of the educational and practical experience of some of the zamindars. But it is known that majority of the zamindars of the region are learned men and enlightened scholars. The liberal Western ideas and western education had succeeded remarkably in moulding the values and attitudes of at least some of the zamindars of this province. Majority of the zamindars promoted cultural, educational, medical and economic conditions of their estates.

From the beginning of its political career, until the Battle of Padmanabham, Pusapati family showed its influence on almost all zamindars of this province. Against to the Fouzdars of Rajahmundry, they safeguarded the interests of the Nuzvid zamindars during the period of Venkatadri Apparao II. When Nooruddin wanted to annex this province, Pusapati Vijayarama Gajapati protested against him with a huge army at Chebrolu near Pithapuram. A number of zamindars of the Visakhapatnam area supported Pusapati's and joined hands with them. As discussed earlier, Kakarlapudi Gopala Payak Rao, the zamindar of Anakapalli and -Satyavaram, heroically fought along with his two thousand Boya Fouz, and killed Nooruddin in the battle.[3] Except the zamindar of Bobbili, almost all the zamindars had their friendly alliances with Vizianagaram.[4] The people, the zamindars and even the trading Companies of the Europeans accepted the supremacy of the Pusapatis in this entire province.

The political situation in the Northern Sircars disturbed when Sulbat Jung became the Subedar of the Deccan. In his Aurangabad Firman, he has given this part of the country also to the French, in gratitude to the help in enthroning him as a Subedar of Deccan. Under the leadership of Mr Bussy, French tried hard to occupy the provinces in between Rajahmundry and Chicacole, the present Srikakulam. To prevent the French in annexing those provinces, Pusapatis spared no efforts and tried by all means to trouble them.[5] The English, who concentrated in strengthening themselves in Tamil areas, were not in a position to come over here and to safeguard the interests of the Pusapatis and other zamindars. Vijayarama Raju and his team immediately changed the strategy and negotiated terms with the French, as it was very difficult to restore them in those critical circumstances. Jaffer Ali Khan, the Fouzdar at Srikakulam by not satisfied with this act of Vijayarama Raju and other welcomed the Marathas of Nagpur to come and conquer these provinces. The joint armies of the Maratha and Jaffer Ali Khan created a great havoc in Northern Andhra.[6] That havoc in this province was described by Gogulapati Kurmanadha Kavi in his Telugu poetic work *Simhadri Narasimha Satakamu.*[7] The joint armies of those zamindars and of the French attacked the Marathas and Jaffer Ali Khan at the Battle of Tummapala which is adjacent to Anakapalli in A.D.1753.[8] Thus, this entire province under the zamindars became a bone of contention between the French, the English the Marathas and the Fouzdar of Srikakulam. Almost all the zamindars of this province were under the directions of the Pusapatis and thus tried hard to safeguard their interests.

But very few chiefs like those of Bobbili and Pachipenta continued their traditional hostility with the Pusapatis. Gopala Krishna Ranga Rao of Bobbili and Virappa Dora of Pachipenta left no occasion to trouble the Pusapati chiefs.[9] When the French armies marched from Rajahmundry towards Bobbili through Kasimkota and Oddadi, Vijayarama Raju welcomed them only due to that rivalry.[10]

In the Battle of Bobbili which has taken place on January 24, 1756, hundreds of the sepoys of Bobbili heroically fought and lost their lives to the battle ground.[11] Gopala Krishna Ranga Rao was killed in the battle. But in revenge to it Tandra Papa Rayudu, one of the Sardars of Bobbili murdered Vijayarama Raju at mid-night. The Telugu literary sources state that the French felt happy for the death of Pusapati Vijayarama Raju.[12]

A letter dated March 8, 1758 sent by Visakhapatnam Chief to the Governor of Madras states thus:

"Some people imagine the assassination of Vijaya Rama Raju at Bobbili was perpetrated by Rama Rao's relations out of revenge. Others think that the French at the bottom of it."[13]

The seven years war between French and the English showed their repurcussions on their Indian Companies also. Under the leadership of Bussy, the French captured the forts of the English one after another. On June 27, 1758, he occupied the, fort of the English at Visakhapatnam too.

But shortly after that, in the changing political conditions and alliances, on September 2, 1758, in support to English and in protest to the French, the local zamindars like the Godes and the Kakarlapudi family, under the directions of the Pusapatis recaptured the fort at Visakhapatnam, removed the Flag of the French and raised the Flag of the English in its place.[14] This incident at Visakhapatnam testifies to the authority as well as the over-lordship of the native zamindaras and chiefs over the navigating ports in their locality.

But in the agreements like that have taken place between John Andrews and the Pusapati Ananda Gajapati, the ports and the income on the ports belongs to the English Company. Ports like Pudimadaka and Visakhapatnam of this area comes under that agreement. But even the Company was not entitled to sell, mortgage or hand over on the grounds to any agency without the prior permission of the local chiefs.[15]

When the relations between the English and the Pusapatis became so close, the French waged war against the Pusapatis and other local chiefs or jamindars at a place called Chendurti near Pithapuram, on December 7, 1758.[16]

After the death of Ananda Gajapati, China Vijayarama Gajapati became the chief of Vizianagaram. But his step-brother Sitarama Raju who was an aspirant for the throne revolted against China Vijayarama Gajapati captured him, put him in the prison and began to administer the estate.

Owing to the differences with the Kakarlapudi chiefs, he occupied some fertile lands irrigated by river Sarada, and made Kasimkota as his centre of activities.[17] He has constructed a 'Thana' and 'Poolbagh' at Anakapalli. Owing to their cordial relations with the Pusapati zamindari, the English has given the authority over the other zamindari estates like Jeypore, Madugula, Golugonda, Anakapalli, Kasipuram etc., to the Pusapatis; and demanded extra peshkash. Thus, all the local zamindari families, which until then worked under the leadership of the Pusapati zamindars were either against the French or English, and had to accept the authority of Viziaganaram.

But some of the local zamindaras and Muttadars under the leadership of the Kakarlapudis and Bhupati Chiefs were against to the temperament of Pusapati Sitarama Raju and protested against his supremacy. As the English Company was not in a position to collect the peshkash without the co-operation and help of Pusapati Sitarama Raju, decided to suppress their revolt.

By rendering military support to the Pusapaties Samuel Johnson, who was the in-charge of the Council at Visakhapatnam, decided to extend military help under the leadership of Captain Richard Mathew to Sitarama Raju. On March 18, 1775, the joint armies of the English and the Pusapatis began to suppress one after one all the revolted chiefs of Jeypore, Salur, Makkuva, Sangamvalasa, Kurupam, Kasipuram, etc., Anticipating this danger from the English and Sitarama Raju, the Bhupati Chiefs of Madugula and Golugonda, and the Kakarlapudis of Anakapalli and Satyavaram decided to unite in challenging the enemy.[18] Being known it, Sitarama Raju strategically moved his army towards Tummapala near Anakapalli of the Kakarlapudi's and thus checked the mutual support of the enemical armies. The joint armies of the English and the Pusapatis marched towards Madugula and occupied it under the captainship of Sagi Narayana Raju. Its ruler Ling Bhupathi and his diwan Vidhyadhara Jogi Raju, escaped to a place called Pandrangi and began to trouble the Vizianagaram troops. But at last, not in a position to withstand the Vizianagaram and English forces, retreated into the agency. The army stationed at Tummapala marched towards the fort of Anakapalli, killed the Kakarlapudi chiefs, Appala Payak Rao, and his son Ramabhadra Payak Rao and captured Anakapalli.[19] According to one tradition, Sitarama Raju who was not in a position to withstand the forces of the above Kakarlapudi Chiefs, in the battle brought a wizard by name Anappindi Visanna from

Anathavaram and through him poisoned Appala Payak Rao and Ramabhadra Payak Rao.[20]

The zamindari of Anakapalli and Satyavaram of the Kakarlapudi family were 'annexed' to the zamindari of Vijayarama Raju. In view of the 'heavy balances due' from it with a condition that he had to pay annually to the Company a sum of ninety thousand rupees and for the maintenance of the family of the deceased Payak Raos, a further sum of ten thousand annually.

Thus, when the Permanent Settlement was formed in 1802-03 the estates of Satyavaram and Anakapalli were sold along with the other haveli lands and purchased by the Pusapatis of Vizianagaram who in 1810 transferred them by a private agreement to Gode Suryaprakasa Rao. When the armed revolt of the Payak Rao began, the Acting Collector, Smith, in his letter to the Board of Revenue dated July 24, 1832, attributed these disturbances to the 'unconciliatory spirit' and unpopularity of the zamindars of the estate in that neighbourhood, and particularly of Gode Suryaprakasa Rao and of his brother Narayana Rao.[21] But, Russell after enquiry into the matter concluded that the Acting Collector was mistaken.[22]

The severe steps taken by the English Company and the reaction of the revolutionary hill zamindars and local chiefs were already discussed in the relevant places. When the zamindars of Golugonda and the Kakarlapudi Chiefs revolted against the policies of the English government, marshal law was ordered in the entire area. To suppress all such insurrections, different steps were taken by the English. Some were captured, some were imprisoned, some were executed, and their family members were prosecuted and were trialed by the military courts. Some of the zamindars and their families had no option except going on exile; and their zamindaris were forfeited.

By the Permanent Settlement, the authority of the Visakhapatnam zamindars over the hill chiefs was affected. The hill chiefs were recognised as independent land-holders and this recognition offended the zamindars of the plains very much. In additions to this frequent attachment and sale of the zamindaris for the default of revenue payments became common. One reason for this was the proprietary right of the zamindari was limited only to fifteen per cent of the cultivable land and of the waste kabds, which he could bequeath mortgage or alienate, while with the rest, he could not dispose of so easily. Another reason was the revenue policy pursued by the company fixing a high peshkash, allowing the accumulating of arrears to enormous amounts, then demanding immediate clearance and then proceeding with the sale of erstwhile estates in lieu for a relatively smaller sum due and appropriating the estates in auction for almost a song. Some of the estates which suffered from this highhanded policy of grab were Golgonda zamindari with an annual yield of 10,000 was bought by government for 10 Sterlings in 1837. This proved to be the causes of letter insurrection.[24]

In 1835, Sir Frederick Adam, Governor of Madras, visited this province and emphasised the expediency of exempting the hill zamindaris from the general regulations.[23] After the experience of such revolts in the other areas also, Russell in his Reports recommended the Agency System. Those recommendations were approved and they formed the basis of the Act XXIV of 1839. Vizianagaram, Golugonda, Kurupam, Madugula, etc., were the estates exempted by this Act from the general regulations.

At the time of the capture of Anakapalli, Pusapati Sitarama Raju sent one Ramachandra Raju with a huge army to conquer Golugonda chiefs. Ramachandra Raju killed Mallabhupati, the Chief of Golugonda by some mischief. Being roused with this, the Sardars of Golugonda killed Ramachandra Raju.[25] Under the leadership of Virabhupati and Bhairava bhupati, those hill chiefs continued their revolt against the Vizianagaram Zamindari which was supported by the English Company. But in course of time under helpless circumstances, one after another all those chiefs had to accept the supremacy of the Pusapatis. With those conquests, Pusapati Sitarama Raju emerged as a strongest chief in this entire province and did not care for the alliance with the English Company.[26] Moreover, he is intended to reduce the influence of the English on his estates.

But due to the internal disputes within the zamindari family his position was disturbed for a short period. After consolidating his position, he began to take revenge on all those who had not supported him in that dispute. As a part of it, he controlled Gode Jagga Rao the zamindar of Visakhapatnam who was acting as the 'dubasi' of the

Company, by not allowing him to visit the Governor at Madras.[27] Being angered with such an act of the Pusapatis, the English Company ordered Col. Braithwaite to occupy the Vizianagaram fort.[28] From February 1778, i.e., when Rambold was appointed as the Governor of Madras, the English availed the family disputes of the Pusapatis for their benefit.

It is during this period, i.e., in 1780, a historical incident has taken place in Visakhapatnam. For the first time in Indian history 'Sepoy Mutiny' has taken place in Visakhapatnam.[29] To suppress Hyder Ali and Tippu in the Karnataka battles, the Madras Governor asked their Council at Visakhapatnam to send the troops from here also. But in Visakhapatnam the troops of the Company, majority being the Muslims, vexed with the policies of the British were reluctant to go to fight with Hyder Ali and Tippu. They strongly decided to disobey the orders of the commanders. Under the leadership of Sher Mohammad Khan, some military officers were killed and their offices were captured for sometime. But probably due to the fear towards the English Company none of the chiefs or zamindars of the area supported those revolutionaries. As a result, the revolutionaries were captured and killed when they were moving towards Payakrao Peta.[30] Gajapati Dev, "the dismissed" zamindar of Kimedi under surveillance at Visakhapatnam dissuaded the mutineers and thus rescued the Company's troops.[31]

On January 10, 1781, though the Board of Directors ordered to appoint a Circuit Committee to look over the situation in this province, due to differences in the Madras Council, it was not established until April, 1783. Morgan Williams, Edward Sanders, Edward Frowd, William – Oram, Hugh Maxwell were the members of that Committee,[32] and they have submitted their Reports related to Visakhapatnam division on September 12, 1784 and on Kasimkota division on October 11,1784. In those Reports the details of the haveli lands, economic position of the provinces under the estatedars, taxation procedure in those areas were studied, to and suggested some measures to regularise the administration and thus to improve the revenue in this province.[33] The estates like Madugula, Anakapalli, Visakhapatnam, Golugonda, Kasipuram, etc., were included in the study of that Report. The Company pressurised the chiefs to minimise the budget by reducing their armed people and thus to raise the peshkash.

Russell, the Chief at Visakhapatnam frequently filed complaints against the local zamindars who were neither ready to pay the additional peshkash, nor to reduce their personnel. Moreover, showing the revolts of the tribal chiefs and zamindars at places like Golugonda, they involved into the internal affairs, of the zamindars and forced some prominent Chiefs like the Pusapatis to surrender some of their provinces in their estates as debt.[34] To damage the prestige and honour of some significant zamindari families, the Company at Visakhapatnam charged some allegations of theft of the Company property on the loyal servants and even on the family members of those families, and arrested them. When such an incident had taken place at Anakapalli, Pusapati Vijayarama Gajapatiinvolved into the matter released them by dispatching his troops.[35]

Some of such incidents widened the gap between the local zamindars and the English Company. In fact, the English Company wanted to take this province into their direct control, as the neighbouring provinces like Orissa and Madhya Pradesh were under the hands of their enemies, the Maharashtras. Moreover, this province of Kalinga Andhra which was blessed with rich natural resources naturally tempt anybody. They also noted that it was a very place of provisions abounding with all sorts of goods.[36]

To put an end to the rule of the Pusapati family which was very significant and influential among all the local chiefs, the Company troubled them in many ways and paved way for the Battle of Padmanabham which has taken place on July 10, 1794. This was the unique battle in the history of modern Andhra, which was fought by a local zamindar against the English East India Company. An inscription on the pillar of the temple of Padmanabhaswamy in the village, where the battle was fought, recollects that historic event thus[37]

> "Atyakta Sainikavaram pratibhati samya
> Gadyapi divya nripa vaibhava Lanchchana Sri:
> Samantha viratanu brinda samavritassan
> Sri Padmanabha dharani dhara parsva bhage"

After that battle, all the lands of the zamindari estates like Kasimkota, Kotavuratla, Kothakota, Anakapalli, Kondakarla, Uppalam and Satyavaram became haveli lands of the Company Government. The estates of Potnuru, Bhimilipatnam, Narava, Oaddadi, etc., were added to Vizianagaram Zamindari.

With the introduction of the Permanent Settlement in 1802 – 1803, in this province, Waltair, Anakapalli, Kasimkota, Munagapaka, Kondakarla, Melipaka, Dimili, Rayavaram, Panchadharla, Sarvasiddhi, Nakkapalli, Srirampuram, Upamaka, Uratla, Kothakota, Vemulapudi, etc., were put to auction and assigned to those who will pay the highest peshkash. Madugula Chiefs were allowed to continue on payment of the required peshkash by the Company.

Early in 1803, the then Visakhapatnam District consists of 16 zamindaris and 23 proprietary estates under a single Collector, Leveston Granville Keith Murray.

The Company introduced Permanent Settlement during the years 1802-03, to remove "all the generated evils of unsettled principles of revenue administration," to "reform and establish it on a firm and efficient footing not less to the advantage of the people than to the security of the revenue"; suppressing "rebellion and insubordination" which was conspicuous, by 'annihilating' the troops of the zamindars and bringing them to subjection, and "acknowledge and submit to the principle, that as they must be indebted to the beneficiance and wisdom of the British Government for every advantage they were to receive, so, in like manner, they must feel indebted solely to its protection, for the continuance and enjoyment of them."[38]

There was a fundamental condition that the zamindars should not be allowed to retain troops; order and tranquility is being reserved by the government. As noticed by M.S.R. Anjaneyulu, no consideration was given to those ancient zamindars wherefore the aristocracy, so turbulent and habituated to independence, could not reconcile itself to the new power which was vigorous and determined to control them.[39] In the view of the English Company, "these Rajas are indolent, ignorant, superstitious, expensive, dissipated, haughty, suspicious of Sircar Officers and they wish to consider them-selves rather tributary chiefs than common subjects."[40] Until Permanent Settlement, these zamindars were treated as the Rajas, the Chiefs or the Feudataries. Authority over the land, maintenance of law and order, exercises of hereditary rights, etc., were considered as their chief privileges. But after the Permanent Settlement, they were stripped of the ruling powers, and their estates were liable to the attachment for the default of peshkash. Just like in other areas, in this province also, during the period under study, many zamindaris were attached several times.

Though the government strived hard not to infringe the principles of Permanent Settlement and Regulations, the "local circumstances" in the zamindaris and continued dislocation in the district did not permit them to be vigorous. The Permanent Settlement was introduced at an unfavourable time and in hurry. The low price of grain, want of specie, stagnation of the Company's investment, adversity of seasons, internal feuds among the hill zamindaris, their strong posts, the fatal climate of the hills, the inadvertency and indolence of the zamindars in general and the obstinacy of the hill zamindars in particular, contributed the failures of the Permanent Settlement.

The authority of the hill zamindars in collecting the revenue could not be checked "for every ryot knows that the consequence of disregarding the zamindar's orders in such matters will be the plunder of his property, the burning of his house and perhaps personal imprisonment and outrage."[41] Throughout this period, the zamindars, chafing at their reduction as mere landholders and aided by a wild and unhealthy country, kept the district in continual ferment with their recalcitrance and feuds. The disturbances, which entirely resulted from their own feuds, impoverished them and made them defaulters. Then they became defaulters and subjected to debts to the government. When the zamindars misused the liberty, the government has to show that they were "resolved to release the peshkash even by sale of the zamindaries and that they were able if necessary to ensure a sale by purchasing and keeping them in their own hands."[42] To have a salutary effect on the other zamindars they sold some zamindaris like Madugula. When there arouse a struggle for succession, and when the successor was a minor, such zamindaris were placed under the 'Court of Wards.'[43] There were a number of such examples to that extent in the zamindaris in this province during this period.

At the time of Permanent Settlement in *fasli* 1213 (1803 A.D.) the total *jama* paid by the zamindar of Madugula was Rs 30,000, Golugonda Rs 11000 and Kasipuram Rs 1200. After the introduction of the Permanent Settlement slight modifications were done, and the total *jama* paid by the zamindars of Madugula was Rs 25000 Golugonda Rs 10000 and Kasipuram Rs 600.[44]

In fact, the defiance of British authority in the Northern Sircars was as old as the British rule itself. Whether one agrees or not, that the anti-British struggle was a continuous process; only the participating class changed from time to time. Before 1857, serious attempts were made in the Northern Sircars as in many parts of British ruled India, to resist unjust policy decisions of the ruling power. The Company sepoys at Visakhapatnam – Masulipatnam and at few other places, the tribals in the agency tracts of Godavari and Visakhapatnam districts, and the zamindars at one time or the other expressed dissent to the oppressive nature of the British rule. Unfortunately, all their efforts were, however, sporadic and not well-co-ordinated.

In the Visakhapatnam Province, and in general in Northern Coastal Andhra, the local landed class under the zamindaris was the important social group. The achievements of those families and the details of those zamindaris have been the subject of many studies. A Vadivelu,[45] Robert Eric Frykenberg,[46] A.V.D. Sarma,[47] Y. Sudershan Rao,[48] C. Ramalakshmi,[49] C. Surya-Lakshmi,[50] D.S. Krishna[51] and B. Syamsundar Raju[52] have in their studies highlighted the general conditions in the zamindari areas. The resistance of native aristocrats is the main theme in the works of M.S.R. Anjaneyulu,[53] B. Kesavanarayana[54] and I. Mallikharjuna Rao.[55] In many other zamindari areas too, there were uprisings on similar lines during the English Company Rule. There is a necessity to bring the events connected with them and also to obtain a comprehensive picture of native resistance, an important phase in the fight against the Company Government's exploitation and tyranny.

Prior to the entry of the European Companies into these provinces, the late medieval chiefs enjoyed a unique status in different aspects of administration. They were supported to be the natural leaders of the country and provided direction to development in their respective fields from the Muslim period. They became a law unto themselves in practice. Some of them were ancient and turbulent. They had been enjoying semi-independent power as well as long established privileges in their respective areas. The British rulers themselves had provoked opposition to their rule. The Company's government determined to make its rule real and imposed on them certain decisions. Naturally these chiefs grouched and grumbled and finally protested against such exploitative policies of the government. Over one-third of the zamindars were provoked to take up the cause of open rebellion which underlines the fact that the discontentment among them as widespread and explosive.

Various policies were carefully crafted and executed by the Company Government to curtail the economic and political powers of the zamindars. It chiefly concerned with extension and consolidation of power, guided certain well conceived considerations. The first was to plant the authority of the government upon a permanent basis by reducing the native aristocracy to submission. The second was to economically weaken the zamindars by extorting more and more money as State demand and collecting the same by a resort to strong-arm methods. Expansion of political power and revenue collection went hand-in-hand. For promoting political interests by executing schemes of empire-building, revenue was required, and political authority was needed for removing all the potential obstructions for the collection of revenue. To accomplish this double task, the government resorted to vigorous coercion and even deployed troops against refractory zamindars. These methods had succeeded in the end. The zamindars were economically ruined and politically weakened, and finally became thoroughly dependent on the Company's gesture of goodwill and generosity for sustenance. We can see all these examples, in the strategies of the British against the zamindars of the province also. But to achieve this, the British had to sweat and toil for many years.

In this context, the recent interdisciplinary approaches related to this aspect are to be discussed briefly. From the last few decades attempts were made by the some scholars to study on the ethno-histories of some kingdoms located in different part of India. The Hollow Crown, the ethnohistory of an Indian Kingdom, by Dirks; and Little Kingdoms in Kalinga, Ideologies, Legitimation and Politik regionaler Eliten by Georg Berkemer (Little Kingdoms in Kalinga by Georg Berkemer) etc., belongs to that category. Such works were well received by the scholars and they paved way for a lively debate on that aspect. The Hollow Crown was critically reviewed by David Ludden in the

Journal of Interdisciplinary History (1989); and "*Little kingdoms in Kalinga*" was reviewed by Burkhad Schnepel in the Journal of the Economic and Social History of the Orient (1986).

The Hollow Crown deals with the various aspects related to the South Indian little kingdom Pudukkottai located in the present Tamil Nadu. Little kingdoms in Kalinga by Georg Berkemer though published in German language, the content of that is available in articles and book reviews. Those studies have thrown significant new light on much debated questions such as the conundrum of the Hindu King's authority and the nature of the caste system. These types of anthropological and historical approaches are undoubtedly fruitful in the pursuance of knowledge. It concerns the impact of colonialism and the "modern state" on South Indian society, closing the flashback historically and historigraphically. It is meant both as contributions to colonial history and as a way of critiquing colonial historiography, in which little kings were at worst rebels and at best landlords and in which the Indian state was deconstructed and the nature of India society misconstrued. Paradoxically, as commented by Dirks 'colonialism seems to have created much of what is now accepted as India "tradition", "Including an autonomous caste structure with the Brahman clearly at the head, village based system of exchange, the ceremonial residues of the old regime state, and fetishistic competition for ritual goods that no longer play a vital role in the political system'.[55A]

Berkemer's study has an interesting politico-geographical focus as commented by Burkhard Schnepel. He studied the little Kingdom of Kilinga, as "an intellectual challenge" by adopting historical and anthological approaches. He enriches his scholarly analysis of temple inscriptions and copper-place grants, which provide the main bulk of his data by also consulting poetical accounts, various kinds of documents containing local histories, and the family chronicle (*vamsavali*) of some of the royal dynasties under consideration.[55B] His analysis of the historical role which ritual activities in the temples, have played in the pursuit of political power and in the legitimation of royal authority, is undoubtedly thought provoking and interesting. V. Yasodadevi,[55C] C.V. Ramachandra Rao,[55D] K. Suryanaryana,[55E] L.V. Pradeep[55F] and other have utilised all such information in their studies. The temple inscriptions at places like Simhachalam (600 Nos),

Srikurmam (204 Nos), Juttiga, Chodavaram, Panchadharla, were noticed in *Annual Reports of Epigraphy* (A.R.E) and were published in South Indian Inscriptions Volumes (S.I.I. Vols, IV, V, VI and X). Later N. Ramesan has edited the inscriptions of Srikakulam District with the title *Inscriptions of Srikakulam District*; and N. Mukundarao edited the records Simhachalam with the title *Simhachalam Inscriptions*.

But those Inscriptions at Simhachalam and Srikurmam are not useful for the study on the history and contribution of the zamindars of this province under study. All those records dealt with the medieval madalika ruling families like the Chalukyas of Elamanchili and Srikurmam, the Reddi rulers of Rajamumdry, the Velamachiefs, the later Eastern Gangas, the Matsyas of Oddadi, the Surbhis, the Telugu Chodas, the Haihayas, and the Gangas of Jantarnadu etc. After A.D. 1599, all those madalika families disappeared from the political seen due to the attacks of Bairamlaman Mulk. Until then all those chiefs were under the subordination of the later Eastern Ganges and the Suryavamsi Gajapaties of Orissa. An inscription dated A.D. 1599, at Srikurmam, (A.R.E.No.1312 of 1896) records that the army of the Qutb Shahis killed majority of those mandalikas in the battle at Chitapalligandi, a place identified with that of the same name in the present Visakhapatnam district. Interestingly, none of the mandilika chiefs who ruled in the earlier centuries in this region appeared as chiefs or zamindars either in the Qutab Shahi armies or under the regime of the English Company. In the hundreds of inscriptions at Simhachalam and Srikurmam only four inscriptions were issued by these zamindars of this province. Those families had no antiquity or earlier connections with the Visakhapatnam province (or with any part of Kalingandra province). As such this had no comparison with the Poligar system of Tamilnadu which originated during the Vijayanagara emperors of Hampi and continued up to the English Company period.

Berkemer's endeavour to retrace the structures of political power of Kalinga from around 600 to 1700 A.D., is interdisciplinary in character and undoubtedly thought provoking and interesting.

Kubja Vishnuvardhana, the Eastern Chalukyan ruler who came from Badami established a strong kingdom in the Visakhapatnam region

A.D. 624 and it continued roughly for four-and-a half centuries, which extended from Mahendragiri down to Nellore. All his early inscriptions are found in the Visakhapatnam region. Roughly a century earlier the Eastern Gangas established a kingdom here and gradually expanded towards Orissa; and later succeeded by the Gajapaties. But later the disappearance of the Vengi Chalukyan kingdom the Mdhyamakliga (Visakhapatnam region) went into the hands of a number of mandalika families whose inscriptions appear on the walls and pillars of the Simhachalam temple. All those mandalika chiefs suffered a lot from incessant troubles, as this was bordered on two great powers, the Reddies and the Gajapatis.

This is the Mandilika phase of Andhra history in general and of the Kalingandra in particular. As correctly noticed by Berkemer in the English summary to his work, the position of such little kings is determined through his relationship to the overload as a necessary part of an opposition, just as he himself is determined through his own role as king with his own perfection of power in relation to his own subjects and through his own role in relation to other little kings within the same as well as within other pyramids of legitimisation. But as stated already, my subject under study belongs to succeeding periods and all those zamindars emerged during the late Qutab Shahi and English Company periods. Even then that is applicable in a way to these zamindars also, as caste or religion never came in the way in selecting them to those positions. After came to power, naturally they claimed antiquity and higher status.

A majority of zamindars were in the financial crisis by 1778 itself. Their position had so alarmingly deteriorated, that they were hardly in a position to support their families with dignity. They had to maintain a number of servants (sibbendy) to help them in the collection of revenue, and in the maintenance of Law and Order. At the time of natural calamities like famines and droughts, they failed to meet their obligations. Majority of them were in debt, and in arrears to the government. Their commitments forced them to borrow money from money-lenders or Company's servants themselves, paying exorbitant rates of interests. Despite weak financial position, they were not prepared to remain quiet when their honour was at stake, and their interests endangered by alien government's actions. In a desperate bid to save their honour and retain their position, the badly effected zamindars protested and created disturbances.

No uniform measure was taken to deal with the rebellious zamindars or chiefs who did not comply with government orders. Extreme measures were applied in respect of those zamindars that had resources, influence and capacity to plunge the area in a state of insurrection and turmoil. Their explanations for delay in the payment of enhanced peshkash were not at all accepted. The punishments included deposing zamindars and installing their nearest relatives in their places, employing military operations to drive out rebel chiefs from their forts, assuming temporary charge of management of estates directly by government, and later resorting them to members of the original family, publicly auctioning and selling away of estates, and arresting the ring leaders and executing or transporting them to distant places.

All these normal policies that were implemented by the British towards the chiefs and zamindars throughout the country were implemented effectively in the Visakhapatnam province also. Such of their policies had given rise to a type of discontent among the zamindars. Some of the decisions like annual enhancement of the peshkash reduced the prestige and importance of the aristocracy. At the regulation of the payments, the Madras Governor granted no relief to the zamindars, and on the contrary, certain terms were compulsively extracted from them. Twelve and half per cent was arbitrarily added to Jumma of most of the zamindars on the ground that the lands were inadequately assessed.[56] The government never thought it essential to inquire into their grievances. The revenue innovations of the Madras Government also caused economic distress among majority of the aristocratic families and created in them, a feeling of general aversion to the British rule. Experiments like annual settlement, triennial settlements, quinquinnial settlements and permanent settlement were tried at regular intervals. Every time, a new settlement was made, the opportunity was utilised to hike the tribute and claim as State demand, a considerable portion of the produce of the country.

The growing discontent among the zamindars became more intensified when their lands were threatened to be taken away from them even for delay in the payment of tribute. This attitude of the government struck a blow at the hereditary basis of their estates and their authority. The maintenance of bands of military retainers was also anathema to the government. The official circles were under the impression that if the armed followers were reduced or completely disbanded, considerable amount could be saved and the zamindars would then be in a position to pay their peshkash utilising the amount thus saved. The zamindars were not mentally prepared to accept this view as their power ultimately rested on the possession of armed men in their service. Further, family disputes in some zamindaris provided an opportunity to government to claim increased revenue and demand its payment. Against their backdrop the spirit of rebellion and insubordination became more prominent and distinct among a number of zamindars of the Visakhapatnam Province, and led to a series of rebel activities gravely disturbing peaceful political climate and hampering revenue collections.[57] Even the introduction of Permanent Settlement, which was expected to restore peace and increase in prosperity, had very little impact for disturbances in the Visakhapatnam province. One significant feature of such revolts was the hold of the native chiefs over the local people. People held them in great regard and respect in all the areas. Local support was overwhelmingly available to rebel zamindars. Bound by the sentiment of loyalty, the people took-up arms in support of their Rajas or zamindars, and fought against the government troops. This bond could not easily be broken. Ironically inspite of numerical superiority, the zamindars lost in the contest for local supremacy.[58]

The vigorous measures by the British government had given raise to a type of discontent among a number of zamindars in the Northern circars also. As a result, a number of zamindars at places like Nuzvid,[59] Mylavaram,[60] Mugaltore,[61] etc., revolted against the British. To that extent the zamindars in the Visakhapatnam province was also no exception.

Of all the native chiefs in the Visakhapatnam district, as stated already, the most powerful were the Pusapati zamindars of Vizianagaram. The Chief and Council of Visakhapatnam (established in 1769) endeavoured for about two decades to cultivate friendly relations with Vijayarama Raju. But when the English government made serious attempts to assert their authority, their relations got stained. In 1788, Vijayarama Raju was instructed by the Company Government to reduce his forces.[62] The Zamindar was not prepared to act accordingly.[63] The government then granted a new lease enhancing the peshkash from three lakhs to nine lakhs, on the ground that Anakapalli, Uratla and Satyavaram estates were added to his zamindari. Partly because of his careless management of the estate as well as other similar reasons, the zamindar fell into heavy arrears with his peshkash, which stood at 6½ lakhs in the beginning of 1793. Between June and August, of that year events moved swiftly changing the entire scenario. The zamindar was directed to assign an adequate portion of his country for the discharge of all arrears. He was warned that in case of failure to comply, his lands would be attached and put under government management.[64] Before any reply from the zamindar was received, a detachment of Europeans had in fact, been ordered to move under Lieutenant Colonel Prendergast to enforce the measures.[65] The zamindar simply ignored the direction, but in a letter sent to the authorities intimated his willingness to clear the arrears in installments by February, 1794.[66] The offer was rejected in August, 1793, Sequestration was effected and the fort occupied by Colonel Prendergast[67]. Despite loss of power, the influence of the zamindar in his country remained to be the same as before. No person came forward with proposals to rent the *paraganas*. The Company officials were convinced that as long as the Raja remained in the land it would be difficult to effect revenue collections and manage the estate. Therefore, Vijayarama Raju was directed by the Government to leave those areas and proceed to Machilipatnam. The zamindar viewed the order "as the greatest indignity that could be offered to him" and "expressed himself convinced that his total ruin was intended."[68]

He, however in contravention of the order, retired with his followers to a nearby place Padmanabham.[69] Most of his soldiers joined him here and the fighting men reached 4000 figure. Emboldened by the response from his people, the zamindar declined compliance with the summons immediately. Colonel Prendergast and 7½ companies of sepoys proceeded against the Raja to secure his person and attacked his army at Padmanabham on July, 1794.[70] In a severe conflict lasting for about three-quarters of an hour, the zamindar and no less than 309 of his followers lost their lives.[71] Narayana Raju, son of the killed zamindar became the rallying point for all armed men who organised the defence of the country and carried out other measures to supplant the Company's Rule.[72] These unexpected developments made the government to adopt a temporising attitude and to proclaim Narayana Raju, as the zamindar of Vizianagaram. The political authority of the estate was thus finally broken.

A number of disturbances flared-up in and around the areas of Visakhapatnam after the Battle of Padmanabham. Some anti-governmental revolts broke out in some of the zamindaris in different parts of the vicinity. They continued an open fight, did not disband armed personnel nor remit the revenue as directed by the District Collectors. The zamindari families at places like Palakonda, Anakapalli, Kasipuram and Golugonda belongs to such group.

As discussed earlier, the Kakarlapudi family which stood next to Pusapati family in prestige and glory in this vicinity had the zamindari, comprises the estates of Anakapalli and Satyavaram, which extends from river Sarada to river Tandava. The government disapproved the adoption of a distant relative by one of the widows of Appala Raju, and discontinued maintenance allowance to the family. The estate was sold away in 1802. Three decades after, Jagannadha Raju, a cousin of the adopted boy espoused the cause of the family, appeared at the head of armed followers, assumed the family title of 'Payak Rao' and exacted contributions. The insurgents could not be easily put under control, forcing the government to place the area under martial law.[73] Hotly pursued by the Company's forces at the beginning of 1834, how Jagannadha Raju fled to the Rampa agency and how the local chiefs betrayed him etc., is discussed in the earlier chapter. He was captured and executed at Payakraopeta, on the banks of river Tandava.

The relations of the Golugonda hill zamindars with the British Company are somehow different. The environs and the nature of administrative set-up in the agency or hilly regions are entirely different. The causes as well as the course of their rebellion, is already discussed in the history of the Golugonda Zamindari. Internal feuds in the Golugonda Zamindari disrupted the normal life making the task of revenue collection difficult. In 1802-03, the Jumma of the estate was fixed at Rs 10,000 in perpetuity. The hill sardars neglected payment of revenue. Consequently, Krishna Bhupati failed to pay peshkash regularly after 1805. The District Collector therefore sequestered the estate. Difficulty of access to the heart of the mountainous zamindari region, unhealthiness of the climate, and loyalty of the local people towards their feudal chief rendered all attempts at forcible interference abortive. In such circumstances the Collector tried 'Judicious remonstrance' and favoured Naganna Dora, 'diwan' of Anantha Bhupati. The murder of the diwan in 1833 was followed by the period of increased disturbances.[74] Displaying firmness, the government attached the zamindari and auctioned it in 1837.

Similarly, in the other neighbouring hilly estates of the Sringavarapukota area (Jantarnadu Sima of the medieval centuries), the English Government intervened into the internal matters of the estate. Originally that Sringavarapukota estate, which was also known as Kasipuram estate, the neighbouring province of Visakhapatnam, originally belonged to the Chiefs of the Mukhi family. In course of time, the Pusapatis of Vizianagaram drove that family and merged that estate with Vizianagaram.[75] In A.D.1793, Raja Bhupala Raju of the original family forcibly occupied the estate of Kasipuram defied the government and made revenue collections himself. But the District Collector intervened, taken over and managed the estate for a short time and handed it over to the Vizianagaram Zamindars in 1796 A.D.[76] Virabhadra Raju, son of Raja Bhupala Raju was retained as one of the principal retainers on an allowance. Narayana Raju, the zamindar of Vizianagaram had left for Banaras in 1827 and the Government prepared a list of retainers eligible for allowance. The list did not include the name of Virabhadra Raju. This provoked the Raju, to lead a body of adventures and create disturbances, demanding his pension.[77] Martial Law was declared and about 1200 Company's troops were assembled for an attack on the rebel centres. The troops burnt Kasipuram and chased Virabhadra Raju into the hills. He was captured in 1833, tried by Court Martial and sent to Gooty in the Rayalaseema area to serve life term sentence.[78]

The relations of the English with Visakhapatnam province need special attention in this context.

Being an important port town in the East coast and the Chief centre of trade, Visakhapatnam played a prominent role in the history of the colonial period. The English East India Company established a Factory at Visakhapatnam in A.D.1682.[79] It seems that they had no political ambitions or interests on this province up to 1752, and hence limited their activities only to promote their trade and commerce. Without involving in to the local disturbances, they followed a policy of neutrality. But, when the French company obtained these Sircars by the Treaty of Aurangabad in 1753, they were possessed with increasing opportunities of trade in this province, and it brought them an enormous prestige.[80] This event brought a significant change in the attitude of English East India Company. The disappointed English Governor at Madras cautioned the Council at Visakhapatnam thus:

"We are more concerned that surprised at this event when we consider what influence they have at Aurangabad by means of their troops. The possession of these countries will put in their power greatly to hurt the company's investment and we imagine they will lose no opportunity of doing it."[81]

They established their power firmly in this province by maintaining their friendship with zamindars, particularly with the Pusapatis. Even though the English confined themselves to affectionate advices and promises, the Pusapatis assured them of their loyal friendship.[82] Determined to dislodge the French, the Pusapatis and the other zamindars urged strongly for the English help. But due to lack of timely help from the side of the English, Visakhapatnam surrendered to the French on 27th June A.D., 1757. All attempts were made by the local zamindars under the leadership of the Pusapatis to get the help of the English. Exasperated Pusapati Ananda Raju wrote fantically to the Governor of Madras: "In short, I meet with ruin in your friendship."[83] Later, when the English realised that the friendship with the local zamindars of this province was beneficial on both sides, they deputed John Andrews, the chief of Machilipatnam to Visakhapatnam.

As stated already on 21st November A.D. 1758, John Andrews came to an agreement with the Pusapatis, of this province to the extent "that all plunder should be equally divided; that all the countries which might be conquered should be delivered to the Rajah, who was to collect the revenue; but that the sea-ports and towns at the mouths of the rivers should belong to the Company with the revenues of the districts annexed thereto; that no treaty for the disposal or restitution, whether of the Rajah or of the English possessions should be made without the consent of both parties; that the Rajah should supply fifty thousand rupees a month for the expenses of the army and six thousand to commence from their arrival at Vizagapatnam for the particular expenses of the officers."[84]

On 7th December 1758, as discussed in the earlier chapter, the combined armies of the zamindars of this province as well as of the English Government defeated the French armies at Chandurti near Pitapuram in the East Godavari District. The significant role played by the Kakarlapudi Zamindars in this battle is well attested to in the Telugu literature of this period. Though almost all the local zamindars participated in this battle against the French, the Pusapatis were benefited by this as they acquired much influence over all the local zamindars.[85] Recognising the Pusapatis as the head of the local zamindars the English came into fresh agreement with them. Accordingly the company agreed "that whatsoever sums the Raja might furnish should be considered as a loan and that the revenues of all the countries that might be reduced on either side of the Godavari, excepting such as belonged to the French either by establishment or granted in property should be equally divided between him and the English."[86] Thus, by this new treaty, the English were entitled to half of the territories South of the Godavari under the French influence.

Even under the British authority the Pusapatis, tried hard to restore their Independence until 1749 A.D. The English established their full-fledged authority in their province when they defeated the Pusapatis in the Battle of Padmanabham in A.D.1794.[87]

Thus, the English Company which established a Factory at Visakhapatnam in A.D.1682, carried a precarious trade up to A.D.1753, and changed its attitude under the pressure of the disturbed political conditions.

They utilised the time properly, acquired land possessions of the zamindars and established their authority in the Visakhapatnam province.

Thus, the zamindari families of the region entered this province earlier as military entrepreneurs or foujdars and then gradually acquired large estates. But in due course of time, all of them were reduced to the positions of estatedars and zamindars.

As discussed earlier, the Pusapati family which claimed ancestry from Madhavavarma of the early centuries of Christian era stated that they belonged to the Kshatriyas of Solar race. In the far later centuries, one Pusapati Madhavavarma, a trusted lieutenant of Sher Mohammad Khan, the Foujdar of Chicacole, was honoured by the Qutab Shahi's of Golkonda for the loyal support in that province. At the time of the transfer of Northern Sirkars to the English Company, they acquired the whole of the Sirkars by subduing the other powerful zamindars and gradually became predominant in that province. The Military strength of the Pusapati's was undoubtedly more in comparison to the other zamindars of that province; and the same status was continued up to the Battle of Padmanabham.

In suppressing the revolts at places like Mylavaram, the Gode family loyally and sincerely supports English company and showed extra ordinary courage. Having acquired Mylavarm province to the company, and also by pacifying the rebellious populace of the region, they were taken into confidence of the company administration. The court of Directors from England was impressed and appreciated the timely uncommon assistance of the Gode family.[88] The various privileges, honours and other royal insignia that they have received by the East India Company were described in works like *Satyavati Parinayam.* They also claimed solar descent and were even called as 'Maharajas'.

Similarly, the Kakarlapudis also began their career as Foujdars under Qutab Shahis of Golkonda and gradually emerged as zamindars. The other zamindars like those at Madugula and Gudem claimed their origin in the Odhara Country, and joined hands with the Kakarlapudi in revolting against the army of the English Company which was supported by the Pusapati army. All such incidents clearly state that the zamindars of this province maintained armies as per their requirement, in the beginning. But after the Permanent Settlement they were stripped of the ruling powers, and their position was reduced. Thus, all the zamindars were not of the same category and of contrasting specimens. At last all of them suffered the same fate under the company.

The administrative policies of the British like the Permanent Settlement gradually transformed the chiefs or zamindars as mere land-lords. At the time of the Permanent Settlement, there was sixteen zamindaries and they were confirmed to the zamindars perpetuity conditionally. The assessment necessary varied according to extent and local conditions. There was a fundamental condition that the zamindars should not be allowed to retain troops, order and tranquility being reserved by the government. No consideration was given even to the biggest zamindaries like the Pasapaties.

Before Permanent, these zamindars were treated as feudatories rather than as mere farmers of the revenue, rather as captains of the borders, lords of the marches, chief of the hills, than as private landholder's and the government was conducted through them, some of them having the responsibility for the hill tribes.[88A] But now, they were stripped of the ruling powers, their estates were liable to attachment for default of peshksh, the British policy system substituted the zamindari on and civil and criminal 'Judicatories' set up, which were complex and vexatious with the hardships, unknown in the 'good old days'. The Permanent Settlement ruined the ancient zamindaries which were auctioned off the heirs. Soon Permanent Settlement proved counter productive in all respects. As the zamindaris fell in unending litigations in the new courts established for the purpose. Besides the new judicial system, the Permanent Settlement also introduced a new system of police administration to aid and assists the civil authorities.

The disturbed stage of this province can be understood by the reports of the British officers like Sir. Thomas Munro, George Russel, Smith, Sir. Frederiek Adam, etc.[88B] In some areas it became very difficult to project some of its officers. As stated already Kasturi Appaya Puntulu, the collector's Sheristadar, while he was returning from his office, was murdered. The British government understood that the administration in general and revenue administration in particular, was not possible without the support of the zamindars. As a result, to protect the interests of the native aristocracy, Madras Importable Estate Act was passed in 1904. Section 2(2) of the Madras Impartable Estates Act, 1904 (Madras Act 2 of 1904) defines an "importable estate" as an estate descendible to a single heir and subject to the other incidents of impartible estates in South India. It is an act to declare that certain estates are Impartable and that the proprietors of such estates cannot exercise unrestricted powers of alienation in respect thereof.[88C] It sees that this Impartible Estate Act has no impact on small zamindaries or estates of the Visakhapatnam Province. By the time of the application of the Act some of the muttadars and hill zamindars of this region turned as rebels against the British. Legal heirs were identified and were nominated by the Agents or the Collectors as muttadar; and the rebels who were struggling to the position were caught and punished under IPC Section 176. In the case of Madugula zamindari, though the Government of Madras involved in its affairs, recognised Mukundadev as well as Rajendra Mani Devi, the grand-daughter of Krishna Bhupati Dev II, as the joint heirs, and divided Madugula zamindari between them.[88D]

Similarly, in the case of the Gode zamindari, as there no male succession the daughters Kamala Devi and Rukhmini Devi succeeded to the zamindari. The Pusapati zamindari of Vizianagaram continued its legal disputes for partition claiming their share in certain properties, as in the case of other bigger zamindaries like that of Venkatagiri.

In this context, it is not irrelevant to discuss about an important Port town nearby to Visakhapatnam in this province. Bhimilipatnam, otherwise known as Bhimili, a sea port on North of Visakhapatnam was the headquarters of an 'Amin' of the Pusapati zamindars of Vizianagaram. In the seventeenth century the Dutch came over there and made it as their settlement by constructing a fort and a factory. Their neighbourhood was frequently referred to in almost all the early records of the English Factory of Visakhapatnam. It was brought to their control under the 'furmans' granted by the Nizam and confirmed by the Mughal Emperor bearing various dates from A.D. 1628 to A.D. 1713.[89] It was granted by the Kowle issued by Hajee Housson in A.D. 1734 and A.D. 1752 and by Jaffer Ali Khan in A.D. 1752. Housson and Alikhan were the deputies (naibs) of the Nizam that looking after the matters of the Sircars.

In A.D. 1754 the Dutch factory at Bhimili was burnt by the Marathas under Raghuji Bhonsle and robbed of several chests of treasures.[90] It is in the same year the Vizianagaram zamindars granted *pattas* to the Dutch renewing the permission formerly given to build a fort, possess a washing-green for bleaching cloth and to establish a mint. On the outbreak of the war in A.D. 1781 between the English and the Dutch Bhimilipatnam was seized and destroyed by the English East India Company.[91] But in accordance with the peace of A.D. 1784, it was restored in A.D. 1785. Again war broke out between the two powers one decade later, and Bhimilipatnam was surrendered to the English. In 1819, it was restored by Mr. John Smith, the Collector, to the representative of the Netherlands Government in consequence of the convention of the allied powers in A.D. 1814.[91A] It was held by the Dutch until 1st June 1825, when under the operation of the Treaty of March A.D. 1824 between England and Holland, it was made over to the East India Company. Since then that place has been the British territory and government property.

Some of the Dutch, who managed the factory and the fort left their bones in the cemetery lied there. This contains 13 tomb stones made of the local garnetiferous gneiss, bearing Dutch inscriptions and Court-of-Arms and ranging in date from A.D. 1661 (the oldest tomb in Northern Sircars) to A.D. 1720. After the Dutch finally relinquished Bhimilipatnam, it rapidly decayed and it was turned as a miserable fishing village.

Later a number of European communities came over there, established Jaggery factories and later Jute Mills, and did much for the town. They supported the Voluntary Municipal Association started in A.D. 1861. They organised subscriptions for a hospital, a school and a church. The other details of the Bhimilipatnam, the industries there, and other economic aspects will be discussed in the next chapter.

(ii) Mutual Relations of the zamindars

The Pusapati family of Vizianagaram, the Zamindars of Nandapuram and Jeypore, the Velamas chiefs (Raos) of Bobbili were the foremost among the near by major zamindaris, which showed their impact on the province of Visakhapatnam. Besides them, a number of other zamindars as well as estatedars like Kurupam, Chemudu, Golugonda, Madugula, Satyavaram, Wadhwan, etc., maintained their relations with this area due to their marriage alliances and other Kinship.

The Pusapati family of Vizianagaram which originally claims its ancestry, from Vishnukundin Madhavavarma of Sixth Century A.D. was the significant zamindari which exercised its authority in the entire Northern Coastal Andhra. It is supposed that they hailed from the village Pusapadu in the Guntur District.[92]

During the period Proudha Devaraya of Hampi Vijayanagara, one of the ancestors of the Pusapatis, Rachiraju-I conquered the ruler of Malwa kingdom and acquired the title Manne Sultan[93]; which became the family title of the Pusapati Chiefs. Aurangazeb who was supported by this family presented them 'Julphicar' (double edged knife) which adorned the flag of the Pusapati chiefs. In A.D. 1713, the foundation was laid for the fort of Vizianagaram. One Madhava Varma of that family, who became a trusted lieutenant to Sher Mohammad Khan who was appointed as Fouzdar of Chicacole (modern Srikakulam) by the Qutb-Shahis of Golkonda in A.D. 1652. Thus, they served the Qutb-Shahis of Golkonda under the Fouzdar of Chicacole. They received a number of honours, titles and inams under the Qutb-Shahis. In course of time, they established themselves as strong power by subduing the other powerful zamindars of the province. At the time of the transfer of Northern Sircars to the English, the Pusapatis family was in the possession of the whole of the Sircar. Their policies and activities determined the course of history of this region. The French and the English, who had factories in this region, craved for their favour and friendship. The attitude of the Pusapatis titled the scales of fortune of those European Companies. With their diplomacy, statesmanship and military superiority, the zamindars of Vizianagaram gradually carved out a big zamindari. There is no exaggeration to say that the history of this region was directly and indirectly influenced by the political activity of this Pusapati family in that period. They exacted tribute from the other zamindars, undermined the power of the Faujdars and emerged as the foremost power in the Sircars.

In the struggle for succession that took place after the death of Nizam-ul-Mulk in A.D. 1748, the French and the English took sides to promote their selfish interests. Nizam Salabad Jung who succeeded to the throne issued a sannad by recognising Vijayarama Raju as the Raja of Vizianagaram in April 1760. Immediately after coming to the power he has taken initiation to release the zamindar of Nuzvid Venkatadri

Appa Rao II from prison and made him as the zamindar of Nuzvidu. At the time of the accession of Vijayarama Raju, his elder-half-brother, Sitarama Raju who was aspiring for the throne, raised the banner of revolt. The succession dispute, the ambition and duplicity of Sitarama Raju, his highhanded and oppressive nature of administration, had a baneful and destructive effect on the fortunes of the Vijayarama Raju and made his rule unpopular.[94] The mutual rivalry between the two brothers weakened the power and prestige of the Pusapatis and made things easier to the English to assert their power in that province. The English Company after acquiring this province in A.D. 1766 began to feel strongly that their interest suffered as a result of the unscrupulous and intriguing activities of Sitarama Raju. From 1766 to 1769, the Company allowed the existing system of administration to continue. In 1769, the native agency was discontinued and the Sircars were placed under the charge of provincial Chiefs and Councils.[95]

In 1776, a Circuit Committee was appointed to investigate the problems of administration of the Northern Sircars. In 1784, the Committee was able to submit its Report on the Kasimkota division. Regarding Vizianagaram, taking into consideration the extensive influence, ambition and oppressive systems exercised by the Rajas, it recommended the reduction of the humilitary strength of Vizianagaram and doubling its Jama.[96] The peshkash to be paid by the zamindar was increased from rupees four lakhs to rupees nine lakhs which was discussed earlier. Vijayarama Raju accepted this increase with the greatest reluctance. This was a turning point in the history of the relations between the English and the Pasupatis and in the fortunes of the latter. Gradually the Madras Government became very active, constituted the Board of Revenue, and began to "keep a straight eye over the conduct of Vijaya Rama Raju."[97] Vijayarama Raju was enmeshed in the Court politics and went under the control of Sitarama Raju. The expensive "mode of life, the State that is thought necessary to be kept up his numerous train of attendants and dependents...the support of family connections, religious charities and sibbemdy charges absorbed immense sums."[98] The natural calamities, particularly the severe famine of 1790-91 thrashed the economic position of the zamindari. The corrupt and weak administrative machinery and economic dislocation causing arrears exposed Vizianagaram to the Company's domineering policy.

The affairs of the zamindari of the Pusapatis became very severe by 1793. The government directed the Chief and the Council to demand the immediate payment of the lakhs of arrears and to summon him to the chiefship to communicate its requisition. In case of his refusal to immediate compliance, the Chief and Council were instructed to demand the surrender of the zamindari "to hold the Company until their demands upon it were fully discharged."[99] The Government directed them to use force if necessary.[100] The Government rejected even the proposals of Vijayarama Raju to clear the arrears in installments, as stated earlier.

The sequestration of the Vizianagaram Zamindari by the government commenced on August 9, 1793; and it was the death-blow to the prestige and honour of a greatest zamindari in this part of the country. After sequestration, necessary measures were taken to set-right the revenue administration in the zamindari by appointing three Collectors. Vijayarama Raju was allowed to stay at Visakhapatnam with an allowance of Rs 12,000 per month. Sitarama Raju who stayed at Madras received Rs 5,000 monthly. When those Collectors decided to enhance the Kowle for the next three years, nobody responded to the advertisements, which are narrated earlier.[101]

The government ascribing the backwardness of the renters and other to tender offers for the proposed rent to "the direct interference" of the Raja insisted upon his departure for Madras or Machilipatnam.[102] Pusapati Vijayarama Raju considered that insistence upon him as the greatest indignity and humiliation that could be done to him. As there was no alternative, with utmost reluctance, on May 10, 1794, Vijayarama Raju set out with his followers to Padmanabham, a small village on the banks of river Gosthani, between Visakhapatnam and Vizianagaram.[103] The Chief and the Council seriously considered this as the violation of the directions of the government; and sent a force under the command of Lt. Kennet to recall the Raja to a proper sense of duty and to insist him to pursue his journey to Madras or Machilipatnam. Without responding and obeying the government orders, Vijayarama Raju continued his stay at Padmanabham. Col. Prendergast marched on the morning of July 10, 1794 to enforce the orders of the government and to take action on Vijayarama Raju. Probably due to his limitations or prevailing circumstances,

Vijayarama Raju was not ready to fight with the English forces. When the English forces began the attack, he has not given orders even to protest the enemy. He thought that at maximum the English forces will capture him alive. But in that Battle at Padmanabham that took place on the banks of river Gosthani, Vijayarama Raju and a number of 'Rachavaru' lost their lives. This battle ended the power and prestige of the Pusapati family, a significant zamindari family in the entire Northern Sircars, and paved way for the Company's supremacy in this province.[104]

On the receipt of the news of the death of Vijayarama Raju, his family along with his son Narayana Raju of 8 years ran to Kasipuram and took refuge under the Mukhi Zamindars.[105] Raya Bhupala Raju of the Mukhi family treated them with utmost respect and safeguarded them and sent them to Makkuva, still further North in the hills. Under the leadership of Raya Bhupala Raju, a number of hill zamindars in the province united themselves against the British and stood for the cause of Narayana Raju of the Pusapati family. They collected rents from the ryots on his behalf and kept up the resistance against the British.[106]

As it was difficult to face those hill zamindars, the Chief and Council at Visakhapatnam decided to restore peace and order in the area by recognising the claims of Narayana Raju. As a result of negotiation for some period, the government has given a new 'Kaul' to Narayana Raju and the Pusapati family accepted the authority of the Company. An allowance of Rs 12,000 per month was fixed and restored him to "the Zamindari of Vizianagaram proper" upon several hard conditions.[107] But the conditions imposed upon him were very unfavourable and untolerable to him. He was called upon to pay at once the arrears of some lakhs of rupees; and a number of zamindaris like Jeypore, Bobbili, Palakonda, Kurupam, Merangi, Sangamvalasa, Chemudu, Saluru, Andra, Golugonda, etc., were taken away from him and kept under those who were brought forward to the direct control of the British Government. Thus, the Company on one side reduced the extent of the zamindari, and on another side increased the peshkash, and required Narayana Raju to pay some lakhs of rupees towards arrears "for the whole extent of the country." This harassing hardship shattered the finances of the Vizianagaram zamindari, and they were forced to contact loans from the money-lenders.[108]

As this much was the ill-treatment given to a major zamindari like the Vizianagaram, there is no need to state about the fate of other zamindars of this province.

It became a chronic feature making the zamindaris vulnerable to the drastic steps of sequestration, attachment and humiliating treatment of the British Company. With the introduction of Permanent Settlement in 1802-03, all those zamindars lost much of their former glory and significance.

It is also stated that the selfish attitudes and mutual rivalries among some of the zamindars were the causes for political turmoil of the period. The Reports of the British officers refer to such non-cordial relations among the zamindars. Mr. Smith, the in-charge Collector of Visakhapatnam, stated that the noncordial relations maintained by Gode zamindars Suryaprakasa Rao towards the Kakarlapudi family, as one of the causes for the revolt of Kakarlapudi Jagannadha Payak Rao in A.D. 1832.[109] This type of allegations shows the nature of at least some of the officers, towards the zamindars. Later enquiries made it clear that the report of Mr. Smith as a mistake.[110]

After the establishment of Permanent Settlement in this province, the entire area was formed into seventeen sub-divisions like Anakapalli, Kasimkota, Kondakarla, Munagapaka, Dimili, Sarvasiddhi, Melipaka, Rayavaram, Panchadharla, Srirangapuram, Nakkapalli, Godicherla, Uratla, Vemulapudi, Kotthakota, Uppada and Waltair.

Inter-sales and inter-exchanges with the permission of the Company was a normal feature in between the zamindars. The Anakapalli Zamindari consists of thirteen Jirayathi villages and three *Srothriyam* villages. This zamindari was first purchased in auction by the Pusapatis of Vizianagaram and later sold it to Gode Suryaprakasa Rao of Visakhapatnam. Besides alliances and exchanges of support, there occur a number of disputes for power and property, among those zamindars and estatedars.

Pusapati Sitarama Raju aimed to occupy Anakapalli Zamindari with the support of Richard Mathews, the Captain of English army. In a battle that took place in A.D. 1776, Appala Payak Rao and his son Ramabhadra Payak Rao were killed which resulted in the end of the

Kakarlapudi Zamindari. British Company declared all the lands under that zamindari as the Company's haveli lands and given them under 'kowle' to Pusapti Sitarama Raju. As discussed earlier, in this deal, Company came to an agreement with the widows of Appala Payak Rao and Ramabhadra Payak Rao, Sitayamma and Rajayamma to pay an annual maintenance allowance of Rs 10,000 (ten thousand) and entrusted that responsibility to Pusapati Sitarama Raju, who has taken that zamindari to 'Kowle'. But gradually the Pusapatis as well as the English Company evaded the maintenance allowance to the queens of the Kakarlapudis which act pushed those ladies into debts and financial problems.[111] In such miserable circumstances, Sitayamma passed away in A. D. 1804, and Rajayamma died in A.D. 1814. Even the adopted son of Rajayamma, was not recognised by the English Company as her heir apparent.

When all the hopes were shut down the Kakarlapudis broke a revolt in A.D. 1832, under Jagannadha Payak Rao. That revolt which continued for more than two years resulted in a devast in the areas of Anakapalli, Visakhapatnam and Golugonda as known from some *Chatu* Verses.[112] But 'the divide and rule policy' of the Britishers costs the lives of Jagannadha Payak Rao and Venkatapati Raju of the Kakarla-pudi family. The strategy of the English divided the alliance of the Kakarlapudis and Golugonda Bhupathis, which incidence was discussed in the earlier chapter. Naganna Dora, the diwan of Golugonda being influenced by the English cheated the Payak Raos by informing the strategies of the revolutionaries against the English.[113] In accordance with that, the English played a timely role in breaking the unity of the various zamindars, when they stood against their interests. Later, in due course, the Kakarlapudi family came and settled at Bhogapuram with the kind support and co-operation of the Pusapati Zamindars.

The National Movement in this area progressed in certain significant and well marked stages along with the other provinces in the country. The first stage was the reaction of the upper classes of the society like the chiefs and the landlords against tyranny and oppressions of the early British administration in this area. The revolts of the zamindars and estatedars at places like Sringavarapukota (Mukhi family), Anakapalli (Kakarlapudi Family), and Gudem (Bhupati family), in the first half of the nineteenth century and the various 'fituries' of the muttadars and tribal-leaders in the early decades, had already referred to. Some of the zamindaris continued to exist even after the shorn of their political and military strength. At the time of the dwindling of the possessions of the estates, they used to mortgage their estates or land-holdings either to the Company or to the other zamindars of the province. Thus, gradually their estates and zamindari lands were divided and purchased by others.

There are a number of examples to that extent in this part of the country. The acquisition of Anakapalli estate which was originally belongs to the Kakarlapudis, by the Pusapatis and later by the Godes; and the acquisition of some of the tracts in the Madugula estate by the Pusapatis of Vizianagaram, and the Zamindars of Jeypore etc., belongs to that category. Chronic financial instability led to the appropriation of more and more territories by the British. At the time of the succession of the minors, and on the occasion of the struggle for succession, the estates were used to place under the Court of Wards. On some occasions the English Company it self-managed some of the estates for short periods for different reasons.

The marriage alliances between the zamindari families paved way for strengthening themselves politically. The Relations of Godes with other zamindars is already referred to. Similarly, Kakarlapudi Payak Rao is the co-son-in-law of Pusapati Ananda Raju I of Vizianagaram. Due to this relation, they supported each other in invading the Faujdar of Srikakulam (chicacole), in occupying the military camp of Nizam at Kasimkota, and in attacking the Factory of the English East India Company at Visakhapatnam. These successes infused self-confidence and they joined hands in heroicly killing Nooruddin, the Faujdar of Rajahmundry, at the battle of Chebrolu in 1734; in protesting the joint armies of Jaffer Ali, the Faujdar of Srikakulam and the Marathas in the Battle at Tummapala in 1753; and in the treacherous Battle of Bobbili which has taken place in A.D. 1757, and in a number of battles at places like Chandurti, Rajahmundry and Machilipatnam fought against the French. Thus, their mutual support benefited each other either in establishing or strengthening their power against the Muslims, the Marathas and the French.

But during the period of China Vijayarama Gajapathi, his step-brother and diwan Sita Rama Raju administered the Zamindari of

Vizianagaram with the support of the English and suppressed some Zamindars like the Kakarlapudi Payak Rao of Anakapalli. That tragedy of the Kakarlapudis was already narrated while describing their history. Thus, the selfish attitude of Pusapati Sita Rama Raju, as well as the 'divide and rule policy' of the English costed the lives as well as the lands of some of the zamindars of this province.

References

1. *Viziagapatam District Records* (V.D.R), Vol. 3771, p. 18.
2. *Ibid,* Vol. 6449, p. 114.
3. *Kakarlapudi Vamsavali,* p. 3.
4. Narayana Kavi, Dittakavi, *Rangaraya Charitra, Asvasa I,* Stanza – 38.
5. Sudershan Rao, Y. *Andhra between the Empires,* p. 51.
6. *Ibid,* p. 55.
7. Kurmanadha Kavi, Gogulapati, *Simhadri Narasimha Satakamu,* Stanza No. 28.
8. Anjaneyulu, M.S.R., *Vizagapatam District,* 1769-1834, p. 93.
9. Narayana Kavi, Dittakavi, *Op. Cit.,* Stanza 88,
10. Sudershan Rao, Y., *Op. Cit.,* p. 57.
11. Narayana Kavi, Dittakavi, *Op. Cit.,* p. 81.
12. *Ibid., "Raju Chavukunanta Parasu Balamu Santasam Bande".*
13. Letter sent by the Vizagapatam Chief to the Governor of Madras on 8-3-1758.
14. Col. Malleson, *Decisive Battles of India,* p. 57.
15. Captain Arthur Brooms, *"The History of the Rise and progress of the Bengal Army"* Cited by T. Satyanarayana Murthy, A.P.H.C Vol.XII, pp. 213 and 214.
16. *Samalkot Kaifiyat,* Mackenzie Mss. Oriental Manuscript Library, Madras.
17. 9th July 1794, V.D.R. (3700:332).
18. Anjaneyulu, M.S.R., Op. Cit., p. 70.
19. Proceedings of A.P.H.C., Vol. XII, p. 222.
20. Satyanarayana Murty, T., *Padmanabha Yuddham* p. 86.
21. July 24, 1832, V.D.R., (4744:305-14).
22. Russell, *Reports on the Disturbances in Parlakimedy, Vizagapatnam and Goomsoor,* in 1832-36, (Madras, 1856), Vol. I, p. 5.
23. Anjaneyulu, M.S.R., *Op. Cit.,* pp. 71-72.
24. *Ibid.*
25. Francis, *Vizagapatam District Gazetteer,* p. 249.

26. Satyanarayana Murty, T., *Op. Cit.*, p. 37.
27. Anjaneyulu, M.S.R., *Op. Cit.*, p. 70.
28. *Proceedings of A.P.H.C.* Vol. XXVI, p. 114.
29. Kesavanarayana, B., "The Sepoy revolt of Vizagapatnam 1780" *Proceedings of A.P.H.C*, 14th Session Warangal *1990*, p. 181.
30. On the hillock adjacent to the sea in the Old Town of Visakhapatnam, behind Masjid, the local people show an old grave as the burial of Sher Muhammad-Khan, who led that 'Sepoy mutiny' at Visakhapatnam in A.D. 1780.
31. Kesavanarayana, B., *Op. Cit.* p. 181.
32. Letter from Presidency to Vizagapatam, October 6, 1783, V.D.R., (3686:435-439).
33. *Ibid.*
34. Letter of Vizagapatam Chief to Vijayarama Raju, dated April 26, 1793, *V.D.R* 3699:64.
35. Venkata Satyanarayana Murty, Kavikondala, *Vijayarama Gajapati, Ramanuja Charya Samithi,* Vizianagaram. pp. 111-114, cited by M.S.R. Anjaneyulu, p. 93.
36. RFSG: DEE, *Op. Cit.*, p. 74.
37. The following is the Stanza in the Pillar Inscription of Padmanabha Swamy Temple at Padmanabham.

    "Atyakta Sainikavaram Pratibhati Samya
    Gadyapi Divyanripa Vaibhava Lanchchana Sri
    Samanta Vira tanu brinda Samavri tassan
    Sri Padmanabha Dharani Dhara Parsva bhage!!"
38. Revenue Letter from the Court of Directors to Fort St. George, February 11, 1801, W.F., Firminger, *Op. Cit.*, p. 51.
39. Anjaneyulu, M.S.R., *Op. Cit.*, p. 62.
40. Carmichael, D.F., *A Manual of the District of Vizagapatam*, p. 223.
41. August 16, 1827, *V.D.R.*, 4740: 122.
42. Letter of Sub-Collector to B.O.R., October 15, 1834, *V.D.R.*, 4746: 359-60.
43. Letter of Collector to B.O.R., November 9, 1829, *V.D.R.* 4741: 328.
44. Anjaneyulu, M.S.R., *Op. Cit.*, pp. 58-61.
45. Vadivelu, A., "*The Aristocracy of Southern India*", Vol. I and Vol. II, Delhi, 1984 Edition.
46. Frykenberg, Robert Eric., "*Guntur District, 1788 – 1848*", (Oxford, 1965).
47. Sarma, A.V.D., "*Integration of Andhra and Orissa, Cultures,*" Delhi. 1986.
48. Sudershan Rao, Y., *Op.Cit.* Hanmankonda, 1991.
49. Rama Lakshmi, C., "*The Northern Circars under the East India Company (1766 –1857)*" (Unpublished Thesis of Andhra University).

50. Surya Lakshmi, C., "*Zamindari Economy: Life in Bobbili*". (Unpublished Thesis of Andhra University).
51. Krishna, D.S., "*The Vatsavai family of Peddapuram*". (Unpublished Thesis of Andhra University).
52. Syama Sundar Raju, B., "*Vizianagaram zamindari in Colonial Andhra*". (Unpublished Thesis of Andhra University).
53. Anjaneyulu, M.S.R., *Op. Cit.*, 83.
54. Kesavanarayana, B., *"British Imperialism and Native Resistance in India: A Case Study of Nuzvid Zamindari, 1766 –1802"*.
55. Mallikarjuna Rao, I., *Native Revolts in the West Godavari District, 1785 – 1806,* (Unpublished Ph D Thesis of Andhra University).
55A. Nicooles Dirks, '*The Hollow Crown*', *Introduction*. p. 8.
55B. *Journal of Economic and social History of the Orient,* Vol. 39, No. 1(1996), pp. 69-72.
55C. Yasoda Devi, V., *History of the Andhra Country: Subsidiary Dynasties, J.A.H.R.S* Vol. XVIII to XXVII.
55D. Ramachandra Rao, C.V., *Administration and Society in Medieval Andhra (A.D.1038-A.D.1538) under the later Eastern Gangas and the Suryavamsi Gajapatis,* Nellore, 1976.
55E. Suryanarayana, K., *History of the Minor Chalukya Families in Medieval Andhradesa*. Delhi, 1986.
55F. Pradeep, L.V., *History of the Mandalika Rulers of Kalingandra* (Unpublished thesis submitted to Andhra University, 2005).
56. Kesavanarayana, B., *Op. Cit.*, p. 163.
57. Anjaneyulu, M.S.R., *Op. Cit*, p. 69.
58. Satyanarayana Murty, T., *Op. Cit.*, p. 42.
59. Kesavanarayana, B., *Op. Cit.*, p. 110.
60. Sudershan Rao, Y., *Op. Cit.*, p. 14.
61. Mallikarjuna Rao, I., *Op. Cit.*, (Unpublished theses, Chapter III, p. 10).
62. Satyanarayana Murty, T., *Op. Cit.*, p. 51.
63. *Ibid,* p. 53.
64. Letter of Vizagapatam Chief of Vijayaramaraju, dated 26th April 1793 *V.D.R.* 3696: 64.
65. Chief to B.O.R. 14 May 1794, *V.D.R.*, (3700: 151-52).
66. 18 and 24 January 1794 February, V.D.R., (3699: 55 and 67).
67. Chief's Minute, 3 September 1793, V.D.R (3696: 479).
68. Anjaneyulu, M.S.R., *Op. Cit.*, p. 106.
69. *Ibid,* pp. 82-116.
70. Carmichael, D.F., *Op. Cit.*, pp. 208-237.

71. Chaudhuri, S.D., *Civil Disturbances during the British Rule in India, 1765-1857,* pp. 116-118.
72. Letter of Representation from Narayana Raju to the President and Members of B.O.R, dated 14 November 1809, 17 November 1869, V.D.R. 3746 – 271.
73. Russell, G.E., *Op. Cit.,* p. 6.
74. Anjaneyulu, M.S.R., *Op. Cit.,* p. 71.
75. Chief to B.O.R, 9 July 1794, V.D.R. (3700 – 336).
76. Anjaneyulu, M.S.R. *Op. Cit.,* p. 15.
77. *Ibid,* p. 216.
78. *Ibid.*
79. *Ibid,* p. 14.
80. Saunders to Richard Bouchier (Governor of Bombay) RFSG: Diary, 24 September 1752, pp. 43-46.
81. RFSG : Letter from Fort St. George (F.S.G), 12 January 1754, p. 3.
82. RFSG : Country Correspondence (CC A.D. 1754, p. 28).
83. RFSG: Country Correspondence (C, 1758, pp. 40-41).
84. RFSG: Letters to FSG, 14 December 1758, pp.127-29, see also L. Forde Lord *Clives Right Hand Man* (London 1910), pp. 190-191.
85. Samalkot Kaifiyat, Mackenzie Mss. Oriental Manuscript Library, Madras.
86. L. Forde, Op. Cit., pp. 71-72.
87. Satyanarayana Murty, T., *Padmanabha Yuddham,* p. 8.
88. Carmichael, D.F. Op.Cit. 334.
88A. Francecis, W. Op.Cit.
88B. Anjayeyulu, M.S.R., Op.Cit, pp. 66-96.
88C. Madras Impartible Estates Act, 1904; amended as Tamilnadu Act, No.II of 1904.
88D. Vedivelu, A., Op.Cit, p. 193.
89. Bimili was granted by the Farmans of Nizam barring various dates from 1628 to 1713.
90. In 1754, Raghuji Bhonslae (Marathas) robbed and burnt Bimili.
91. In 1781, Bilimi was seized and destroyed by the English.
91A. Francis, W., *Op. Cit.,* p. 227.
92. Satyanarayana Murty, T. *Op. Cit.,* p. 1.
93. *Narsa bhupalarajiyam,* p. 5, cited by T.S.N. Murty in *proceedings of A.P.H.C.,* Vol. XII, p. 271.
94. Edward Cot Ford's letter RC 4A, p. 1485 referred to by M.S.R. Anjaneyulu, *Itihas*, Hyd. Vol. XVIII, 1992.

95. Firminger, W.F., *The Fifth Report from the select committee on the affairs of the East India Company,* Vol. II, Madras Presidency, Appendix-13, p. 3.

96. Report of the Committee of Circuit on the Kasimkota Division of the Chicacole Circar, October 11, 1784 (Printed in 1914).

97. Letter from the Secretary, White (Fort St. George) to Vijayaramaraju (VC), October, 30, 1778, V.D.R. 3692, pp. 323-324.

98. Letter to Fort St. George, August 30, 1783, V.D.R. 3686, pp. 384-386.

99. To the B.O.R dated May 15, VDR 3696, p. 200; Letter from the B.O.R dated June 3, enclosing on extract of a letter from the government and a letter to Vijayarama Raju dated May 22, VC, June 11, 1793, pp. 227-234.

100. Letter from the Government dated June 6, VC June 14, VDR 3696, pp. 236-237.

101. Collector to the B.O.R, February 21, and 22, 1794, p. 142; Chief to the BOR dated February 11, p. 99; and Collector to the B.O.R, February 13, p. 104 and February 20, 1794, p. 138, VDR, 3699.

102. VC April 15, VDR, 3699, pp. 380-388.

103. Vijayarama Raju to the Chief, dated May 9, VC, May 10, 1794, VDR 3700, p. 118 and pp. 120-121.

104. Ananda Gajapati III, Vizianagaram Treaty of November 15, 1758, Madras.

105. Intelligence from Padmanabham, July 13, 1794; V.D.R. 3701, pp. 273-275.

106. Letter from Prendergast, August 22, V.D.R. 3701, pp. 273-275.

107. Government Consultation, June 30, 1796, General Reports of the B.O.R, Paras 35-37.

108. Anjaneyulu, M.S.R., *Op Cit.,* pp. 111-112.

109. July 24, 1832, *VDR* (4744 : 305 – 14).

110. Anjaneyulu, M.S.R., *Op. Cit.,* p. 70.

111. *Ibid,* p. 69.

112. *"Payaka Rao Tupakigunduche Kalage Visakhapattnamu, Kampamu nonde Golugonda".*

113. Russell, G.E., Report on the Disturbances in *Parlakimedy, Vizagapatam and Goomsoor,* Vol. I, p. 6.

Chapter - 4

Society and Economy

Even upto to A.D. 1871, considerable section of the people, i.e., about 33.8 per cent were engaged only in agriculture and allied occupations, while those in government services and personal services did not exceed 5.0 per cent. The period between A.D. 1891 and A.D.1901 witnessed an increase in the urban and the rural population, by 25 per cent and 5 per cent respectively, and was caused by emenities and opportunities of urban life. A noteworthy shift of population from rural to urban areas occurs from the early decades of twentieth century, and this province under study is not an exception.[1] Visakhapatnam, Vizianagaram and Anakapalli, etc., were developed as urban centres. It was not just the growth of those towns that was noteworthy, but rise of Visakhapatnam as an important port that earned the approbation and appreciation of numerous officers and town-planners like Goddes. He believed that Visakhapatnam was an excellent example of town planning and house building efficiency, which was traditional in India. He observed: "I have heard Waltair repeatedly described as a Brighton, but the comparison is quite inadequate. It corresponds rather to the fine portion of the Riviera."[2]

Social Groups and Migrations

Majority of the social groups that belongs to various castes and sub-castes came over to this province from different parts of the country in different periods for various purposes. Some of the communities and sub-communities connected themselves with this province.

The Dravidas which was an important sub-group among the Brahmins of this area claims of different origins. Arama Dravidas were stated to have hailed from the Aramas; Peruru Dravidas claim their origin from Peruru, where as Dimili Dravidas claim that they originally belong to Dimili of this province, which village was referred to by Enugula eeraswamayya also in his "*Kasiyatra Charitra.*"[3] Some of the scholarly families were brought over here by the zamindars. The grants of agraharas, *srothriams*, and inams made those donee Brahmins to come over to those respective areas. Almost all the zamindari families that connected themselves with this province liberally granted land fiefs and villages to scholars and Brahmins, who came over here from elsewhere and settled here.

In granting such villages, some of the zamindars renamed those villages in the name of their parents, which was noticed in the case of Gode family, who renamed the granted villages as Subhadrapuram, and Suryanaryanapuram.[4] The Bhupathi family of Madugula particularly the Krishna Bhupathi granted a number of land grants to scholars and same was the case with other zamindars also. Pusapati Sitaramaraju has given an agrahara to the Vemula family and brought them to Anakapalli area. Majority of the Niyogi brahmins hailed from the Godavari districts. The Sistu karanam or Patnaik families had their original home in Orissa. Golukonda Vyaparis originally belong to Telangana areas came over here along with Kakarlapudis.[5]

A number of families which claim themselves as Kshatriyas spread throughout this area by establishing their own settlements begin with Vizianagaram upto Payakaraopeta. A number of villages consist of Kshatriyas in good number. Tangedu, Oaddadi, Koppaka, Darlapudi, Kondala Agraharam, Rachapalli, Rambilli, Melipaka, Alamanda, Jonnavalasa, Rakodu and a number of other villages of this province are well-known for the Kshatriya population. Sagi, Vatsavai, Penumatsa, Datla, Chintalapati, Gottumukkala, etc., were the surnames of those Kshatriyas of this province.

Gollalu, a shepherd community which constitutes a majority population in this area, claims that they originally belongs to this province and they bore the surnames like Panchadharla, Elamanchili and Upamaka, the names of some of the villages of this province.[6]

Koppula Velamas, a sub-caste in the Velamas which is a dominating section in the population of this tract had their origin in the Velanadu area and came over here gradually by settling at various places in the entire Nothern coastal Andhra.

The Arya Vaisyas who consider themselves as pure Vaisyas settled in this province from earlier times and traced their origin somewhere at Penugonda, referred to in their communal history (*Kula Purana*) *Vaisya Puranam*. They were the worshippers of Kanyaka Parameswari, and they used to construct temples to that Goddess in all important towns where, they reside. Some of the Vaisya families who bore the surnames like Tadikonda, Uppara Boggavarapu, Tammana, Immedisetti, seems to come over here from the present Telangana portions of Andhra Pradesh.[7]

Besides the above, a number of other castes and sub-castes that lived in different occupations appear here during the period under study. Because this area consists of a good coast line, a number of fishermen villages existed throughout the coast of this area. Konada, Bhimunipatnam, Visakhapatnam, Mutyalapudu, Gangavaram, Appikonda, Pudimadaka, Revupolavaram, etc., were the centres of fishing community, Reddikas, who now claimed themselves as Reddis were also found in and around Visakhapatnam.

As this entire area experienced Muslim rule and subjected to a number of Muslim attacks, there was no wonder in noticing a number of Muslim Settlements throughout the area. A number of Dargas and Masjids were found at a number of places. It is already stated how the Muslims played the significant role, in the 'Sepoy Mutiny' at Visakhapatnam in A.D. 1780, which may be credited to be the first war of Indian Independence.[8]

It is already noticed that how during the period of the Godes the Church activity of the Christians gradually increased in this area. Owing to the cosmopolitan nature of Visakhapatnam it attracts a number of Colonial agencies who established Churches, and began their Missionary services here. Besides urban and rural centres they extended their services to the hilly regions and tribal areas like Paderu and Madugula of the district. As such the population of the Christians is also not less in this area.

A very important community that needs special study in this part of the country was the Gavara community. Though this community was a minority in the total population of the area, their customs and systems made them a unique community. This community was located only in this area and even those communities that migrated to other areas claimed this area as their original home.[9] Discussing on this significant community Suravaram Pratapa Reddi, traced their origin in Bengal and thought that they came over here during sixth-seventh centuries A.D.[10] E.H. Thurston in his *Castes and Tribes of Southern India* considered Gaaras as a sub-division among the Vaisyas; and also complimented them as the best agriculturists of the area.

In literature, though this community had no specific mention in the early centuries, they were referred to in the *Sukasaptati* written by Palavekari Kadiripati of Seventeenth Century.

The word 'Gaura' or 'Gavara' is a 'desi' word which means a Vanija or businessman. The *Sukasaptati* states that Gavaras formed a separate community which had business as its profession. Just like any other community, Gavaras originated on the basis of profession and religious practices. Gavaras lived particularly in the areas around Anakapalli, pudimadaka of this province. Gowridevi or Gouramma was their tutelary deity. As in the case of other communities, the Gavaras had also some traditional stories about their origin. The historicity and other details of those traditions (though not unquestionable), resembled the stories of other communities like the Vaisyas, the Sadhusettis, the Balijas and the Perikis. In addition, some of the surnames and *gotras* of the Gavaras coincide with those of the Sadhusettis, the Perikis and the Vaisyas. It is also believed that it was one among the ex-communicated division of the Vaisyas, as narrated in the *Kulapuranas* of the Vaisyas.[11]

Basing upon the inscriptional evidence that refers to the construction of a temple of Papavinasana Deva at Panchadharla of this area in A.D.1432, it is surmised that this community made this area as their settlement at least from Fifteenth Century onwards. Aitamsetti, Adari, Alla, Kanisetti, Karri, Kalla, Kandregula, Komila, Konatala, Koyilada, Korubilli, Tarahsya, Chadaram, Tanakala, Dadi, Doddi, Parim, Petakamsetti, Pilla, Paila, Polamarasetti, Polimera,

Pentakota, Budda, Boddede, Malla, Maddala, Madeti, Marisetti, Molleti, Yallapu, Rapeti, Rajagiri, Villuri, Yalaga, Vegi, Sarakanam, Silaparisetti, Sarise, Surisetti, Tekkali, Bisetti, Vadisetti, etc., were the surnames borne by the Gavara families. The surnames like Pilla, Konatala and Vegi traced their connections with the areas of Tamil Nadu and Vengi.[12] A majority of the surnames had the honorary suffix 'Setti'. It is interesting to note that some of the same surnames and *gotras* were known to the communities like Kapu, Balija, Sadhusettis and Perikis. As E.H. Thurston noticed, even today, the community of the Gavaras made agriculture as their main profession. Being hard working people, they succeeded in the field of business also. In implementing new agricultural methods and in cultivating commercial crops, the position of the Gavaras was unique one.

It is stated, that the Payak Raos of Anakapalli zamindar encouraged this community due to their expertise in the cultivation of sugar-cane.[13] Even the ladies of this community, were skilled in agriculture and business. They were against to the unhealthy practices like smoking, etc., and interested in group living. Until recent times, the ladies of the Gavaras had their own fashion in wearing the neck-ornament named Kuttiganta; heavy gold rings to nose and ears; and big-sized single bangle, named Kadiya or Chanda to forearms. It was a regular custom in this community to install the idols of the ancestors, after their death. Construction of temples and performance of the festival of Gauri were their normal practices. They were enterprising and were interested in exploring into new fields. They spread as far as Burma, Malaysia, Mauritius and South Africa; and wherever they have gone, they proved themselves as an intelligent and dynamic community acquiring name and fame not only to their community, but to this province also, which they claimed as their motherland.

Thus, there lived different communities in this province by adopting various professions during the period under study. As this province is adjacent to highway in the East Coast that connecting the North and South, travelogue literature like '*Kasiyatra Charitra*' of Enugula Veera Swamayya gave more information about this area. He has stated those fourteen lakhs of rupees income was derived from Visakhapatnam district during the time of his journey. The entire land in the district is stated to be under the control of zamindars.

Twenty five per cent (25 per cent) commission was taken by the zamindars from their revenue collections. The revenue of the district is stated to have much affected by dacoits.

Redocher (Jeguru) colour was painted and white dots were designed in rows to beautify the walls of the houses in the villages. Door jombs of the houses were decorated with turmeric and Kumkum. Usage of Tambula and Tabacco smoking was common.

Sabbavaram near Anakapalli is also referred to by Enugula Viraswamayya. Zamindars granted an agrahara to Vennakota (Vinna Kota?), Brahmin family to maintain there a choultry which is stated to have well-maintained.

Referring about the pilgrim centre Simhachalam, he informed that two hundred houses located there. Veeraswami described that the entire highway was surrounded with thick jungles and with the movement of tigers.

Some superstitions and believes existed in the villages. It is stated that in the village Dimili, an agrahara, though all the Brahmins were the rich, they used to live only in the thatched-houses due to a curse of a Saint!

It is stated that sheep, buffaloes, etc., were more in number in Panchadharla Elamanchili, Upmaka and Nakkapalli areas.[14] (This was probably due to the predominant population of the Shepherds like Gollas, of this area which was also evident by the *Kulapuranas* like *Yedavapurana*. Otherwise know as *Katamaraju Kathalu*).

Veeraswami described the ladies in the Visakhapatnam Province as they were very beautiful and with good facial features.

Population

In 1861, the population of Visakhapatnam was 16,758; and the then population of Vizianagaram was 17,019. By this it was understood, that due to a number of occupations and patronages the population in big zamindaris was comparitively more. But due to the trade activities of the Company, from next decade there occured a change and the population gradually began to increase in Visakhapatnam Bhimilipatnam, which consisted a population of 5,912 the first municipality in the entire Madras Presidency on 09-02-1860 and it is second one in India.

The following tables indicate the population position of the then district as well as of the important towns in this area:[15]

Table 4.1: Population of Visakhapatnam District

Year	*Population*
1871	21,59,199
1881	24,85,141
1891	28,02,261
1901	29,33,038
1911	31,89,821
1921	31,92,229
1931	36,07,948
1941	38,45,944

Table 4.2: Population of Important Towns in Visakhapatnam District

	1871	*1881*	*1891*	*1901*	*1911*	*1921*	*1931*
Visakhapatnam	32191	30291	34487	40892	43413	44711	57303
Vizianagaram	20169	22577	30881	37270	37650	39299	44696
Anakapalli	13044	13341	17010	18539	20625	20360	23376
Narsipatnam	6160	7767	9785	10589	11268	11531	14005
Elamanchili	3648	4649	6296	6536	7036	10441	11763
Bimilipatnam	8744	8582	9827	10212	9314	7495	9629
Madugula	7428	7612	9133	8952	6611	5966	6346
Chodavaram	4475	4601	7729	7931	8242	5853	6624

Visakhapatnam

Visakhapatnam was the smallest taluk in the district and next to the ordinary tracts in Palakonda; it was the most densely populated. Its inhabitants increased at a relatively higher rate than those of any other taluk, in this province. It contained more number of Muslims and

Christians than any other taluk, and its people were also better educated than those of any other area. Probably it was due to the connections with the zamindar, the company and the Christian activity.

It is a picturesque tract. The coast line is broken by the bold headland called the Dolphin's Nose (1,174 feet above the sea), the hills which run down to the shore by Lawson's Bay, just North of Waltair and the Sugar-loaf hill which separates this from the Bay just beyond it, and inland stands the Simhachalam range of rounded red hills and its continuation Northward towards Bhimilipatnam.[16]

Immediately North of Dolphin's Nose, was a small river called the 'Upputeru' (canal into which back waters flow).[17]

The Dolphin's Nose is known to the natives as 'Blackmore's hills'. In 1801, Captain Thomas Blackmore, of the Artillery stationed at Visakhapatnam, obtained a grant from the Company for 44 acres of land on the hill (on which, 'some years before', he had built a house) and also permission to occupy, enclose and embellish the declivity of the hill next the sea'. This house was perhaps the building of which the ruins still stand on the very top of the hill. The remains of foundations by the neighbouring flag-staff seem to show that there was also once a battery there. It is stated that there was once a light-house here,[18] and that it was blown down in the cyclone of 1876.[19]

Lower down the Dolphin's hill, on the side facing town, Mr J.W. McMurray, Treasury Deputy Collector constructed a bungalow in 1886.

To save the coast from the sea erosion, a series of loose stone grains (still visible) were put down in 1844, Sir Arthur Cotton.[20]

Mr A.T. Mackenzi of the public works department made a report in 1899 on "Viziagapatam Harbour Investigations" which was is an authoritative account of the difficulties involved in the harbour, and the remedies for them.

Dabagardens, the, residence of Ankitam Venkata Jagga Rao contains the Observatory of Gode Venkata Jagga Rao, originally established in 1841. He erected the existing flag staff on the Dolphin's Nose, the flagon which used to be hauled down precisely at 9.00 a.m. to set the time for the station. After his death his daughter,

Mrs A.V. Narasinga Rao, and her husband added largely to the equipment of the Observatory. The institution began the contribution to the Bengal and Government of India Meteorological Departments of the series of observations which was continued upto 1884 A.D. In A.D. 1884, Mrs. Narasinga Rao proposed to endow the institution with a fund of three lakhs and hand it over to trustees under the control of the Madras Government. That government did not find themselves able, to accept the position, but eventually in 1895, the Government of India vested the Observatory under the management of a committee. Subsequently A.V. Jagga Rao regained control of the Observatory and its endowment.The instruments there include six-inch equatorial, a three-inch transit instrument, a sidereal clock and a photographic telescope. That observatory was the prestigious institution of the Visakhapatnam zamindars.

Besides English officers, the local zamindars tried hard for the growth of Visakhapatnam. Gode Narayana Gajapati and his wife donated Rs 10,000 to clear and level the site adjacent to Dabagardens which was later developed as Maharanipeta.

Most of the lands in the Waltair area were the haveli lands, and sold by auction in 1802. As such, the details of various constructions in Waltair were not properly recorded. The present Kailasagiri hill, West of Waltair also known as 'Thomas Folly', on the top of which Mr E.C.G. Thomas, the then Judge of Visakhapatnam, made it as his residence in 1871. The Pusapati family of Vizianagaram, the original owners of the hill constructed a permanent house for Mr.Thomas, the remains of which are stated to have visible for a long period.

In between Maharanipeta and Dabagardens there was Suryabagh, the residence of Rani of Wadhwan. Just North of it, there was 'the Regimental Lines Cemetery, which was known as *Mors Janu a Vitoe Cemetery*, Consecrated by Bishop Spencer in 1847. The Protestant cemetery, near the present Municipal office was consecrated by Bishop Gell in 1864. Some learned men and business people formed a group in 1858 as "Voluntary Municipality Association of Vizagapatnam" to act voluntary on behalf of the people in the maters like education and health. It is mere a voluntary organisation and in the entire Madras Presidency, it was first voluntary Municipal organisation.

That association is transformed in 1866, as Municipality of Vizagapatnam. Due to the District Municipality Act of 1884, its name was changed as Municipal Council of Vizagapatnam.

Majority of the zamindars in Northern Coastal Andhra have their palaces in Visakhapatnam. Hawa Mahal, Godavari Devidi, Chemudu Rani Palaces, palaces of Kurupam Zamindar, and Vizianagaram Palace, were of such type. Some of the zamindars donated their palaces for endowment purposes, charitable organisations and for educational and medical institutions.

Central Jail in Visakhapatnam was constructed in 1908 (and it was recently shifted to Mudasarlova area situated back to Simhachalam hill).

It is not beyond context to discuss about some of the revolts against British administration that have taken place in this province. The memories of some of the revolutionaries were still there in different areas. At Chodavaram, hanging from a tree in the Deputy Tahsildar's office compound was one of the old iron cages in which the bodies of revolutionaries used to be gibbeted after execution. It was formerly suspended from a gallows, but this rotted to pieces and it was then brought to its present situation. It was made for the body of one Asi-Dora, the mokhasadar of Pedda Madina, who was hanged in March, 1840 for the murder, on the night of March 6, 1837, of Kasturi Appayya Pantulu, the Collector's Sheristadar, as he was returning from office in a palanquin. It appears that after the Vizianagaram estate was placed under the management of the Collector in 1827, endeavours, in which the Sheristadar was very active, were made to assess to Kattubadi (payment), the numerous mokhasas and inams which upto then had escaped rent-free. The murder was a result of the unpopularity which the Sheristadar incurred in consequence.[21]

One important tribal revolt in the Visakhapatnam province was the revolt of Korra Mallayya at Saluru in 1900. Korra Mallayya was a tribal leader. He had strongly opposed the forest policies of British government. He had distributed bamboo sticks to his followers, who used the sticks as rifles and raided over, the district authorities. Nearly 5,000 tribals were imprisoned. Korra Mallayya had passed away in the prison itself. This revolt was ruthlessly suppressed.[21A]

The 'Sepoy Mutiny' of 1780, at Visakhapatnam which was the first of that type in Indian history is discussed already in the earlier chapters. Kingsford Verrner, a Cadet of 19 was killed in the Sepoy Mutiny of 1780 at Visakhapatnam and he was burried in the old cemetery.[22]

There were occasional fights between the English and the French, and on September 18, 1804, John Dykes, a young seaman was killed in stirring fight in the Visakhapatnam roads by a French man.[23] In honour of the police or revenue officers, who lost their lives in the tribal revolts, memorials were constructed in the Sub-Collector's office at Narsipatnam, with the details as stated hereunder on those memorials:

IN MEMORY OF

CAPTAIN JOHN JAMES GIBSON

26TH REGNNCNTNI

WHO DEPARTED THIS LIFE ON THE 30TH

DAY OF JANUARY, *1849*

AGED 52 YEARS AND 2 MONTHS

THIS MONAINETI SEETED BY

HI SAI FLTETED WINDOW

BLEFHED ARE THE DEAD WHICH

DIE IN THE LORD

IN MEMORY OF

PARTY FOR THE SOUL OF

CHRISTOPHER WILLIAM SCOTT COWARD

ASSISTANT SUPERINTENDENT INDIAN POLICE

BORN - 29TH MAY 1895

WHO WAS KILLED IN AN AMBUSH ON THE DAMANAPALLI

GHAUT ON 24TH SEPTEMBER 1922 DURING

THE REBELLION IN THE GUDEM HILLS

HE WAS A RENOWNED SHI KAR AND A FINE

LEADER OF MEN

IN MEMORY OF

NAME - LIONEL, NEVILLE HAYTER
- HELDEST SON OF HARRY HAYTER
OF THE DAMANAPALLI GHAUT ON 24 SEPTEMBER - 1922
DURING THE REBELLION IN THE
GUDEM HILLS
- HE WAS BORN ON 11th SEPTEMBER 1896 AND AFTER
HAVING SARVED IN THE BRITISH AND INDIAN
ARMIES FROM 1914 TO 1920 WAS SARVING
TEMPORARILY
- AS AN ASSISTANT SUPERINTENDENT IN THE INDIAN POLICE

All such revolts and killing of government personnal, testify to the avengence of some people against the British Policies.

The Municipality of Visakhapatnam with a view to improve the sanitation of the place acquired the house sites of the fishermen there, and ordered them to remove themselves to some other place far away from the town. Soon after this was done, Vairicherla Virabhadra Raju of Kurupam, in the course of his usual visit to the poor, comes across a number of sick beds near the new site, granted to the fishermen by the municipality. As they always lived near the sea, and as they suddenly removed to swampy places, more than half the number died from the effects of the change. The Raja of Kurupam came to the rescue of the survivors by purchasing a suitable site for them at his own cost, near the beach.

British Burma, with its extensive uncultivated barren lands, attracted much of the labour from this part of the country in general and from Visakhapatnam province in particular. Large streams of working class began to flow out to Rangoon and Moulmein, in search of living. While women from this area worked as prostitutes in the Burmese Sea Boards, men went mostly as labourers and a few as traders. The long-standing British-India Steamer Circuit, Kakinada-Visakhapatnam-Gopalpur -Rangoon, contributed greatly to familiarizing the people of the area with the idea of Burma and so stimulated an emigration flow thither. The anti-Indian agitation in Burma which showed itself in the violent riots in Rangoon sent back to their native land a good many Indians apprehensive of future worse developments.[24]

Migrations due to Droughts or Famines

A number of droughts disturbed the economy as, well as the normal life of this province. In the years 1824, 1871-72, in 1876-78, 1885-86, 1889, 1896-97, this area witnessed severe droughts and famines; and in 1870, 1878, these areas were effected with floods. Owing to those natural calamities, a number of artisan groups, as well as cultivators were forced to migrate to other areas.

Public Health and Hospitals

This period witnessed the spent of substantial funds on public health by the zamindars. Small Pox and Cholera are the seasonal diseases generally prevalent in different parts of this province. Still more prevalent disease in this part of the country was fever, which appeared in mild form. This fever characterised by congestion of the brain, liver and spleen caused effect upon the nervous system, the digestion was also impaired and the disease frequently passed into typhoid state terminating to death. The worst season of the year for this disease was undoubtedly the rainy season and the least unhealthy period was from November to April.[25] The zamindars were so sympathetic towards the people in their zamindaris and tried to save them from those epidemics. To enlighten the people and to realise the benefits of vaccination, some of the foresighted zamindars published pamphlets of lectures of the Principal Inspector-General, in Telugu.[26]

The government servants also started a hospital to offer treatment to Company's servants as well as to people who lived in and around Visakhapatnam. The 'Vizagapatam Civil-Dispensary' originated in 1845, was located in the centre of the town in an old building. By the end of 1857, it was shifted to a new building which was constructed at a cost of rupees 17,200, in which the government sanctioned an amount of Rs 6,975; and the rest of the amount was collected by the Gode zamindars. That hospital maintained a poor ward and its expenditure was met by the subscription of the people. But it became difficult in course of time to meet the expenditure of Rs 70 to Rs 80 per month. To create a permanent fund and to relieve the government from this burden the Civil Assistant Surgeon, C.A. Andrews convinced Pusapati Vijayarama Gajapati, to donate huge fund for its maintenance. Vijayarama Gajapati with his noble ideals and for that noble cause gave property to the value of Rs 20,000 for the permanent support of the Civil Dispensary at Visakhapatnam.[27]

And the Raja stipulated that "the sum should be invested in the name of Collector for the time being"; and that the committee appointed to supervise the administration of the funds should consist of public officers of the government.[28] In accordance with his wish the Governor appointed a Committee consisting of different government officers, viz., Collector, Civil and Sessions Judge, W.C. Clark, Paymaster, Ankitam Venkata Narasinga Rao, Deputy Collector and C. Poorushottamayya, District Munsiff, Visakhapatnam, to supervise the administration of the endowment of the Poor Ward of Civil Dispensary.[29]

In recognition of his high character in these respects, his Excellency the Viceroy and Governor-General John Lawrence bestowed on the zamindar of Vizianagaram the title of "Maharaja" in the sannad of 1864.[30]

Later, in 1913, the English Government handed over that hospital and allotted 36 acres of land for it. The construction of new buildings of the hospital were completed by 1923, at an expense of Rs 4,97,910. As the Country was under the rule of Emperor George V, that hospital was named after him. The then Chief Minister of the combined Madras State, Raja Panuganti Ramarayudu inaugurated it on July 19, 1923. That was the present King George Hospital (K.G.H) in Visakhapatnam.

The medical services of the zamindars were not limited to the urban centres; they extended those services to some selected villages also. At Sabbavaram and Chipurupalli, the Pusapati zamindars established hospitals.

The Vatsavai Zamindars, whose estate boardered that of the Kakarla pudis also showed much interest in taking care of the health of the people. Some of them showed much faith in Ayurvedic medicine. They prepare excellent drugs, mixtures and used to give them away free to the people. They had English, Ayurvedic and Unani medicines with them; and maintained an establishment for preparing and administering them.

In A.D.1883, Mental Hospital was established in a big garden in China Waltair, at Visakhapatnam.

In A.D.1894, Gode Narayana Gajapati purchased a Dutch Bungalow where in it a hospital for ladies in the name of Empress Queen Victoria as "Victoria Gosha Hospital"was established (It is adjacent to Kodanda Rama Swamy temple in the old town).

Rani China Janakamma, the wife of Gode Narayana Gajapati has not satisfied with the medical facilities of the estate, and in consultation with the government, established a Medical School appended to the King George Hospital, which in course of time developed as Andhra Medical College.

Education: Another important aspect that closely relates with society, next to medicine is education. The zamindars of this province, majority of them being educationalists, extended their services for the promotion of education also. Besides, missionaries also encouraged education.

In the first half of nineteenth Century, this much is the information on education in the then Visakhapatnam District:[31]

> Population – 9,14,001, Schools in the District - 914, Hindu students-9,618 (girls - 303), Muslim students - 97 (Girls - nil), Total number of students - 9,715.

In fixing the salaries of teachers in schools, a Committee of Government in A.D. 1832 recommend thus: English headmaster Rs 300 per month; Arabian and Parisian teachers 70 per month; Telugu, Kannada and Tamil teachers Rs 15 per month; Sanskrit teachers Rs 70 per month.

At Visakhapatnam there were some liberal officers like Patric, B. Smollet who served as Agent of the Company. During 1855-56, he reported to the government to increase the salaries of Indians and to multiply them up to three times.[32]

By 1855, London Missionary Society established an English medium school and girls' school at Visakhapatnam. Lord Patric B. Smollet in his report deliberately commented how due to the politics of the Company, majority of sections, educated as well as peasant groups were suffering.

Sir Thomas Munro noticed that how the education was neglected in the British administration. He despatched letters to the District Collectors seeking information on the number of schools in their respective districts, type of education, methodology, asked suggestions without involving into the religious sentiments of the people and the necessity of the financial support.

Warren Hastings reviewed the educational conditions of this province, and suggested a number of reforms to be implemented. He noticed the necessity of encouraging native education. He recommended to establish a Hindu Higher Education Institution at Simhachalam, and a Muslim Madrasa at Chicacole (Srikakulam); and to grant a sum of rupees one lakh annually for their maintenance[33], but the government has not followed that recommendation.

A very important question that demanded the attention of experts in matters of education was whether any instances existed in which government institutions of high academic status had been closed or transferred, to the management of local bodies, as contemplated in the Despatch of 1854, and what were the chief reasons, why more effect had not been given to that provision. Most of the authorities were not aware of any such instances; it being impossible to find local bodies willing to take over such institutions, and the Commission had to consider that the country generally, was not yet ripe for voluntarily bearing any educational burden. Yet nearly half a century ago in Visakhapatnam, Gode Narayana Gajapati actively promoted a movement, the pioneer of such enterprises in the Presidency, which resulted in the establishment of the Hindu College at Visakhapatnam.

Narayana Gajapati headed an undertaking with a view to promote female education under the auspices of D.F. Carmichael, the Collector and Agent to the Governor at Visakhapatnam, which led to the opening of the 'Visakhapatnam Caste Girls School' (now under the management of the sisters of St. Joseph's Convent). It is solely supported by the Gode family. Janakayamma, wife of Gode Suryaprakasa Rao, was most appropriately elected the first patroness of what was the first institution of the kind in Southern India. There was also an adult caste Girls school at the same place called the "Maharani Gajapati Rao Ladies Institution."

Besides granting donations and monthly subscriptions to many charitable and educational institutions of all denominations, Narayanamma Gajapati was the donor of several prizes and of the "Carmichael medal" awarded every year by the Hindu College at Visakhapatnam. He founded a Sanskrit Prize for the University of Madras, known as the 'Godevari Sanskrit Prize'. As a member of the Senate, he took a great interest in educational matters.[34]

Gode Narayana Gajapathi was responsible for the starting of Anglo-Vernacular School in Visakhapatnam in A.D.1860, which later developed into Hindu College and was finally christened as Mrs. A.V.N. College.

After Janakamma's death, her daughter, Ratnayamma, the wife of Gudivada Lakshmi Narasimharayulu maintained the school. Along with the teaching of English and Telugu, Fine Arts useful to women such as painting, music, knitting and other crafts were taught in the school. In the very first year of its inception there were 38 girls studying in the school.

Prior to the zamindari regime in this province, the education of the people of this province was not on Western lines. The schools were run purely by Brahmins, imparting classical literature and traditional education. The education on modern lines has not received attention upto Nineteenth Century. It was zamindars of this province that established schools and colleges for the spread of education in this part of the country, as at other places.

In the second half of Nineteeth Century, the British administration encouraged the zamindars, to involve in spreading education with liberality and to take measures for the establishment of educational institutions. Christian institutions and Churches of different European countries liberally opened educational institutions to spread education as well as Christianity. The wide knowledge secured by some of the zamindars under the civil servants and their attachment with the learned people at places like Madras and Calcutta, widened the minds of some of the zamindars to contribute for the promotion of education.[35]

With the enlightenment they got they thought it wise and auspicious to establish schools.[36] They established schools not only in their zamindari areas, but also at important parts of the country like Madras, Visakhapatnam and Rajahmundry. For example, Pusapati Vijayarama Gajapati of Vizianagaram liberally contributed funds to the Anglo-Vernacular School at Visakhapatnam which was established in 1860 by Grant, inspector of Public Instructions, for many years.[37] Some of the zamindari families have created facilities for the promotion of higher education. Poor people were offered a free boarding as well. Some of the zamindaris like Pusapatis established an institution for the promotion of Sanskrit learning. As said earlier, the zamindars of Vizianagaram, Bobbili and Jeypore also showed keen interests for the promotion of education in Visakhapatnam province. Pusapatis established three scholarships for those students of higher education in Madras University who originally belongs to this province. The value of scholarship was Rs 15 and it was raised to Rs 20 after a student passed his F.A. examination. Two years will be allowed for passing F.A. examination, and three years for the Degree of B.A. or B.L. and the zamindari also bore all the expenses for their passage to Madras.[38]

Vijayarama Gajapati III was known for his liberal activities; and he donated several places in and around Bimilipatnam for the public purpose. He donated land close to the adjoining Municipal Reading Room at Visakhapatnam, and at the entrance of the town, from Vizianagaram to Visakhapatnam for the construction of Anglo-Vernacular school buildings by the municipality with the assistance of subscription of its inhabitants.[39]

In 1857, Roman Catholic Missionaries established an English School at Visakhapatnam. During the period of Queen Victoria that school was recognised and it served the needs of only the English and Zamindari families.

A number of private schools run by private agencies as well as by missionaries were recognised and grants were allotted during the period of Queen Victoria.[40]

Chilakamarthi Lakshmi Narasimham in his autobiography states that in 1881, Alexander Munro was the Inspector of Schools at Visakhapatnam.[41]

As stated already Gode, Narayana Gajapati with the support of local nobles established Anglo-Vernacular School at Visakhapatnam in 1860. Later, it is affiliated to University of Madras in the name of Hindu College. In 1892, Ankitam Venkata Narasinga Rao donated Rs 1,15,000 (One Lakh Fifteen Thousand) and changed its name in memory of his wife, Achichayamma as Mrs. Ankitam Venkata Narasinga Rao College. From A.D. 1892 to A.D. 1943, students were trained in that college only upto F.A., i.e., course equivalent to Intermediate.

Andhra University which was originally established at Vijayawada on April 26, 1926, was shifted to Visakhapatnam on September 5, 1930, with the zamindar of Bobbilli as Pro-Chancellor. Almost all the zamindars of this province extended their helping hand, and liberally contributed for the procurement of the site, and for the construction of the buildings for the University. During the Non-Cooperation Movement, in protest to the arrest of the national leaders, Cattamanchi Ramalinga Reddi, the Vice-Chancellor of the University resigned to his position; and re-elected for second time on May 20, 1936 and continued upto December, 1949. During the period of Second World War on April 6, 1942, Japan bombed on Visakhapatnam and at that time temporarily Andhra University was shifted to Guntur and brought back in 1946.

The Hindu Reading Room which was established in a building with the financial support of the Narayana Gajapati became very old, and in 1909, it was shifted by Vikrama Deo Varma, the Jeypore Zamindar, and others to a place called 'Dharmasramam' which is adjacent to Gosha Hospital. Later the eldest daughter of Narayana Gajapati, Sitabai the Rani of Wadhwan financially supported it and constructed a new building in 1917, in memory of his father "Maharaja Sir G.N. Gajapati Rao Hindu Reading Room." It was inaugurated on February 24, 1917 by the then Madras Governor, John Baren Pentland.

In token of the completion of 50 years, and latter 60 years of Queen Victoria's regime, Golden Jubilee celebrations and Diamond Jubilee celebrations were organised throughout the country. Majority of zamindars encouraged their court poets to write songs, *prasastis and kavyas* in praise of Queen Victoria; and have established a number of buildings, statues and halls in her name. During the period of Narayana Gajapati Rao such celebrations were held at Visakhapatnam also. After his death under their heir-apparent Ankitam Venkata Jagga Rao on May 24, 1904, a statue of Queen Victoria was inaugurated in a four road junction, by the then District Collector, H. Campbell. (It is now situated at Old – Post Office in the Old Town).

ECONOMY

Landholdings in the Visakhapatnam Province:

The state is the proprietor of the soil and it raised the greater portion of its revenue from the landed classes, whether directly from the cultivating ryot, or from the zamindar who holds large estates as middlemen, or direct owner subject to the land tax. The right of holding land is subject to the payment of customary rents and taxes.

The following is the average extent of holding in acres in the Visakhapatnam district, in different decades.[41A]

Table 4.3

Years	*Acres*
1866-1876	81,618
1876-1886	86,288
1886-1896	1,25,644
1896-1906	1,74,796
1906-1916	1,79,238
1916-1926	1,81,694
1926-1936	3,12,789
1936-1941	5,17,887

This clearly shows how in the different decades land holding gradually increased. It increased 15 per cent in between 1886-1896; it went upto 72 per cent in between 1926-1936, and 65 per cent in between 1936-1941. Probably it was due to land reclamation. This increase in the extent of land holding resulted in the increase of assessment also, which will be shown in the same chapter (Table 4.3).

Land Revenue

The whole question of the Land Revenue Settlement formed the subject of a very animated discussion in the early years of the last century (1807-1820), the Madras System being the occasion and the focus of the discussion.[42] Land revenue is derived from (i) peshkash or revenue from permanently settled estates, (ii) *shrotriam* Jodi or quit-rent levied on *inam* villages, (iii) assessment, including water rate, on lands held under the ryotwari system, and (iv) the Miscellaneous revenue.[43] The principal land revenue paying classes of the Presidency are the zamindars, whole inamdars, minor inamdars and ryotwari pattadars.[44]

Ownership of land is an age old question. Conflicting ideas prevailed about the status of land. While Cornwallis believed that the State was the proprietor of the soil, some others like John S. Mill contended that land was private property subject to payment of revenue.[45] Some like Sir Charles Wood, in 1864, stated that the assessment was revenue and not rent. Contrary to expectations, the government accepted that assessment was rent. The difference between rent and revenue was obvious to the cultivator under the rent theory, these payments were a portion of his gross produce, limited by the condition of his first paying wages and profits; under the Ryotwari, they were unlimited either way except by the mercy of the government.[46]

Initial settlements having been carried out in all districts throughout the Presidency, the operations to be carried out in the future will be almost entirely re-settlements. A re-settlement consists in a revision of the rates of assessment which were calculated not on holding, but on fields which may then be in the same or in different holdings. In revising those rates, changes in prices, in means of communication, in the accessibility of markets and in the quality of the irrigation sources since the original settlement are taken into consideration, together with any other indications of economic progress or retrogression. A re-settlement may also be made by remodelling the original settlement by a reclassification of soils and the application of a new set of money rates based on a fresh calculation of grain out turns, cultivation expenses etc.[47]

Under the Ryotwari Settlement, the soils are classified and grouped according to the source of irrigation available and for each of the classes of the soil a grain value is adopted which represents normal gross produce which is then converted into cash by the application of a commutation rate. The basis of this system is the division of the whole area into fields by a cadastral survey, each field being valued at a fixed rate per acre and the assessment settled there on. In the Ryotwari system, the revenue is assessed on individual cultivators; and there is a single headman, generally hereditary, who is responsible for order and for the payment of the government dues.[48]

Ryotwari lands were upto 1864-65, classified under the Madras Revenue System into lands assessed as dry, wet and garden.

Zamindaris or landed estates held under a sanad or title-deed showing proprietorship as against the government and paying a land revenue or peshkash fixed in perpetuity. Zamindars hold under a deed termed a "Sanad-i-milkeut istimrar" and give in exchange a corresponding Kabulyait or acceptance.[49] Zamindars and persons registered as 'Proprietors' under the Limited Proprietors Act IV of 1911 have the power to appoint the village officers employed in the villages of the estate according to a sale approved by the Collector and the Board of Revenue.[50]

Inam land, which is wholly or partially free from assessment, comprises fields which have been given to individuals at various times, as rewards for services, or as funds for the support of pagodas, choultries (or resting places for travellers), and other charitable purposes; or from motives which were merely personal.[51]

In 1941, Visakhapatnam District had 1,187 Inam villages, which consisted of an area about 5,04,022 acres of land.[52]

A Kowle is a grant of land free of assessment for a certain period, or subject to favourable assessment gradually rising to full assessment. Until the full assessment is imposed, the holder is subject to the terms of the contract contained in the Kowle. The Kowle tenure is usually granted to induce ryots to bring under cultivation unpromising waste lands or to plant trees or shrubs for green manure. The terms of a Kowle reserve to government the power of re-entry on breach of its conditions.[53]

Though ryotwari tenure was introduced in several of the hilly tracts inhabited by the tribals, in the interior hill valleys, the Malguzari, Muthadari, Izara or the renting system were found to be in vogue. The principal features of the tribal system of land tenures consisted of joint village ownership and inalienability of land without the previous sanction of government.[54] In some areas, a considerable extent of land was fully or partially exempted from the assessment under the designation of Asalmiah Lands, *pati peradus*, Badi Badlands...These were alienated lands by the zamindars to the relations, whose origin of the tenure was lost in obscurity. Long prescriptive enjoyment, either free of tax or on favourable terms, gave them the right to continue.[55]

The British Government preferred re-assessment land every 30 years on the basis of a moiety of its net produce computed into money at an average of the prices ruling during a certain number of assessment years.[56] Survey operations were begun in many districts from 1859 to determine the exact extent and value of land under various categories. The following is the average assessment in rupees by the plains in the Visakhapatnam District between A.D. 1866 and A.D. 1941.[57]

Table 4.4

Year	*Amount Rs*
1866-1876	1,89,094
1876-1886	2,07,072
1886-1896	3,21,580
1896-1906	4,63,902
1906-1916	4,82,396
1916-1926	5,61,834
1926-1936	6,76,442
1936-1941	10,62,696

In 1864, the Madras Board of Revenue decreed that no ryot could be rejected from his holding, so long as he paid, or was willing to pay, the established rate.[58]

A new provision was introduced into the Rent Recovery Act VIII of 1865 enabling the government and the zamindars to enhance rents on grounds which never permitted them to have recourse under the law that was in force till 1865. In 1882, Ripon laid down the rule that in districts which had been surveyed and settled, there should be no enhancement of the land revenue except on the ground of an increase in prices.[59]

The main principle of the Madras Estates Land Act of 1908 was that every cultivator admitted by the landholder to the cultivation of the estate lands has the status of an occupancy ryot who is protected against eviction so long as he continues to pay the prescribed rates of rent; enhancement of rent being allowed only on certain clearly defined grounds and a non-occupancy tenant acquiring occupancy rights under certain conditions.[60]

In Visakhapatnam Distrct, Golugonda and Sarvasiddhi taluks were settled during 1880-1900. Of the total survey area of 88,332 acres and 1,56,051 acres in Sarvasiddhi, and Golugonda respectively, the extent of *inams* was 16,115 acres or 18 per cent Sarvasiddhi and 18,429 acres or 12 per cent in Golugonda.[61]

The result was an increase of Rs 5,055 in Golugonda Taluk against the increase of 13,579 acres of 36 per cent in area and in Sarvasiddhi, a decrease of Rs 6,132 or 16 per cent against a decrease of 5,407 acres or 20 per cent in area. The revenue net average in Golugonda and Sarvasiddhi was Rs 5-3-5 and Rs 5-5-1 against the settlement average of Rs 4-11-8 and Rs 5-1-11 respectively.

Agriculture

There are three distinct agricultural seasons, viz., *Punasa* (from April to August when the staple dry grains are sown), *Peddapanta* (the wet crop season from August to December) and *Pairu* (January to March).

Out of the total area of 20,67,976 acres, 7,13,169 acres or about 34 per cent were arable and the whole of this extent is under occupation. The area cultivated is 6,12,148 acres, or about 86 per cent of the occupied area. The area cultivated in the last decennium was 3,34,463 acres. About 76 per cent of the total area under cultivation is devoted to the production of food-grains. Cereals occupy 64 per cent and pulses occupy 12 per cent. Paddy, cholam, cumbu, ragi and samaxi were the chief crops among cereals. The bulk of the area under cereals was occupied by dry crops, the extent being 7,35,256 acres. The area under other cereals was greater than the extent under paddy in Sarvasiddhi and other taluks. The area under paddy is 8,83,644 acres. That was the chief food crop of lower middle, middle and higher classes.

Red gram, greengram, blackgram were the most important of the pulses. The area under pulses was the greatest in the Golugonda, Narsipatnam and Sarvasiddhi areas. The extent under fruit trees and vegetables was largest in the Golugonda, Sarvasiddhi, Gudem, and Vizianagaram areas. Gingely was cultivated in Golugonda, Sarvasiddhi and Gudem areas. Cultivation of cotton has not drawn the attention of the ryots here. The District Collector remarked that the chief cause why the ryots of Visakhapatnam did not grow cotton more largely was because it did not pay; eight months were required to produce a cotton crop, whilst two crops of gingely, and other dry grains, might be produced from the same lands within the same time, securing a larger profit to the grower.[62] Cotton was cultivated in some areas of Golugonda and Sarvasiddhi taluks. Jute was cultivated in Bhimilipatnam, Sringavarapukota and Vizianagaram areas. Tobacco was cultivated mostly in the Sarvasiddhi taluk. No need to mention that sugarcane was cultivated in the Anakapalli-Elamanchili provinces.

Much of the tract of fertile land in the Anakapalli area was watered from the channels of river Sarada, and grows excellent sugarcane; other parts of it were dotted with wells and the patches of garden crop they irrigate, and the prevailing tree throughout the whole was the palmyra, which stands in grows along the boundaries of all the fields and grows in clumps in every hollow.

Probably due to the attention of Gode zamindars in the promotion of sugarcane production in the Anakapalli area, the neighbouring zamindars of the later period like Vairicherla Virabhadra Raju, the zamindar of Kurupam who married the second daughter of Gode Narayana Gajapati, introduced sugarcane plantation into his estate, and worked it upto a success. He has taken great interest in the study of botany and horticulture. He has fine gardens attached to his mansion.

Some of the zamindars like the Vatsavais of Peddapuram gave advance money to the ryots for the purpose of the cultivation. During the time of calamities like famines they made large remissions and hence those ryots never migrated to other places.

Paddy, ganti, chodi, jonna, mokkajonna, sugarcane, onion, chillis, mango, groundnut, coconut, guava, plantain, all types of pulses, gingeli etc., were the general crops; and in some areas, jute, cashew, sarvey, plantation were made. In the hilly regions of Madugula and Gudem the crops like pippali, tamarind, ginger, and turmeric were cultivated in plenty.

The most common method of manuring was to pensheep in lands for several nights; and to apply farm yard manure which was made-up of ashes, sweepings and other refuge stored in pits or heaps. *Vempali* (wild indigo) which was ground growing luxuriantly in sandy soils was applied to sugarcane and other garden crops as green manure. Sunhemp which was grown commonly as a mixture with cumbu, ragi and onions in the *punasa* season in wet lands was incorporated in the soil, while puddlings in the wetlands. Here and there *pillipesara* was sown in wetlands after the harvest of paddy for a dual purpose during the *pairu* season, i.e., from January to March; one or two cuttings are taken and fed to milch cattle and later in the *punasa* season it was incorporated into the soil as a green manure. Dry lands and garden lands were usually manured with tank silt whenever available.

The implements of husbandry in use throughout the district were primitive. They consist chiefly of a wooden plough with an iron share, a flat board called 'patti' used for breaking colds and levelling. Another flat board with a lever or handle arrangement called 'Nolla' was used for levelling puddled plots, or levelling uneven plots. Besides these a *'para'* (spad), *'boriga'* or *'tollika'* (hand hoe), *'gunapam'* (pick-axe) and *Kodavali* (a sickle) formed the main implements in use.

This province was mostly dry and was always dependent on rainfall for the successful cultivation of crops. But owing to the erratic behaviour of the monsoons of late, there were series of failure of crops. To tide over this difficulty and to get some assured crops a number of wells were dug and thus increased the area under garden cultivation.

Regarding the other data of cultivation regarding the extent of land, varieties of crops etc., one have to depend upon the records of the village officers like Karanam, which were checked by the revenue officers and Tahsildars, which may be taken as approximate figures. Accurate figures were not possible to get for zamindari and other *inam* lands; and it can be assumed that same state of things prevailed in those areas also as in the ryotwari villages.

Irrigation

The most important sources of irrigation were the channels from rivers like Tandava, Varaha; Sarada, Sarpa, Nagavali and Gosthani. Besides, there are big tanks having an ayacut of more than thousand of acres, which were constructed by the earlier ruling powers or later date zamindars. Penjervu at Vizianagaram, Lakshmipuram Cheruvu near Oaddadi, Ramasagaram and Pedda Cheruvu near Sarvasiddhi, Penjervu at Elamanchili etc., belonged to that category. Besides there were considerable number of small tanks and wells, that supply irrigation to this province.

Rain water, wells, tanks and the rivers above mentioned were the chief sources of irrigation. Referring to the agricultural production of this province, Radha Madhavakavi in his *Vishnumaya Natakam* states:[63] "*Kalinga madhya dikhandambu langula saradanadulache jala bandu.*"

Doddigallu Kaifiyat refers to that Appala Payaka Rao of the Kakarlapudi family, who helped the cultivating families by liberally giving lands on the agreement of fifty per cent share in annual produce (Dharma Kowle).[64] His successors also spared no efforts for the promotion of agriculture besides traditional crops like rice, fruits and pulses; commercial crops like sugarcane were also promoted to the maximum extent. As referred to earlier the sugarcane varieties like *Rayagada* and *Dubbukeli*, as they were subjected to diseases, were replaced by Maritious variety by Gode Suryaprakasa Rao in A.D. 1839. By giving loans as well as by giving training in the preparation of jaggery, Pyari Company encouraged the cultivation of sugarcane and preparation of jaggery among the cultivators.[65] From thence onwards until now Anakapalli became very famous for the jaggery industry and the jaggery market. Besides this, weaving and glass industries also were developed in this province.

Across the rivers Varaha and Sarada, there constructed a number of anicuts for irrigating the lands in Sarvasiddhi, Golugonda and Anakapalli taluks. There were some private dams, beloned to the zamindars, through whose estates the rivers flow. The regulator constructed across the Gokivadagedda in the limits of Gokivoda, a ryotwari village in the Sarvasiddhi taluk, diverted the water of the gedda into" the river Sarada. This diversion was made for the irrigation of the ryotwari lands situated in the lower Sarada basin of the Sarvasiddhi Taluk. The anicut across the river Sarada near Anakapalli supplies water to the Kondakarla Ava. The Peddakattu across the river Varaha diverts water into the Komaravolu Ava. Those two were the fresh water lakes in the Presidency never entirely dry-up and although not of great depth when full have proved themselves to be very useful irrigation sources. They irrigated some thousands of acres of ryotwari land in the area. Besides, there are many government tanks and some small rivers that irrigating both ryotwari proprietary villages.

Position of Cultivators during the Last Stages of the Zamindari System in Coastal Andhra

In spite of the various efforts of some of the zamindars, to improve the irrigation facilities and other benefits to the ryots in their respective provinces, the tax burden as well as the natural calamities did not permit the peasantry class to live in prosperity. To the maximum extent they became the victims of poverty, hunger, floods and further overburdened with mountaining debts. 'Land to the tiller of the soil' and 'relief to the man behind the plough' etc., remained the only remote dream, per the poor ryots in this province also. They survived with mere skin and bone and sheltered in huts.[66] Till the end of the Nineteenth Century, the ryots were rather satisfied with what little they had; and continued to live amidst of all the problems. But generally it is blamed that the backwardness of the ryots was due to their class distinction and other superstitious beliefs.[67]

The Western ideology and the British policies provided the necessary base for the spread of socialistic ideas during this period. They instigated the poor ryots that the zamindars formed only a minority in the country, and they were enjoying the benefit at the expense of the majority. They described the wealthy as those people who know nothing of what soil, misery, unemployment, and hunger was.[68] They began to bargain for an equitable distribution of land, improvement in productivity, proprietary right of the land, abolition of tenancy system, better living conditions and reorganisation of the agrarian system on modern scientific lines. It gradually undermined the very existence of the zamindari system.

As it is already discussed in the earlier chapters, there are two classes of zamindars in this province, viz., the hill zamindars and the zamindars in the plains. The lands in this area were also divided into zamindari lands and *haveli* lands. The hill zamindars were descendants of the ruling class of Orissa or Kalinga Andhra, entrusted with the protection of the province from the incursions of robbers and wild beast and with the suppression of internal commotions.[69] The zamindars in the plain were the revenue agents, who were employed by the Muslim conquerors or the British Company in the management of their acquisitions.[70] The *haveli* lands were otherwise known as Crown lands reserved for the support of the governors of the provincand members of the royal family and their immediate dependents.[71]

When the English power was established in Visakhapatnam Province along with other parts of the Northern Sircars in 1769, the Presidency of Madras described the zamindaris here as land held by certain rajas or chiefs as their hereditary estates, paying a certain tribute to the government and being subjected to suit and service in a manner very similar to the ancient feudal tenures.[72] They held the view that the zamindars were hereditary landlords similar to the ancient feudal lords in England, but later on they understood that they were not lords or proprietors.[73]

Normally it can be said that zamindaris were mere offices of trust and those zamindars were just accountable managers and collectors. "The nature of money they paid to the government instead of being in the nature of a tribute or mere acknowledgement of subjection or fealty was no other than a jumma or revenue, annually calculated upon the produce of the several zamindars, that as a check upon the conduct of zamindars". The duty and responsibility of the zamindars as prescribed in their sannads of appointment was to superintend that position of the country committed to their charge, to do justice to the ryots or peasants to furnish them the necessary advances for cultivation, and to collect the land rent and other taxes of the government.

As already stated earlier, the Permanent Settlement was introduced in the Visakhapatnam Province in 1803;[74] and the duties of the Commissioner were transferred to the Board of Revenue. On the basis of the average collections of the past years, two-thirds of the gross produce received by the zamindars was fixed as a share of the Sircar (*Peshkash*). In this province, though it resulted in the increased facility and regularity of revenue collection, undoubtedly it undermined the rights of the cultivators and left them practically at the mercy of the zamindars.[75] The agricultural community is reduced to the status of serfs. The English Government lost its direct contact with the people and the intermediatary, namely the zamindar, became very conspicuous. The preamble of the Patta Regulations glorifide that the very purpose of the Permanent Settlement was the emancipation of the cultivators from tyranny and, oppression of the officials employed to collect revenue. To liberate the cultivators from arbitrary imports by superiors, the government wanted the zamindars to give *pattas* as per the regulation of 1802-1803. It suggested measures to rectify the irregularities prevalent in the methods of division of shares of the produce between the ryots and the government and the zamindars.

But in practice, the condition of the ryots continued to worsen even after enactment and implementation of the regulations. The zamindars altered the rent from time to time without considering the pitiable condition of the ryots. The government could not intervene on behalf of the ryots and left them to the tender mercies of the zamindars. Just like in the other areas of the contemporary period, majority of the zamindars of this province also assumed themselves the overlords of their respective areas and regular by the conviction that they would do whatever they liked.[76] The ignorance of the cultivators, the non-issue of the *pattas* and the disproportionate increase in the rate of rents, compounded their misery. At the time of natural calamities, at the time of over-expenses, and at the time of clearing the revenue arrears, the normal cultivators were forced to borrow money from the money-lenders at huge rate of interests.[77] In 1822, Sir Thomas Munro visited some of the areas and understood the pathetic situation of the cultivators, and became very sympathetic and considerate to the cultivators.

In the interest of the cultivators, he cherished the idea of purchasing the estate whenever possible and converting them into ryotwari lands.[78]

The vast difference of the rent was mainly due to the fact that the lands were not measured and assessments were not fixed on scientific lines. Similarly, the assessments continued to increase three to four times after the introduction of Permanent Settlement on the coast.[79] The Settlement officers took no notice of the difference between the sterile and fertile lands and levied kists in an arbitrary manner.[80] In 1856, though the Madras Survey and Settlement Department was established, it failed to effect delimitation in the boundaries of villages and in preparing field maps and village maps.[81]

The Rent Recovery Act of 1865 was intended to protect the cultivators from the arbitary evictions and to regulate the relations between the cultivators and the zamindars. But in practice majority of the zamindars continued to lease out their estate villages to the middlemen and collect half of the produce as tax.[82] The Estate Land Act of 1908, have given relief to the ryots. It conferred upon the cultivators the permanent right of occupancy of the land. It protected the cultivators from the eviction from their holdings and from the enhancement of the land rents.[83]

But the original attitude of some of the zamindars of this area had not changed and it paved way from 554 to 892 litigations in the Visakhapatnam Province.[84]

Being sufferers, the ryots have taken an uncompromising stand against the general nature of the zamindars as well as the zamindari system. It may be viewed as a part of the universal struggle capitalism versus socialism. The leadership of some eminent socialists further emboldened the peasants to continue their uncompromising struggle till the abolition of the zamindari system. The ryots of this province also were awakened and resolved to liberate themselves from the hands of the zamindars. The All India Kissan Conference held at Palasa, which is situated in the then Visakhapatnam District, in March, 1940 passed a series of anti-zamindari and anti-congress resolutions.[85] Voices were raised from all corners for the abolition of the zamindari system. The District Zamin Ryots Conference held at Visakhapatnam also adopted a similar resolution.[86] When the agitations gathered momentum, the Government of Madras appointed the Estates Land Committee under the chairmanship of Tanguturi Prakasam, the then Revenue Minister of Madras Presidency. The Committee made it clear that the tenant is the real proprietor of the soil and the zamindar has no right of ownership. The Indian National Congress also declared that the tillers of the soil should be made its owners and there should be no intermediary between the government and the tenants.

As it is well-known, just like majority of the zamindars of the country, the zamindars of the Visakhapatnam Province were pro-government. In the contemporary politico-economic set-up, it was not at all possible to differ with the English Government to any zamindar. The incidents like the Battle of Padmanabham, the revolts of the Kakarlapudis and hill zamindars, and other similar events that taken place in the province clearly indicate the fate of the zamindars, who stood against the English Government in this area. In the then circumstances, those zamindars had no option except to support the government if they want survival. Under such circumstances some of the zamindars supported the government even in suppressing a number of revolts including the first armed struggle (Sepoy Mutiny) that occurred at Visakhapatnam in A.D.1780.

Except few, majority of the zamindars of this province were very sympathetic and provided a good number of facilities to the cultivators as well as to the general public of this province. But they, in no way, protected them against the protest movement against the zamindars.

When the public opinion gathered momentum against the evils of the zamindari system, the leaders of the Indian National Congress also condemned the government pro-zamindari policy. In 1936, when the Indian National Congress formed its ministry in the Madras Presidency, they began to take a number of welfare measures for the benefit of the ryots. The Madras Estates Act of 1908 was amended in 1936 to provide protection to the ryots.[87]

To give relief to the ryots from the unsettled disputes with the zamindars, in 1942 the Congress Ministry of the Madras Presidency appointed a Special Tribunal to clear all such cases. In addition, in 1945, the Madras Estates Act of 1908 was again amended to empower the District Collector to settle all such disputes.[88] But all such measures had not brought any improvement in the fate of the ryots; and as such the Congress in its Working Committee meeting in 1945, moved towards the abolition of the zamindari system.

The year 1947, which marked the beginning of a new era of total liberation and equality, served the death knell to the feudal system which reduced a major section of the people to serfdom. When matters gathered momentum and the venue got ready for the ultimate collapse of the system, the zamindars prepared themselves for the final round of the struggle. They moved all levels of the Court from the Privy Council to the Lower Courts and also the Forums of Assembly. Knowing the pulse of the people, the government followed an uncompromising stand and proceeded to abolish the zamindari system. The zamindars reaffirmed that they had proprietary rights over the land that they held. In support of their stand, the zamindars cited the various judgements, pronounced by the Subordinate Courts, High Court and the Privy Council.[89] Amidst the continued criticisms and objections, the Bill was passed with certain amendments in November, 1948 and it became law on April 19, 1949. It forfeited the honorific titles and the enormous sources of wealth of the zamindars.

Forest

The government reserved forests of the combined district of the Old Madras Presidency covers an area of about 2,57,553 acres. All those reserved forests exist well inland at the foot of the ghats in Golugonda, Sarvasiddhi and Gudem taluks with the exception of an area of approximately 23 square miles in the neighbourhood of Elamanchili. Without exception, they were found on the low hills where the soil was unfit for agriculture. The forest growth in this district will just serve the purpose of supplying fuel and bamboos to the villagers besides preventing erosion of the rocky hill slopes. Except for the absence to teak, other valuable common species are available in those forests although they never attain to any very big size.

In the agency tract, the system of shifting cultivation, or podu, was mostly responsible for such state of affairs, while in the plains, the demand for firewood and the enormous flocks of goats kept in many villages have caused the denundation. Forest conservancy in the district was yet in its infancy, having been practically non-existent before 1890.

Guggilam (Robusta), Tangedu and Konda-Tangedu (Xylia delabriformis), Billu, Billudu (Chloroe ylon Suietenia), Sirimanu, Yellama (Anogeissus, Hatifolia), Pachi (Anogeissus Accumiriata) Yegisa (Pterocarpus Marlepium), Maddi, Nallamaddi (Terminalia tomeniosa), Somi Somide (Soymide tobrijuga) were the common species of wood available in the forests. Bamboo was also plentily available, and a very large proportion of the forest revenue was derived from this source. The trade in minor forest produce at the coastal towns was almost entirely from the agency, where the forests were extensive.

The Forest Committee of 1912, emphasised the need for reducing to a minimum the contact between the forest subordinate and the villager, and recommended that reserved forests should be classified according to their nature and situation and the objects which they were intended to serve. They recommended that the management of forests which were mainly intended to ensure a continuous supply of grazing, fuel and agricultural requisites, should be entrusted to panchayats composed of resident cattle-owners. In accordance with such recommendations, certain minor forests were transferred to panchayati management in 1914. In 1923, a reclassification was made and minor fuel and grazing reserves which were useful mainly for the supply of the every day needs of the ryots came to be termed 'ryots forests' for the management of which panchayats could be formed. But, as it requires no special technical knowledge, their control was transferred to the revenue department from 1925 onwards.

Climate and Monsoon

The climate of the district varies considerably in different parts. Near the coast the air was moist and relaxing and the temperature seldem rose high. The climate was hotter in land and was hottest in the areas bordering the agency and especially so from February to June. The South-West monsoon which then sets-in, moderates the heat and by the middle of November, there took place a marked fall in the temperature.

Rainfall

Most of the rain is received during the South-West monsoon, that is during the period June to September, the average for this period being fifty inches. There is also a moderate rainfall during the North-East monsoon period (October to December) amounting to 1,108 inches. The rain fall during the South-West monsoon period decreases from the inland taluks to the coast, while the conditions are quite the reverse, during the North-East monsoon. The rain-fall for the remaining part of the year is slight. The district is thus mainly dependent on the South-West monsoon; and the North-East monsoon is of less importance. The rainfall on the whole is scanty, and this factor largely contributes to the fact that this district is not self-sufficient in the food supplies. The rainfall is also characterised by the violent fluctuations in the amounts received in all parts of the district.

The agricultural practice in the district does not differ greatly from that of the other parts of South India, but varies with the soil, rainfall and facilities for irrigation and also with the status of the ryot to invest on agriculture. As already stated, there were three distinct agricultural seasons, namely 'punasa' the period from April to August when the staple dry grains were sown, 'Peddapanta', the regular wet-crop season from August to December and 'pairu' the period from January to March. The year was also divided into 27 *karthis* or stars of the lunar Zodiac and the ryots commonly hold that each of those asterisms as the proper season for certain agricultural operations. They believe that, if owing to want of rain or other cause, the season is allowed to pass the particular operation cannot afterwards be carried out with an equal chance of success.

The agricultural knowledge of the people of this province is well-attested to in the literature of the early centuries. *Sasyanandam* a unique Telugu work of the early centuries that deals with rains, monsoon and agricultural science that testifies to the scientific, knowledge of the people here, is composed at Panchadharla of this district.[90]

Mining

Agriculture remained for a long time, the chief occupation of the people, like in other parts of the Madras Presidency, owning the absence of mineral wealth in this province.

The only mineral, besides salt, which has been providing work for any considerable body of people, is manganese, the ore of which is being worked with good results for exportation at Visakhapatnam.[91] The origin of manganese mining in India dates back to 1892 when manganese quarrying was started in Visakhapatnam.[92] Manganese ore is found in great quantities in the Visakhapatnam District and is mined at Vizianagaram and about 60,000 tonnes a year are shipped to Europe where it is used in the manufacture of steel.[93] Visakhapatnam was the only important manganese producing district till 1922.[94]

The Visakhapatnam manganese deposits are situated near Garividi. Manganese is found there in large quantities, but it is of inferior quality. The Visakhapatnam mines are frequently hampered by water troubles, serious floods being experienced in the rainy seasons. Practically, the entire tonnage of manganese ore for Madras is turned out by the Vizianagaram Mining Company, which holds the exclusive right to mine on the great Samsthanam Estate, or Vizianagaram Zamindari, belonging to the Raja of Vizianagaram.[95]

Iron used to be extensively made from the local ores and is smelted on a small scale in few places on the borders of this district i.e., Jeypore area.[96]

Graphite is also found in some parts of the district but mining for it does not appear to have proved a commercial success.

Regarding precious metals, near Bhimilipatnam there existed, a small silver industry that produces some attractive spoons, broaches, signet rings, etc.

Industry

Industrial activity is regarded as a higher class of employment, and is decidedly more remunerative than agriculture.[97] The industrial development of any province depends partly on the state of its natural sources, partly on its geographical situation and physical characteristics, partly on political advantages and partly on its manufacturing capacity.[98]

Opening of railways, development of communications, expansion of trade with the West, cheap foreign imports, machine products, created a lot of displacement in rural life and industries.[99]

Eversince the British acquired power in India, it has been their systematic policy not to develop and encourage the indigenous industries and trades of India.

There were a number of industries in this district. The Sarvasiddhi area contained the largest number of looms. The oil mills are of a primitive pattern being made locally. Iron mills are used throughout the district for the manufacturing of jaggery in lieu of the old wooden mills. Lead is used for making culinary vessels, bronze and bell metal works were also familiar at Anakapalli. Sugar factories started at Etikoppaka near Elamanchili and Thummapala near Anakapalli. Bhimilipatnam is noted for the extensive sugar works of Messrs Arbuthnot & Co., at Chittivalasa, where the latest English machinery has been introduced, and upwards of 6,000 tonnes of sugar is expected to export annually. There were also three indigo factories at or near Bhimilipatnam.[100]

The quint little branzen figures which was so popular, were manufactured at Visakhapatnam.[101] Weaving was an important handicraft that employed the largest number of people. Neither silk nor woollen fabrics were made in the district on an appreciable scale. Only in Viravalli taluk, silk clothes are woven by Devanga community.

The cotton weaving in this district resolves itself into the making of rugs and weaving apparel for men and women. Cotton rugs and carpets are also manufactured at places like Jami, but they are not of superior variety.

The following are the chief weaving centres in the district:

Nakkapalli	Sripuram (Siripuram)
Payakaraopeta	Bonthalakoduru
Chukkavani Lakshmipuram	Ponduru
Dosuru Venkatapuram	Chipurupalli
Somalingapalem	Budithi
Kailasapatnam	Chapara
Gundupala	Maliputti

The local jute knom as '*Yerra gogu*' and the fibre of the sunhemp plant are spun and woven into gunny cloth at Kondakarla and Melipaka, in the Anakapalli area and they are used in the place of canvas for holding cots and chairs. In the Singannadorapalem, near Vaddadi, cotton tape for use on cots is manufactured on a large scale.

Jute is grown in the vicinity of Chittivalasa, Sringavarapukota, Vizianagaram and Nellimarla. In 1944, the mill at Nellimarla had about 8,800 spindles and 365 looms, and it employed 2,028 workers.[102] Those factories at Chittivalasa near Bhimilipatnam and at Nellimarla near Vizianagaram were established under European management. Gunny bags were manufactured there on a large scale under steam power, and a large number of labourers were employed. The gunny bags manufactured there and sent for use throughout the country.

The manufacture of indigo has ceased to be one of the industries of the district years ago owing to the competition of the German 'synthetic dye'. There were three indigo factories at Bhimilipatnam. Some attempt was made during the First World War period (1914-18) to revive that industry, but it proved unsuccessful.

The chief centre of jaggery trade was at Anakapalli, on the rich wetlands where much sugarcane is grown. The jaggery manufactured at this place is considered to be of the best quality and is being exported to other parts of the country. Jaggery is well manufactured in majority of the villages of this province even today.

Tanning of hides and skins is carried on in several tanneries around Vizianagaram.[103] Lacquer work is done in Nakkapalli and Eetikoppaka in Sarvasiddhi taluk, and also at Lakkavarapukota and Sringavarapukota. Wooden dolls and toys of various designs and colours are manufactured at those places and sold all over the district and in the adjoining districts also.

Bangles of the 'glass' made by melting down alkaline earths are made in several villages round about Anakapalli, Kasimkota, Elamanchili, Chipurupalli, and at Paidipalem.[104]

The ivory work at Visakhapatnam had won international appreciation. Fancy articles and a host of other varieties in ivory frame work, fitted on sandal wood stands were among the numerous articles made here. Purchasers were mostly Europeans, Rajahs, and Zamindars. The ivory required is obtained from Calcutta, Bombay, Travancore, and also from the local Marwari merchants.[105] At Visakhapatnam, two or three firms have manufactured for European clients, fancy articles from tortoises shell, horn, porcupine quills and ivory. The industry was in a flourishing state and is stated to have been introduced by Mr Fane, Collector from 1859 to 1862.[106]

The significant port-town, Bhimilipatnam which flourished under the Dutch during Seventeenth and Eighteenth Centuries came to decadence when they relinquished it in the 1st half of Nineteenth Century. In A.D. 1846, Messers Arbuthnot & Co., having obtained the lease of the Palakonda state, built a factory at Chittivalasa, roughly 5 km. north to Bhimili, for making jaggery from sugarcane, the cultivation of which they set themselves to develop in those areas. They had also undertaken an export business of oil seeds. In A.D. 1867, the factory was converted into a jute mill for spinning and weaving by steam, the local product jute. It was the only jute mill in the Presidency containing 98 looms, and over 2,000 spindles, employing 800 people, and turning out 26 lakhs of gunny bags annually.

The export trade originated by Messers Arbuthnot & Co. quickly attracted other European firms and the town took a fresh lease of life. A number of European merchants constructed their residences for export trade, the ruins of which were called by the local people in their names as 'Lawson Meda', Dawson Meda, and Malcolm Meda, which later became the property of the Vizianagaram Estate.

The total value of the import and export from port Bhimilipatnam by A.D. 1868, had risen to nearly 43 lakhs, and that figure was still about the same for decades together.

The imports consist chiefly of cotton twist and piece goods and the exports consist of gingelly seed, other seeds, tanned hides and skins, raw and manufactured jute, gingelly oil and the produce of the neighbouring hill tracts, such as myrabolams, horns, etc. The town Bhimili owes its importance to the fact that it is the nearest port to Vizianagaram through which all the hill-products comes. More than seven European firms had export agencies at that place at one time.

In 1847, a light house was erected but the light on which was removed and shifted to Visakhapatnam in 1902.[107] A new light house was erected at there in A.D. 1903 which consists of a white dioptric light of fourth order of 750 candle powers flashing four times a minute, and is visible eleven miles out at sea in clear weather. The anchorage is in five fathoms about half a mile from the shore and cargo is landed and shipped by means of masula boats. Mr W. Parkes, an expert sent by the government in 1882 to report on the capabilities of the port, gave it as his opinion that the existence of the river mouth so close to it was a great objection to the undertaking of any permanent works for the projection of the anchorage.

In between Tuni and Elamanchili, on the trunk road, there is a village by name Nakkapalli. In the pre-railway days, it was an important halting place. That was the place of Padmasali the community, of weavers who promoted there the weaving of coarse white clothes. As referred to earlier, very nearer to it there was a place called Etikoppaka which was very famous for lacquered toys which were prepared with the locally available wood of 'Ankudu' trees.[108]

There were a number of ports along the coast in between Tuni and Anakapalli. Pentakota, Polavaram, Vatada, Demili, Pudimadaka, etc., were formerly ports but were closed during this period. Salt factories existed in all those ports.

Though unsafe in the south-west rains, during the North-East monsoon all those did a considerable export trade. But all those were closed to regular trade in 1881, for the curious reason that they was too far from Visakhapatnam and Kakinada for the European merchants to be able personally to supervise exportation which result in the native contractors so adultrating the exports that the shippers incurred heavy losses.

Small Scale Industries

Anakapalli is known for its brass and iron vessels, made by Kancharis (a sub-sect of Smiths); for its cotton clothes and sheeting woven by Devanga (weaves), for the sugarcane growing conducted by those industrious and enterprising agriculturists, the Gavaras. Glass bangles and coarse white clothes are made in Kasimkota.[109]

In April, 1796, the government included some causes obliging the Pusapatis to pass free of duties all "cotton and cotton thread and to exempt from taxes all weavers to encourage the inland trade carried on by Bunjaries and to prevent the importion of lead, sulphur, salt petre or gun-powder from the neighbouring districts."[110]

In addition a number of conditions were levied on local chiefs. The local chiefs should not levy taxes on the transport of cotton textiles and on those who were working in textile industries. To facilitate the exports and imports from the port towns, to transport commodities from one place to another, the business of the Perikis and Banjaras were encouraged. Lead, sulphur, etc., along with gun powder were allowed into their territories by the local chiefs. Such were the conditions of the agreements between the local chiefs and the English.

Trade activity of the East India Company in Visakhapatnam was permitted by Qutb Shahis and to that extent issued a firman on February 26, 1634. At the flourishing stage of their trade they constructed a factory at Visakhapatnam in 1682. Textile was the main commodity of export and coffee, tea, species, were the main commodities of import. During the period of Aurangazeb, the English East India Company declared war against him, and at his direction, the Fouzdar of Chicacole captured the factory at Visakhapatnam and hanged a number of British Officers there. After severe loss, the English people tendered apologies to Aurangazeb and conditionally continued their business at Visakhapatnam.[111] Being experienced by that lesson, the then in-charge of the Visakhapatnam factory, Hall Cubm fortified it for safety and security. Pusapati Vijayarama Raju supported and protected the interest of the British in all such occasions. In maintaining the cordial relations between the English and Pusapatis, John Andrews played a significant role.

Occasional disputes broke between the zamindars, when there were no natural boundaries or when the authority of those zamindars was not defined by the authority, as noticed by the Chief and the Council.[112]

Basing upon the circumstances, in the initial stages estates were given on rent to the highest bidders or to the neighbouring zamindars, for there is no survey and the situation of the boundaries of villages and *paraganas* and of irrigation sources and aicuts is unknown. To let the havelis in separate lots would lead to constant disputes between renters.

Salt

There were two main systems of manufacture of salt known as the monopoly and the excise systems. As for monopoly system, salt is manufactured for sale to government only under the supervision and control of its officers, and was disposed of by it to the trade. The right to manufacture was confined to certain areas called factories, and to the registered owners or holders of definite portions of the factories called sets of pans. The quantity to be manufactured at each factory is determined yearly by the head of the department, on consideration the stocks in hand and probable requirements of the trade.[113]

Under excise system, the government confined itself to the levy of a duty on salt leaving the factory; and does not interfere with manufacture or storage, except so far as is necessary to facilitate the collection of this duty by regulating storage operations, and by insisting on the works, on which large sums of public money have been spent under the old system, being kept in efficient repair.[114]

The incidence of salt duty in the Visakhapatnam District was apparently low as compared with the interior districts because production of salt from sea water was cheaper than that raised from the mines.

The retail price of salt in seers of 8 tolas per rupee was 10.58 in 1880 and 11.70 in 1890. The main commodity of export from the Sircars was salt. Visakhapatnam purchased salt worth of Rs 2,21,963, in A.D. 1860.

The private merchants were carrying it by road and rail. The government at this stage wanted to have the monopoly of salt trade by their virtually taking it over rather than leaving it to private enterprise in the hope of giving it at cheaper rates to the public, the attempt was deprecated by the Collectors as unnecessary.[115] The salt channels were left in a very inferior state and they had to be cleared for manufacturing salt as the clearing charges too could not be borne by the poor salt makers, who, in the absence of advances from the government, had to borrow at 100 per cent interest very often.

Visakhapatnam had the sale of intoxicating drugs at a premium in Berhampur, Srikakulam and Gumsur.

Trade in Visakhapatnam Province: The trade of the district may be divided into two divisions: (1) Non-Agency Trade, (2) Agency Trade. Non-agency trade may be further divided into two, that carried by sea and the latter by road.

The main exports consist of manganese, groundnut, mirabolam, molasses, and in certain seasons there was considerable coolie traffic with Rangoon. All foreign imports were transhipped either at Calcutta or Madras, none being received direct. In 1902-03, the imports and exports at Visakhapatnam were Rs 3,11,000 and Rs 32,17,000 respectively. One hundred and sixty-four steamers with a tonnage of 3,90,663 cleared the port in 1913-14, and in 1922-23 the figures were 127 and 3,11,205 respectively.

At Visakhapatnam, the municipality ran a ferry on which rates were collected on all traffic by a fixed schedule. The tender was for Rs 150 a year, the municipality accepting to pay the lascars Rs 18 per month, but the expense of keeping the boat in order was decided by the government.

Although Visakhapatnam is a better port than Bhimilipatnam, possessing a still-water channel in which surf-boats can be loaded and unloaded a float directly from the wharf, and although the fact that the railway runs down to it gives it all the manganese trade, yet Bhimilipatnam does a much greater export business for the reason that it lies nearer to Vizianagaram, the point through which all the carts from the Parvatipur and Jeypore agencies must pass as stated earlier. Merchants who have brought their goods by cart all the way to Vizianagaram naturally send them on by cart to the nearest port at Bhimilipatnam rather than transfer them to the railway to be railed to Visakhapatnam. When the Vizianagaram-Raipur line runs through the foot of the Jeypore ghat and on to Parvatipur, produce will travel by it direct to Visakhapatnam Port, and Bhimilipatnam will no longer be able to obtain the lion's share of the export trade.

Of the average value of the imports at the two ports together in the five years ending 1902-03 (Rs.14,97,000), more than half consisted of cotton twist and yarn (for the use of handloom weavers) or cotton piece-goods, and the only other item which amounted to as much as half-a-lakh was glassware.

Of the average value of the exports in the same period (Rs 50,16,000), gingelly seeds and oil accounted for over eight lakhs; other seeds for a similar sum; and jaggery, hides and skins for over seven lakhs each; and the Vizianagaram Mining Company's manganese ore for six lakhs; and jute, indigo and myrabolams, between two and three lakhs each.

Apart from manganese and jute (which are exported by sea from Visakhapatnam and Bhimilipatnam respectively, and so appear in the statistics of sea-borne trade), the cotton fabrics of Rajam, Siripuram and Ponduru (which are sent by rail to Ganjam, Cuttack and Calcutta), those of Nakkapalli and PayakraoPeta (which go to Godavari), the jaggery of Anakapalli (which is mostly exported to the Samalkot distillery) and the tobacco and chillies of Cheepurupalli taluk (which are sent to Ganjam and Cuttack), the chief items in the exports by a road and rail from the plain taluks are the surplus stocks of the ordinary agricultural staples raised within them; while the principal imports are those necessaries of life which the district does not itself produce, such as and kerosene, European piece-goods, sugar and iron and other metals.

The chief exports from the agency are its surplus grain (paddy, ragi, cholam, cambu, and red, green and blackgrams); the oil seeds, gingelly, niger and 'long pepper'; honey and wax; horns, hides and skins; dammar and lac; marking-nut; myrabolams and other tanning barks; end Kamela powder (obtained from the seed vessels of the tree Mallotus philippinensis) and other dyes.

The imports to the agency include salt, and salt fish; chillies, tobacco, and onions; jaggery, kerosene; coconuts, cotton twist and piece-goods; beads, bangles and coral; metals and metal utensils and jewellery. The numerous weekly markets take a prominent part in collecting material for exports, and also in distributing imports to the villages. The best market centres are Kottavalasa, Salur, Palakonda, Parvatipuram and Madugula.

Except Kottavalasa, the reset of these owe some of their importance to the fact that they are situated near the foot of the hills, and so are marts of hill produce. All along the foot of the hills, from Krishnadevipeta, Gudem and Kondasanta in the South (near Narsipatnam), to Palakonda in the north, is a line-of markets at which hill produce is exchanged for the goods of civilisation. In the tribal areas also, there are many markets on the main lines of communication.

Markets and Santas

Local markets were held in some important commercial centres for the purchase and sale of goods. Bhimilipatnam, Vizianagaram, Anakapalli, Chodavaram, Tuni were prominent trade centres. Madugula, Kothakota, Narsipatnam, Salur, etc., were the significant market yards of agency products. Santas or weekly congregations of all merchandize, mostly fruits, vegetables, grains of all varieties, pulses, clothes, twist for weavers etc., were available here. At the time of purchase from the cultivators directly, the bargains were settled in the villages when the Sahukars send their bullocks or boats to get the produce.

Transport is very important to move goods from one province to another province, and stood as the important aspect in trade as well as economy.

First train from Visakhapatnam to Madras began on July 15, 1893. Ships were used as means of transport to some extent. Marepalli Ramachandra Sastri states that in 1893, he came from Kakinada to Visakhapatnam by a ship. Single Ox Cart, double oxen cart, horse-cart, etc., are means of transport

In 1913, railway line is established beween Waltair to Calcutta. In those days train journey is considered as a wonder and some local Telugu songs were popular on trains.[116]

Railways

Visakhapatnam desired the construction of a light railway from the East Coast towards Raipur as nature has provided a cleft in the Eastern Ghats and no pass over these ghats need be constructed.[117] The district is traversed from South to North by a broad gauge line which was built by the State and is worked as far as Waltair by the Madras Railway Company, and later by the Bengal – Nagpur Railway Company. The former section of 100 km (61 miles) was opened to traffic in 1893 and the latter of 126 km (76 miles) in the next year.[118] The railway line connecting Rajahmundry, Waltair, Visakhapatnam, and Simhachalam was laid on July 15, 1893.

Roads

The period under study and in particular, the Nineteenth Century holds significance for modern means of communication and transport. With the exception of a few hill roads and half road in the agency tracts, the roads in this province are in-charge of the local authorities. Village roads which are often mere tracts that can only be used during dry weather are to be managed by the village themselves. Roads and railways together have revolutionised the methods of transport.

A modest beginning was made in the construction of roads in 1851, when the line from Vizianagaram to Bhimilipatnam was by public subscription. Even the great Northern trunk road, which ran right through the district from Payakrao Peta, Anakapalli, Sabbavaram and Chittivalasa, and thence parallel to the coast to Chicacole, entirely belied its high sounding name at this time, being in some places entirely obliterated.[119]

In 1862, the Raja of Vizianagaram contributed Rs 63,500 for the roads from Visakhapatnam and Vizianagaram to Kasipuram, at the foot of the Anantagiri ghat, were undertaken.[120]

In 1862-63 funds were allotted for the construction of the trunk road from Chittivalasa to Chicacole and from Vizianagaram to Chipurupalli.[121]

A road was laid from Visakhapatnam to Anakapalli in 1869. But due to the canals like Upputeru, the traffic was completely closed for several months in the year for both carts and laden cattle, and made it frequently dangerous to poor passengers.

Both Anakapalli and Pudimadaka roads have to be crossed through drainage canals.

Apart from the nothern trunk road, the following roads were prominent.[122]

From	To
Polavaram	Narsipatnam
Pudimadaka	Madugula
Visakhapatnam	Bowdara
Bhimilipatnam	Salur
Ramabhadrapuram	Parvatipuram
Parvatipuram	Srikakulam (Chicacole)
Vizianagaram	Palakonda

The country carts of the Visakhapatnam district are somewhat smaller and lighter than those of the south and usually have only wooden axles. The palanquin is still common in the agency, but may only be used by those to whom the ruler has granted permission. Kavadis (baskets slung on either end of the bamboo carried across the shoulder) are much used for lighter loads, and are so popular both in the plains and the agency that a man will use them even for the lightest loads, (when taking out his dinner to the fields, etc.) instead of carrying them on his head. Manure, etc., is often carried on to the land on a kind of rude sledge made of two bamboos tied together at one end and fitted with a yoke at the other, between which is placed a large basket. The contrivance is pulled along by cattle and is called Sarugudu.

Cycle is stated to have entered into India in 1896 A.D. Ananda Gajapati, the Pusapati Zamindar is stated to have brought eight cycles for the usage in the court.

Shipping

In the Visakhapatnam province there is a large coast-line containing a number of ports – Visakhapatnam, Bhimilipatnam, Pudimadaka, Revupolavaram, Pentakota, etc as stated earlier. A conference was held at Ootacamund in August, 1915 to discuss the question of the construction of the Visakhapatam harbour and it was resolved that plans for the harbour should be prepared by the Bengal-Nagpur Railway Company who are to finance and to work it.[123] Visakhapatnam and Bhimilipatnam are regularly visited by the boats of the British Indian Steam Navigation Company and Clan Line Steamers call at intervals at the former place for the manganese from the Garividi mines.

Within recent memory, a regular fleet of schooners, owned and manned by natives, used to ply from Visakhapatnam, and boats of this class were built in the backwater, but the steamers have later captured all the trade.[124]

Ship building activity is not unknown both to the Andhras and the Kalingas, and there are earlier references about navigation as well as naval battles over the sea in this province, in literary works like *Dasakumara Charitra* by Dandin and *Kavyalankara Chudamani* by Vinnakota Peddana.[125] But ship-building activity has not gained ground in this province until the advent of the Sindhias, in the Twentieth Century. The Sindhia Steam Navigation Company, the only shipping firm to have weathered British shipping interests, was formed in 1919, to take advantage of the post war shipping boom, and later represented 90 per cent of Indian shipping.[126]

Sindhias had launched a ship building venture before the outbreak of the second world war, and obtained a suitable site in Visakhapatnam for a ship-building yard, but due to official obstruction in the form of the government having ordered the removal of all equipment at Visakhapatnam to Bombay for urgent repairing of vessels damaged in the war, it was not until March, 1946 that Walchand succeed in shifting back the equipment from Bombay to Visakhapatnam.[127]

The native trades of Visakhapatnam were assisting the English company in its transactions. Annapurna, Venkata Lakshmi, Lakshmi Prasadam, Muhmmad Bakshi, Venkatesam, etc., are the names of their ships.[128]

Choultries

In the transport particularly on highways, for rest or halting, there were some places with the establishment of Choultries. Construction and maintenance of Chattrams or Sattrams (Choultries) was the normal practice in India from the earliest times. They were maintained mainly by the contributions and donations or as an endowment of the chiefs, nobles and zamindars. Normally they are located adjacent to highways or at pilgrim centres. *Kasiyatra Charitra* of Enugula Veeraswamayya, Village Kaifiyats and local traditions give some information about such choultries in this Visakhapatnam province.

The endowments made by Gode Jagga Rao to a choultry at Banaras, the famous pilgrim centre in India, made him popular. Nakkapalli, Elamanchili, Sabbavaram, Visakhapatnam, Vizianagaram, Maradam, etc., were the popular choultries. The Local Boards maintain eighteen choultries for native travellers, five of which possess with small endowments.

In Visakhapatnam town, near the old parade ground, is the Turner Choultry founded in 1894 as a memorial of Mr H.G. Turner, Collector and Agent from 1881 to 1889. The site was the gift of the late Maharaja Sir Gode Narayana Gajapathi and the sum of Rs 33,000 spent on the building was raised by public subscription. In April 1898, the institution was handed over to the Municipal Council.[129]

The Maharaja of Bobbili, Ranga Rao, due to his respect and admiration towards Mr Turner made a contribution of Rs 6,000 for the construction of that choultry.[130]

As referred earlier, in gratitude towards Queen Victoria, statues, buildings, hospitals, etc., were constructed in her memory by a number of zamindars like the Roads of Bobbili and the Godes of Visakhapatnam. To show their admiration, love and respects for late Queen Empress, some of the zamindars named their children in the name of Victoria.

On the banks of river Tandava, adjacent to Payakaraopeta of the Kakarlapudis, one Zamindar established a choultry, where a large number of people, irrespective of caste, colour or creed were fed every day. A separate establishment was there for the management of the choultry and those who once visited there would be highly satisfied with the treatment they receive at the hands of those in charge of it. On auspicious days, it used to feed hundreds of people.

As Visakhapatnam happened to be the politico-commercial centre, a number of Choultries were established by nobles, chiefs, and charitable persons and institutions. Garudavari Satram, Narasubayamma Satram, Turner Satram, Edunutula Satram, Bairagula Satram, etc., were established in Visakhapatnam.

Gurrala Satram, Uppaluri Guravappa Satram, Gundaalavari Satram, Kanukurtivari Satram, Maharajavari Satram, etc., were the popular choultries in this area.

Vairicherla Virabhadra Raju of Kurupam built a choultry, and a hospital at Kurupam in the name of his late wife, Lakshmi Narasayamma, the daughter of Gode Narayana Gajapathi. He has contributed towards the maintenance of a hospital at Waltair named after her.

The Godevari ward in the Monegar Choultry at Madras is the act of the philanthrophy of Gode Narayana Gajapati.[131]

References

1. *Madras Census Report,* 1911, p. 94.
2. *Report on the Towns in Madras Presidency*, Visited by Mr. Geddas, 1914, p. 15.
3. Viraswamayya, ENUGULA, *Kasiyatra Charitra,* p. 334.
4. Donappa, T. *Andhra Samastanamulu – Sahitya Poshanamu,* p. 134.
5. In the Sub-Caste of Golkonda Vyparis there are surnames like 'Bhagyanagarapu', i.e., that belongs to Hyderabad.
6. Suryanarayana, Kolluru, *Madhyandhra Yuga Charitraka Vyasamulu,* p. 48.
7. Satyanarayana Murty, T., *Proceedings of A.P.H.C.,* Vo. XII, p. 225.
8. *Proceedings of A.P.H.C., XIV* session, Warangal 1990, p. 181.
9. *Ibid,* Vol. XII, p. 271.
10. Pratapa Reddy, S., *Andhrula Sanghika Charitra,* p. 217.
11. *Proceedings of A.P.H.C.,* Vol. XVI, p. 79.
12. Lakshminarasimham, Petakam Setti, *Prachina Gavarala Charitra,* Chapter I, p. 9.
13. *Proceedings of A.P.H.C.,* Vol. XII, p. 271.
14. This is probably due to the predominant population of the shepherds like Gollas of this area, which is also evident by the *Kulapuranas* like *Yadavapurana,* otherwise known as *Katamaraju kathalu.*
15. *Census of India,* 1931, Madras, Part II, pp. 10-16.
16. Francis, W., *Vizagapatam District Gazetteer,* p. 326.
17. On the banks of this Upputeru, Gode Narayana Gajapati constructed a mansion, which was washed away due to the effect of floods. That incident was described by a poet thus:

    "Karuna matha dharunam silpakanam tadhaivacha
    Gode Narayana Dravya mayyo ayyo vridha vridha"!!
18. *Manual of the Administration of the Madras Presidency*, Madras 1885, pp. 111-280.
19. Francis, W., *Op. Cit.,* p. 327.

20. *Ibid,* p. 328.
21. *Ibid,* p. 321.

21A. The Agency Commissoner's report to the Chief Secretary, Government of Madras, October, 24th, 1900, Madras, pp. 36-37.

22. Francis,W. op.cit. p. 331.
23. More particulars of the various graves will be found in Mr. J.J. Cotton's *List of Inscriptions on Madras Tombs.*
24. *Census of India,* 1931, Part I, Report, p. 75.
25. *Administrative Report of Madras Presidency for the year, 1864-65,* pp. 102-104.
26. Proceedings of public Department, July 13, and 14, 1866, Letters from the general superintendent of Vaccination to the Secretary to Fort St. George, dated June 25, 1886, No. 298.
27. *Proceedings of Madras Government,* Public Department October 21, 1863, Order No. 1152.
28. Letter from D.F. Carmichael, Collector, Vizagapatam to A.J. Arburthnot, Chief Secretary to Government, Fort St. George, October 19, 1863, No. 839, Para 5, Proceedings of Madras Government, Public Department, November 11, 1863, No. 51.
29. *Proceedings of Madras Government,* Public Department, December 7 and 8, 1863, Order No. 1349, December 3, 1863.
30. Carmichael, D.F., *Manual of Vizagapatam District,* pp. 279-280 and C.D., Maclean, Manual of Madras Presidency, Vol. I, p. 56.
31. M.J.L.S. No.38 (1850). p. 380, referred to by Arudra p. 74, Vol. III.
32. Patric B. Smollet, *Madras, Its Civil Administration,* London, 1858, p. 133.
33. Firminger, W.F. (Ed.,): *The Fifth Report from the Select Committee on the Affairs of the East India Company,* Vol. II, Madras presidency, Appendix. 13.
34. Vadevelu, A., *Aristocracy of Southern India,* Vol. II, p. 15.
35. *Proceedings of Board of Revenue,* December 26, 1868, No. 398.
36. *Proceedings of Madras Government, Education Department* December 5, 1868, No. 1112.
37. *Administrative Report of Madras Presidency,* p. 97.
38. *Proceedings of Madras Government, Education Department,* July 23, 1867; Letter from the Director of Public Instruction to the Acting Chief Secretary to Government, Fort. St. George, July 17, 1867, No. 1407.
39. *Proceedings to Madras Government, Education Department* April 18, (1866) No. 46-47.
40. Vadivelu, A., *Aristocracy of Southern India.,* Vol. II, p. 14.
41. Surya Rao, Angara, *Rendu Satabdala Visakhanagara Charitra,* p. 43.

41. A Compiled from "*A Statistical Atlas of the Madras Province revised and brought up to the end of Fasli 1350*", Government Press, Madras, 1949.
42. *Sixty Years of Indian Finance,* p. 12.
43. Report on the Administration of the Madras Presidency (1911 –12), p. 118.
44. *Ibid,* (1917-18), p. 26.
45. Raman Rao, A.V., *Economic Development of Andhra Pradesh,* p. 95.
46. Lord Sailsbury's 'Notes on Land Revenue in Madras' (1857), appended to the Report of the Indian Famine Commission 1880.
47. Report on the Administration of the Madras Presidency (1921-22), p. 70.
48. *Administrative Problems of British India* 1910, p. 129.
49. Report on the Administration of the Madras Presidency (1911-12), p. 55.
50. *Ibid,* p. 56.
51. *Hand Book to the Cotton Cultivation in the Madras Presidency,* p. 13.
52. *Statistical Atlas of Madras Province,* p. 6.
53. Report on the Administration of the Madras Presidency (1911-12), p. 58.
54. Raman Rao, A.V., *Op. Cit.,* p. 261.
55. *Ibid,* pp. 203-204.
56. Minutes of Sir Louis Mallet, 1857, Appended to the Report of the Famine Commission.
57. *Statistical Atlas of Madras Province,* p. 8.
58. Proceedings of the Madras Board of Revenue, dated December 2, 1864, No. 7843.
59. Dutt, R.C., "*The Economic History of India*", Vol. II, p. 347.
60. *Introduction to the Study of Indian Economics,* p. 467, Cited by B. Kesavanarayana in *proceedings of A.P.H.C.,* Vol. XVI.
61. *G.O. Order No.* 784, dated September 23, 1899.
62. Mr. Fane's letter, February 15, 1862.
63. "*Kalinga Madhyadi Khandambu Langula Sarada Nadula Che Jala Bandu*" cited in *Proceedings of A.P.H.C.,* Vol. XII, p. 271.
64. *Visakhapatnam Zilla Grama Kaifiyatulu,* Hyderabad - 1990, pp. 3-23.
65. *Proceedings of A.P.H.C.,* Vol. XII, p. 271.
66. Madras Legislative Assembly proceedings, Vol. VI, September, October, 1847, p. 35.
67. *Newspaper Report,* Madras, 1935, *Rastra Bandhu,* January 14, 1935.
68. *Ibid.*
69. *Note on the Permanent Settlement,* Madras, 1940, Para 49.
70. *Ibid,* Para 51.
71. *Manual of Standing Information,* p. 55.

72. *Op. Cit.,* pp. 18-20.
73. Firminger, W.F., *Op. Cit.,* Vol. 11, p. 7.
74. *Early Land Revenue Settlement in Madras,* Vol. II, p. 84.
75. *Manual of Standing Information,* p. 55.
76. *Madras Assembly Proceedings,* Vol. VI, September – October, 1941, p. 1027.
77. Prakasam, T., *Madras Estates Land Committee Report,* Madras, 1938, p. 41.
78. *Index to the Proceedings of the Governor for the purpose of Making Laws and Regulations for the year 1865,* pp. 22-28.
79. *Native Newspaper Report,* 1897, pp. 170-171.
80. Prakasam, T., *Op. Cit.,* p. 40.
81. Noag, G.T., *The Madras Presidency,* 1881, p. 45.
82. Legislative Department G.O. No. 3109, December 19, 1907.
83. *Ibid,* G.O. No. 10, 9th January, 1908.
84. Revenue Department, G.O. No. 612, Madras, dated March 19, 1919, pp. 1-2.
85. Fortnightly Report for the second half of Madras, April, 1940, pp. 24-25.
86. *Ibid,* pp. 41-42.
87. Legal Department G.O. No. 26, dated May 5, 1936.
88. *Ibid.*
89. Madras Legislative Assembly Proceedings, Vol. VI, 1947, pp. 633-634.
90. Suryanarayana, K., *History of the Minor Chalukya families in Medieval Andhra desa.* p. 241.
91. Tozer, H.J., *British India and its Trade,* Harper and Brothers, London and New York, 1902.
92. Rege, D.V., *Report of an Enquiry into Conditions of Labour in the Manganese Mining Industry in India,* p. 3.
93. George Patterson, "*A Geography of India, Physical Political and Commercial*", p. 287.
94. *Census of India,* Madras, Part – I, p. 209.
95. Ralph Stokes, S.G., *Mines and Minerals of the British Empire,* Edward Arnold, London, 1908, p. 23.
96. Bal-Four, E., *Report on the Iron Ores of the Madras Presidency,* Madras, 1855.
97. Visveswarayya, M., *Reconstructing India,* p. 154.
98. Havell, E.B., *Indian Art, Industry and Education,* G.A Natesan & Co, Madras, p. 25.

99. *A Statistical Atlas of the Madras province,* Governor Press, Madras, 1949, p. 86.
100. *A Gazetteer of Southern India,* Madras, 1855, p. 32.
101. *Ibid,* 1905, p. 277.
102. Report of an Enquiry into Conditions of Labour in the Jute Mill Industry in India.
103. *A Statistical Atlas of Madras province,* Madras, 1949, p. 45.
104. Francis, W., *Op. Cit.,* 1907, p. 126.
105. Narayana Rao, *Report on the Cotton Industries of Madras,* 1930.
106. Francis, W., *Op. Cit.,* 1907, p. 128.
107. *Ibid,* p. 309.
108. *Ibid,* p. 313.
109. *Ibid,* p. 309.
110. Government to Webb, General Reports of the BOR, June, 1796, Para 43.
111. Records of Fort St. George, "Dairy and Consultation" cited by T. Satyanarayana Murty, p. 9.
112. Morgan Williams, *Factory Consultations; Vizagapatam Factory,* Volumes 3681, 3689.
113. *Encyclopedia of the Madras Presidency,* p. 441.
114. *Ibid,* p. 442.
115. G.O. No. 79, date: 7-1-1860.
116. *"Rai ani Ranke vesi Kuu ani kuta kusi povuchunnadibandi – Na waltair nundi!"* cited by Angara Surya Rao. p. No. 69. *Rendu Satabdala Visakhanagara Charitra.*
117. Raman Rao, A.V., *Op. Cit.,* p. 253.
118. Francis, W., Vol. I, *Op. Cit.,* 1907, p. 144.
119. Report on Important Public Works for 1854, p. 31.
120. Francis, W., Vol. I. *Op. cit,* 1907, p. 134.
121. *Ibid.*
122. *Ibid,* pp. 133-221.
123. Report of the Madras port Trust, Madras port Department for 1915 – 16, *Statistics of British India Part VIII;* Local Funds.
124. Francis, W., *Op. Cit.,* p. 145.
125. Suryanarayana, K, "Maritime History of the Ancient Kalinga Rulers:" published in *Power to Punch,* Visakhapatnam 2010; p. 3.
126. Asoka Mehta, *Indian Shipping,* 1940, p. 49.
127. *Industrialisation in India,* pp. 96, 101, 103.
128. Dodwell, H., *A Calendar of Madras Despatches,* 1744-1755, p. 25.

129. *"Contribution of the Gode zamindari in the Fields of Agriculture, Economy and Culture in Vizagapatam District"*. Unpublished M. Phil dissertation by B. Anjani Kumari, p. 73.
130. Vadivelu, A., *Op. Cit.,* Vol. II, p. 58.
131. *Ibid*, p. 15.

Chapter - 5

Customary Practices and Cultural Conditions

The customs and practices of any period were decided by the demands, necessities and fashions of that particular period. The Politico-economic, as well as the socio-sultural systems of a particular period was responsible for the customs and practices of that particular society. In the ancient monarchical rule and in the later period zamindari system, majority of the customs and practices followed, were accepted or tolerated as they were suitable only to that particular period in that particular society; and they may not be acceptable to the later centuries. As such the social customs and practices of one period are considered as social evils of the later centuries. The ancient Indian social practices like child marriages, *kanya sulka*, polygamy, devadasi system, dowry system, cocubinage, etc., were followed during the zamindari period also. Thus, the period under this study, on one side reflects the ideology of the ancient feudalistic tendencies. But interestingly with the advent of the European Companies and Western Education tremendous change has taken place, at least to some extent in the ideology of some sections of the society during this period.

Under the rule of the English East India Company, to trail the judiciary cases one Supreme Court was established at Madras; and later its name is changed as Provincial Court. The Judges in those Courts naturally belong to the English and they do not know anything about either Hindu Dharma Sastras or customs and practices of the society here.[1] As such, to assist the judges on such matters, the learned scholars in Srutis and Smritis were appointed in District Courts and in Higher Courts. Basing upon the views and opinions of such scholars, judgments were given on different cases that were trailed in the Courts. Later an English writer Sir Thomas Strange has written a book on Hindu customs and practices by name *Elements of Hindu Law.* Considered that book as an authority, Judgements were given in different cases by the English Judges on Hindu matters. But later, when the son of Sir Thomas Strange, Thomas Lamsdan Strange came as a Judge in the Madras Court and noticed the necessity of revision as well as elaboration to his father's work. He studied all commentaries and different opinions on Hindu *smriti* works, collected the various Judgments on Hindu cases of the different Courts and with that knowledge published a book entitled *Manual of Hindu Law*. That book was translated into Telugu with the title *Hindu Dharma Sastra Sangrahamu* by Paravastu Chinnaya Suri, which was published in 1858.[2] The code of conduct stated in the ancient *Dharmasastras* and *smritis* is included in that work. The detailed information on all aspects related to Hindu society like child marriage, kanyasulka, polygamy, etc., is referred to in that work. The society in the Visakhapatnam Province is not an exception to all such changes.

Child marriages were very common in this province also and the marriageable age for boys was in between 12 and 14 and it was around eight years for the girls. In A.D. 1860, the famous social reformer in the Andhra country, Kandukuri Viresalingam, married at the age of 13 years, when his wife Rajya Lakshmamma attained the eighth year. A number of marriages held in the zamindari families and in their Courts, were child marriages. Even in the beginning of the twentieth century the same system was in practice in this province. This type of early marriages became a cause for a number of social problems and a number of social reformers pressurize the government to abolish child marriages in the society. Sir Hara Bilas Sarada, a social reformer introduced a bill by fixing the marriageable age to boys and girls as 18 years and 14 years respectively. This became an Act in 1929, popularly known as Sarada Act, which creates a great sensation in the orthodoxy society of the then period. To escape from the punishment of this Act, a number of people used to go to Yanam,[3] near Kakinada to celebrate child marriages as it happens to be a French Colony. Panuganti Lakshmi Narasimha Rao described various incidents of the child marriages which were celebrated at Yanam in his drama *Vichitra Vivahalu*, which was written in the year 1929.[4]

A young girl-child was given to marriage in an age-old man after taking some money called 'Kanya Sulka' (cost of the bride) from him. Being influenced by the Western thought and ideology, in the light of Western education the seeds of social reform began and spread during this period. Interestingly the Zamindari Courts of Visakhapatnam province played their unique and significant role in protesting such social practices which turned as social-evils of the day. Gurajada Appa Rao, in his introduction to the famous Telugu drama *Kanya sulkam*, elaborately discussed about this social custom.[5] Owing to the efforts of such writers and their patron Zamindars that practice of *Kanya Sulka* gradually disappeared in the society to the maximum extent in the successive periods.

By child marriages a number of minor girls lost their husbands and became child widows for no fault of them. To set-right the lives of such girls, a society was established in Madras in 1874 by Palle Chanchala Rao. The motto and object of that organisation is to celebrate remarriage to such girls. Such an idea itself is not tolerable to the orthodox society of the times. Within two years, that organisation disappeared.[6]

Maha Mahopadhyaya Paravastu Venkata Rangacharyulu, a resident of Visakhapatnam, a famous teacher to a number of Zamandari families and a great scholar who published a number of books, examined a number of *Dharma Sastras* and proved that widow remarriage is supported by the Sastras. To that extent, he published a small book in 1875, which became an inspiration to Kandukuri Viresalingam who established an organisation for widow remarriage, named "Stri Punarvivaha Samajam" at Rajahmunday. Amidst of strong protests, he supported widow remarriage in his speeches as well as in his articles published in his journal *purushardha Pradayini*. The first bride-groom that accepted for widow remarriage was Gogulapati Sriramulu, a man of 22 years, working in Visakhapatnam. Thus, the people of Visakhapatanam who were inspired by this widow remarriage moment played their due role in making it a success.

Brahmo Samaj Movement

To protect the Hindu Society from the social evils, a new Socio-Religious organisation by name Brahmo Samaj, was established in Bengal by Raja Ram Mohan Roy, Devendranath Tagore and some others in 1828. It showed its impact on the ideology of Andhras in general and the people of Visakhapatnam in particular. The Bengali literature enlightened the people of this province. Writers like Gurajada Apparao, who lived in the court of the Pusapati Zamindari influenced by the ideas of Brahmo Samaj propogated the same in his writings[7]. As some of the members of the zamindari families of this province got their education at Calcutta, which also paved the way for the spread of the ideas of Brahmo Samaj in this province. Gradually that Samaj is considered as the religious sect of the social reformists. The native place of Gurajada Apparao, S. Rayavaram is located in the Visakhapatnam district; and the ruins of his house are still there in that village.

Polygamy

"A male member can marry any number of ladies".

"A lady is not entitled to remarry, though became a widow in her childhood".

These were the rules derived from Ancient Dharma Sastras that were incorporated in *Hindu Dharma Sastra Sangraham*, which was followed as an authority in the Judiciary Courts of the Period. Polygamy was in vogue in this society from the earliest time onwards. Basing upon his richness and social status, a male member can marry any number of ladies as per the existing system of the day. It is stated that in case, if a lady is not co-operative with her husband, or if she revolts against him, or if she is not blessed with children, or if she goes on giving birth to female children, her husband can marry another lady. Even without any of the above causes, her husband can marry any lady, with the approval of his wife.

During the period under study, the same system was in vogue not only in the Zamindari families but also in the noble and middle class families. This system has given rise to a number of problems like that of succession to the estates as well as distribution of properties.

We have seen already how the English Company involved in the succession struggles of the heir-apparents in some of the Zamindari Families[8].

Polygamy is considered as another important social evil and hence a number of social reformers propagated against Polygamy. In fact, they expected its abolition with the involvement of the British government. But the British government never dared to abolish that system of polygamy, as it was the practice in vogue in almost all the royal families and the zamindars, on whose support they are administering the Country. As such, that social evil of Polygamy is not abolished until the British rule was over.

Devadasi System

Though *Devadasis* are different with the *vesyas*, those words are used as synonyms during this period. In the literature of medieval and later medieval centuries the significant role played by the *vesyas* is highly described. That institution also is subjected to a number of changes in the ravages of times. Some of the *sanis* were very rich and maintained good properties. As discussed earlier, in this province, some of the *sanis* purchased estates and emerged as estate owners.[9] In the changing system, their role in the religious services and the temple rituals gradually disappeared. During the occasions of the marriages in the rich families, and also in the annual *Kalyana Utsavas* (Marriage rituals) in the temples, *melas* and *mejuvanis* of the *vesyes* are arranged. But the reformers of the society strongly felt that it was uncultured and not good to encourage such dances on the festive occasions amidst of gents-folk. In a society in which the maintenance of such *sanis* as a status symbol to protest such an act was not that much easy. Social reformers of the period raised their voice against this social evil also. A number of attempts were done by some of the reformers to mould the people's opinion and to divert the people's interest against *'Bogam Melam'*. One such attempt is known by an elaborate letter by a reader to the editor of the journal Vrittantini, which was published on 15th February, A.D. 1841. In the popular drama *Kanyasulkam* that was written by Gurajada Apparao under the patronise of the Pusapati Zamindars of this province, there were references about anti-nautch movement. It was during the same period, that Kandukuri Veeresalingam published a series of articles in *Vivekavardhini*, in protest to this social evil.[10] Under this reformist movement, to show an alternative profession to such *sanis*, in 1902, Marepalli Ramachandra kavi established a dramatic association by name "Sangita Manini samajam" at Visakhapatnam.[11] Similarly, in the light of Western education and Western ideas, some of the zamindars and some of social reformers rendered yeoman services to eradicate a number of other social evils like *Kanyasulka* and *Varakatna*.

Industrial Revolution and Social Change

The English East India Company procured good quality of textile and beautiful handmade artifacts made of wood and ivory, in addition to spices. In that period Visakhapatnam was very famous for ivory industry: and Etikoppaka in the same province, where a special variety of wood by name '*Ankudu*' was available was famous for toys industry. Those industries seem to have continued up to the beginnings of twentieth century. Panuganti Lakshmi Narasimha Rao in one of his articles entitled: "*Swadesi Parisramalu*" published in *Andhra Patrika* dated November 24, A.D. 1920, refered to the ivory-industry and wooden toys of Etikoppaka.[12]

With the discovery of Steam Engines and industrialisation, the economic set-up of the world changed all of a sudden. From the beginning of the nineteenth century, European products dominated the Indian market: and due to that impact, the Indian handloom and artifacts gradually began to disappear. Thus, the European trade and their imported goods thoroughly effected various professions and thus disturbed the economy of the land. As such people of the professions had no option except to turn towards agriculture. With this the number depended on agriculture, increased from sixty per cent to eighty per cent. In the beginning of nineteenth century drought and famine disturbed this province and a number of persons lost their lives. In addition to this a number of desease spread all over the land and cost the lives of the people. In 1881, if the average life span of a Britisher was 56 years, the average life span of an Indian was 26 years. For survival and livelihood, a number of people migrated from Visakhapatnam province to Rangoon.

As per ancient orthodoxy of the Hindus, Sea voyage is prohibited. But majority of the zamindars and educated families of the

Visakhapatnam province seems to have not followed that system. Tanguturi Prakasam Pantulu, who has gone to England in1904, in his autobiography refers to a member of a zamindari family that hailed from Visakhapatnam to England for the purpose of study in A.D. 1854 itself.[13] Thus, the zamindars, nobles and educated groups of the Visakhapatnam province, on one side followed the customs and traditions of the land, and on another side influenced by the Western concepts and ideas welcomed and followed them. It was probably due to the colonial connections of this province, in trade as well as in administration. The liberal attitude of a number of aristocrat and zamindari families of this province due to their own reasons, were responsible for the admixture of culture in this province.

Cultural Activity and Entertainment

Prior to the industrialisation and expansion of European culture in this province, a number of cultural activities existed here. Narration of the Bhagavata and Puranic stories, Pupet shows, and dramas, etc., were the main items of cultural entertainment. In the second half of nineteenth century, being influenced by Kuppuswami Naidu, Adibhatla Narayana Dasu introduced a new type of narrative which became very popular as '*Hari Katha*'. As that narrative '*Hari Katha*' happened to be an admixture of literature, music and dance with folk-touch, it attracted the general public: and that Adibatla Narayana Dasu became very familier as *'Hari Katha Pitha Maha'*. He has given a number of shows in various parts of this province and later a number of his students continued that stage-act.

Another important cultural entertainer was drama. As drama requires a separate hall or place, a team of artists, a number of sets and screens, technicians, orchestra, etc., it is involved with much expenditure. Probably due to that the earliest dramatic associations were originated with the support and patronage of the zamindars and nobles. In Visakhapatnam, the earliest dramatic association "Jaganmitra Natyamandali" received full support and encouragement of the Jeypore Zamindar Vikrama Deo Varma.[14] Later in the end of nineteenth century, another dramatic association named 'Srikalabhilasham Nataka Samajam' was established in Visakhapatnam by the efforts of Marrepalli Ramachandra Kavi and Setti Lakshmi Narasimham.[15]

Another important and interesting cultural entertainment that won the hearts of the people of this province was the 'circus' performed by Kodi Rama Murti, who was appreciated and honoured by the National leaders like Bala Gangadhara Tilak, with the title 'Kaliyuga Bhima'.

In the initial stages of the establishment of the East India Companies in this province, just like in the other provinces in India, as all other commodities, slave trade was at its peak. The Dutch settlement at Bhimilipatnam is known for its slave trade, just like in their other centres like Jagannadhapuram in the adjacent district. Purchasing the slaves for labour, instead of hired labour was found convenient by the Dutch. Hence, the Dutch went for bulk purchases in coastal Andhra. It was in this time natural calamities occurred and we found a number of instances of such victims. The failure of crops and harvests, drought, famine, cyclone, storms, floods in the region bordering the coastal Andhra, enabled them to be successful in having their ships loaded with slaves. Some of the Company officials considered the trade of slaves was more important than textile.[16]

Thus, slavery in nine forms existed in Andhra as noted by the European trading companies: where slaves were purchased, gifted, inherited, pledged, taken in time of famine, a voluntary slave in payment of a debt, voluntarily a slave, voluntarily for a time, and one who sells himself as a slave. Slave-trade carried on by the European Companies in this province, completely based on the needs of the company, its network in Andhra, and on the other socio-economic conditions of the period.

Animal Hunting

As the area under study was filled with thick Jungles and hilly-slopes, hunting of wild animals, became a prestige and fashion to the aristocracy, European officers and nobles.

Sri Ranga Rao Bahadur, the Zamindar of Bobbili in his work *Advice to the Indian Aristocracy*, published in 1905, revealed some of the ideas of aristocracy on such manly sports like animal hunting. It is said in the *Hindu Sastras*, if a man shoots 21 tigers, he is called 'Tiger Slayer'[17]. If a man shoots 100 tigers he is considered to be quite equal to the one who has performed the sacrifice called the Rajasuya.

The aristocracy, nobles and animal hunters considered that shooting and hunting animals is essential, because it teaches them how to grow accustomed to fatigue, to become quick and good shots and it gives them plenty of exercise and makes them watchful. But they should not devote too much of their time to shikari.

It is a common practice in this period to wear necklaces made of tiger nails on their chest by the shikaris and nobles.

Festivals and Jataras

Elamanchili was an important halting station with a number of good Travellers bungalows like Uppaluri Gurappa Satram. Near one corner of it was the shrine of Achchayamma Perantalu, which affords a good instance of the genesis of local deities and their shrines. Achchayamma, a kapu woman committed *sati* on this spot some 200 years age and the reverence which would in any case have been paid to the place in consequence was increased a hundred-fold by the eventual appearance of an ant-hill over it. The hill was duly protected by a small thatched building; and an annual festival is held, vows are paid to the lady, and her resting place is covered with various offerings.[18] Close to the hillock of Elamanchili, there was the shrine of Ramachandramma, the famous village goddess. On the annual festival, buffaloes were sacrificed and she is declared to have appeared in the form of flashes of lightenings in the sky, as in the case of another nearby goddess Paiditalli of Mamidivada.

At Sringavarapukota, the seat of the 'Mukhi' family earlier, there was another important goddess, Erakamma, who is also stated to have committed *sati* and became a *perantalu*. Ballads are sung about her saying that she was the child of Dasari parents and that her birth was foretold by a Yerukala woman who prophesied that she would have the gift of second sight. She eventually married, and one day she begged her husband not to go to his field, as she was sure he would be killed by a tiger if he did. Her husband was not withstanding and was slain as she had foreseen. She committed *sati* on the spot and later emerged as goddess.[19]

At the pongal feast, a large gathering of some thousands of Hindus takes place at the foot of the Buddhist monument Bojjanna Kondalu (with an impression that those stupas as Siva Lingas).

At this feast, the curious stone image standing in the hollow between the two hills also comes in for some attention. It represents a woman surrounded by a border made up of tiny human figures and is locally declared to be the image of the Eirnamma, who used to kidnap children and eat them. Every woman who comes to the pongal feast hurls a stone at her, and she is now all but buried beneath the pile so formed.

At Padmanabham, on the top of the hill which overlooks the place was a small Vishnu shrine reached by a flight of some 1,300 steps, and at the foot of it was another larger temple to the same deity. Tradition says[20] that both were improved and endowed by Pusapati Ananda Raju, the predecessor of Vijayarama Raju, and that a kapu who was previously incharge of the former was induced to relinquish his claims by the grant of a hamlet and on the condition (still carried out by his descendants) that he should do worship every Saturday to the image on the slab which stands by the Dhvaja Stambha on the top of the hill.

A goddess named Sambari lives on the Boda Konda in the Golugonda hills and animal sacrifices were made to her. One day as was said in the story, a man went to her temple just after the sacrifice to fetch a brass pot which he had forgotten and came upon the goddess drinking the blood of the offerings. She was furious at being seen, and fluing his pot two miles away, where it made a deep hole (still shown) in a piece of rock.[21] Since then no native has ventured to go up to the hill. A survey party of Europeans, it is locally declared, laughed at the superstition and set out one fine day to take bearings from the top of the hill. But they had hardly got half way up when they were surrounded by a forest fire which burnt up much of their kit and so frightened a horse they had with them, that it bolted over a precipice and was killed.[22]

At Dimili, the village temple, an unpretentious building, is dedicated to Siva in the uncommon from Nagnesvara, or the naked Siva. The story goes that the rishi Agastya was unable, to his great grief to be present at the marriage of Siva with Parvati, and that the former accordingly promised to appear before him with his bride whenever he wishes it. Agastya expressed the wish at a moment when neither of them had any clothes on, but they appeared nonetheless just as they were, and the temple was erected to commorate the event.[23]

Adjacent to the village Nakkapalli, which is situated roughly 15 kilometres away from Payakraopeta, there is a village Upamaka at which on the hillock there lies on ancient temple of Lord Vishnu. At the bottom of the hill, a temple to Lord Venkateswara was erected by the Kakarlapudi family and by later patronised by the Gode family and the Estatedars of Urtala.[24]

Panchadharla, originally the headquarters of an estate under Pusapati family which was renamed as Chipurupalli estate, was the seat of famous Siva temple, Dharma lingeswara, which dates back to the Chalukyan rule.[25]

Pentakota near Payakraopeta contains the remains of a Fort and Mosque.

Balighattam is a small village adjacent to Narsipatnam on the bank of the river Varaha. It is known throughout the district for its famous temple of Brahmalingeswara, which stands at the foot of a small hill on the other side of the river and at which there is a large festival on the day of Sivaratri.[26] The shrine, like that of Visvesvara at Benaras, faces West, instead of East as usual, and this peculiarity and the fact that the river for a short distance here flows North and South have led to the spot being considered peculiarly scared (uttara vahini). The local Pandits quote with unction, the *sloka* which says "where a lingam faces west and a river runs north, that place is equal to kasi (Benaras), and there, one will surely obtain celestial bliss".

The shrine is almost all quite modern and is not interesting architecturally.[27] It is supposed to have built by Brahma: the river is declared to have been made by Vishnu, during his incarnation as a boar, (Varaha) - hence its name; and some deposits of white clay in the river bank are supposed to be the ashes of a sacrifice performed here by Bali, the demon king from whom the village takes its name.

At Lotugadda roughly 43 kilometers north-west of Narsipatnam among the Golugonda hills, there are ruins of some old granite temples dedicated to Siva.[28]

The most famous, richest and best sculptured shrine in the province of Visakhapatnam is the temple of Simhachalam, dedicated to Narasimha, the man-lion incarnation of Vishnu, which gives the hill its name.[29] In honour to that temple, a number of people of this province are named as Simhachalam, Simhadri, Narasimham, Appanna, Appa Rao, Kondayya, and so on. Pusapati family of Vizianagaram is known to have provided flower-gardens for the temple.[30] They have been wardens of this Shrine from long before and have endowed that temple with more lands. Some of the members of the Gode Zamindari like Chengala Rao made some donations to this temple.[31]

Besides the *Jataras* of village goddesses, a number of other festivals were celebrated in this province. In Visakhapatnam both Muslim and Hindu festivals were celebrated in a magnificient manner. Ramaleela Utsavas were celebrated on Sriramanavami day near beach; and Peerla Panduga, the important Muslim festival was celebrated in the area between fort and Pirlakoneru.[32] Both Hindus and Muslims participated in them and the zamindari families lavishly contributed to them.

Construction Activity

Some of the European officers, to exercise their administrative duties constructed bungalows and other buildings at different parts of the province. Captain W.G. Owen built the divisional officers house at Narsipatnam which was later sold to the Raja of Vizianagaram. The same Captain is stated to have constructed bungalows at Kondakalaava near Anakapalli and at Polavaram.

Pusapati Sitarama Raju is stated to have made the oblong brick-fort with five bastions at Madugula within which is the present residence of the zamindars. The Circuit Committee, said in A.D. 1784 that it had been constructed after the European model by brick layers form Madras and was then garrisoned with a battalion, about 1,000 strong, dressed and armed in the European manner.[33]

At Visakhapatnam just behind the Port-office, are Ross Hill and two other knolls occupied respectively by a Roman Catholic Church, a Hindu Temple, and a Muslim Mosque, all in close proximity. Mr Ross was a sub-Judge who built a bungalow, about 1848, on the hill, which bears his name. The Roman Catholic Mission bought the property in 1867, and erected a Church on the site. This was afterwards enlarged and opened in 1877; the 'Darga' to which the mosque is attached is widely known. It is the tomb of Sayid Ali Madina alias Ishak Madina, and Hindus make vows at it, as often as Muslims.

The Saint is considered to be all potent over the elements in the Bay of Bengal. Mr Carmichael says that when he wrote (1869), every vessel passing the harbour inwards or outwards used to salute the Saint by hosting and lowering its flag three times; that many a Silver Dhoni was presented to him by Hindu Ship-owners after a successful Voyage.[34]

The actual history of the 'Darga' and Mosque was not clearly known. The early records of the English Settlement at Visakhapatnam speak of the frequent visits paid to that place by the Fouzdars of Chicacole.

Once there existed a 'fort' in this southernmost part of the Visakhapatnam. Pharoah's Gazetteer speaks as if it was still in existence by 1855, and says "Within the fort are the barracks for the European invalid soldiers the arsenal, the Officers quarters and various public buildings".

The Waltair Orphan Asylum otherwise known as 'the Vizagapatnam Male and Female Orphan Asylum', originally founded in 1817 by the Rev. C. Church Chaplian was remodeled in 1831. It is intended to afford a shelter and home to destitute children, orphans and foundlings of the Northen Sircars, and to provide for the maintenance of the off-spring and descendants of the men of the Karnatic Veteran battalion who were disbanded in 1842 and who left their children and grand children in a state of destitution.

In 1838, St. Paul's Church was constructed in Waltair, by Captain J.H. Bell. St. Peter's Church was constructed in between 1845-1864. Sacred Heart Catholic Church was constructed in 1850 at Bhimili, and appended to it a hospital and orphanage centre and a school, was constructed later. At the same place in 1876 Doctor Revarend Stanford constructed Andhra Baptist Church with the support of Canadian Christian Mission.

In 1844, Sir Arthur Cotton constructed the St. John's Church. In 1854, St. Anne's Cathedral was erected; and in 1887, Roman Catholic Church of the Sacred Heart of Jesus was built.

During the last years of nineteenth century to commemorate the Diamond Jubilee of late Queen Empress, Town Hall was presented to Visakhapatnam by the Maharaja of Bobbili.

On the sand-hill, buildings were constructed for Civil Hospital, Mrs. A.V. Narasinga Rao College, and Gajapati Rao poor-house were constructed, whose details were already discussed at relevant places.

One Canadian Baptist Church was constructed at Elamanchili during this period.

Kakarlapudi Payak Rao also contributed much by their constructions. They have constructed a fort at Anakapalli. In front of that fort, they have constructed the Bhogalingeswara temple in A.D. 1611 and on the back side of that temple, to protect that fort, erected a temple to their tutelary deity Kakatamma, which later called as Nukalamma, the famous goddess in that province.[35] They have also constructed a shrine to Jagannadha Swami at the same place. Similarly, they have also constructed forts at places like Satyavaram, and Melipaka, and as they were the worshippers of Nukalamma, they constructed a temple to that Goddess at Satyavaram and a temple to Goddess Satyamamba at Melipaka. Even now there is a mound called 'Sattemmadibba' at Milapaka.

The present Venkateswara temple at Upamaka was also constructed by them. They have also constructed temples at places like Sriramapuram at Godicharla.

References

1. Arudra, *Samagra Andhra Sahityam* Vol.III, p. 278.
2. *Ibid.*
3. Surya Rao, Angara, *Rendu Satabdala Visakhanagara Charitra,* p. 66.
4. *Ibid.*
5. *Satyanarayana, K., "Gurajada Appa Rao – A Study"* (An Unpublished Thesis, submitted to Andhra University).
6. Surya Rao, Angara, *Op. Cit.,* pp. 67-68.
7. Satyanarayana, K., *Op. Cit.,* p. 91.
8. The involvement of the Company Government in the Administrative matters, particularly at the time of succession disputes is well-attested to in the case of Madugula, Kakarlapudi, Gudem, Pusapati, Gode and other zamindars that administered the provinces in the period under study. All they suffered due to the intervention of the English people in the succession disputes.
9. Francis, W., *Vizagapatam District Gazetteer,* p. 255.
10. Rama Krishna, V., *Social Reform Movement in Andhra*, p. 118.

11. Surya Rao, Angara, *Op. Cit.,* p. 73.
12. Narasimha Rao, Panuganti; "*Swadeshi Parisramalu*" article published in *Andhra Patrika*, 24th November, 1920.
13. Surya Rao, Angara, *Op. Cit.,*
14. *Ibid.*
15. *Ibid.*
16. Francis, W., *Op. Cit.,* p. 226.
17. Vadivelu, A., "*The Aristocracy of Southern India*", p. 35.
18. Francis, W., *Op. Cit.,* p. 315.
19. *Ibid,* p. 318.
20. Francis, W., *Op. Cit.,* p. 230.
21. *Ibid,* pp. 252-253.
22. *Ibid.*
23. Subba Rao, Ralla bandi (Ed), *Kalinga Sanchika,* p. 269.
24. Sarma, A.V.D., *Kalingandhra Devalayamulu.* p. 39.
25. Suryanarayana, Kolluru, *Puratana Saiva Kshetramu Panchadharla,* p. 3.
26. Francis, W., *Op. Cit.,* p. 252.
27. *Itihas,* Vol. XVI, p. 68.
28. Francis, W., *Op. Cit.,* p. 253.
29. Sundaram, K., *Simhachalam Temple,* p. 27.
30. *Mackenzie Manuscripts,* Local Record IV, pp. 265-269.
31. *S.I.I.* Vol. VI, No. 1192.
32. Surya Rao, Angara, *Op. Cit.,* p. 94.
33. Francis, W., *Op. Cit.,* p. 320.
34. *Ibid,* p. 329.
35. *Proceedings of A.P.H.C.* Vol. XII, p. 271.

Chapter - 6

Literary Patronage

The period under study is a tremendous stage of transition in the patronage as well as flourishment of literature. Almost the succession of the medieval rulers to power came to an end during this period. Advent of the European powers into the country provoked a deep sense of interest and respect towards regional faith and regional literatures among the people. The responsibility of patronage and the enrichment of literature were completely shouldered by the zamindars and nobles of this period. Inspite of their political disturbances and financial problems, they showed much care and interest in patronising scholars and poets. Some members of the princely families themselves composed literature. With the gradual development of the establishment of schools and colleges the literacy rate also increased which indirectly paved way for the outcome of good literary productions. Some of the aristocracy families though thoroughly influenced by Western mind and thought nowhere neglected literary patronage. In fact, the patronage towards literature under this period was in no way less than that of any period in the history of literature of the land. The literature that was composed and patronised under the zamindars of the Visakhapatnam region had its own significance. A number of well-versed scholars and great poets enjoyed their patronage and enriched literature in multi-directions.

Pusapati Zamindars

One of the foremost zamindari family that dedicated completely to the contribution of literature in the contemporary period was that the Pusapatis of Vizianagaram. There is no exaggeration to say that writers like Gurajada Venkata Appa Rao and other who lived under their patronage stood as trendsetters to the ideologies as well as to different styles of writing in the contemporary period. One of the ancestors of this family Mailama Btimana is referred to in the chatu verses of Vemulavada Bhima Kavi. The famous scholarly family of Adidam continued as court poets under the patronage of those Pusapatis. Besides literary patronage, some of their family members of the earlier generations were stated to have composed literary works. One Pusapati Krishnama Raju who became familiar as the founder of the 'Sapta Santanas' made a prabandha entitled *Rukmini parinayam*.

Pusapati Tammabhupala (1620-1670), composed Srikashna Vijayam, which describes the Bhagavara story of Parijatapaharanam. His minister somanamatya composed a Sringaraprahandha called Simantini charitrmu. Venkatapati Raju, the grandfather of Pusapati Ananda Raju composed the famous romatic story of Usaha and Aniruddha and dedicated to god Rama at Ramtirtham which composed Nava Ramayanam which is not available. His son Pusapati Peda Vijayaram Raju, who became the cause of the Battle of Bobbli, was also known as the patron of poets and writers. Thus, majority of the rulers of these Pusapati family were known as poets and literary patrons.

Gogulapati Kurmanatha Kavi: (1720-1790)

Gogulapati Kurmanadha Kavi the court-poet of Vijayarama Raju was one of the famous poets of the period. His work with the suffix 'Vairi Haaramha and Simhadri Narasimha' was composed at the Muslim attacks on the temple of temple of the Lakshmi Narasimhanatha at Simhachalam. In dedication to the Lord of Ramatirtham, he made a prabandha by name Ekantaseva. An Yaksha gana entitled *Mruthyunajaya Vilasam* which described the marriage of Siva with Parvati and the birth of Kumara; *Lakshmi Narayana Samvadam, Tirumangayaalvar Samvadam* were the Vaishnavaite stories composed him. In addition to this type of Bhakti works, he made a Sringara Sataka by name *Sundarimani Satakam.*

He also composed another Sataka with the Suffix "Vijayaram! Ramatirthasraya!!"

Adidam Family

The scholarly family which produced a number of poets and scholars during this period was the Adidam family. Adidam Surakati (1720-1785), a famous poet of this family lived during the period of Peda Vijayarama Raju who fought the Battle of Bobbili, and also during the period China Vijayarama Raju who fought the Battle of Padmanabham. He has composed a number of works and dedicated all those to god Ramalingeswara at Ramachandrapura agrahara near Chipurupalli.

His *Kavijanaranjana prabanandham* which became very familiar as Pilavasu Charitram describes the marriage of Chandramati and Harichandra. Andhra Chandralokamu, the translation, to the Chandralokamu of Sanskrit, and another work *Kavisamsayavichchedamu* were his works on grammar. His *Andhranmaseshamu* was his Telugu dictionary in poetry. His *Ramalingeswara Sataka* strongly criticises the power mongray, mutual rivalries etc., which existed in the ruling family, misappropriation of power by the royal officers, and highlighted the various troubles faced by the people during that period. It is believed that he composed a number of 'Chatu' verses during his visits to the neighbouring estates. Some of his chatus glorifies his patronage to literature and his liberal grants to scholars and poets.

Other Poets Under the Patronage of the Pusapatis

Chatarati Lakshmi Narasakvi who lived under the patronage of Narayana Gajapati wrote a number of works like *Pdmanabhayuddam, Eswari parinayam, Viseshaandhram, Bhandanarati Bhimasatakam*, whose details will be discussed in the succeeding pages.

Rama Yogikavi, and Sarvamangaleswara Sastri, of Nadiminti family were also adorned the court of Pusapati Narayana Gajapati. Ramayogi Kavi has written *Ushaparinayam* and *Bhallana Dandakam.*

Besides poets and writers Pusapati family encouraged and patronaged the art of music and welcomed a number of musicians to their court. Pdeda Gururaya a famous musician and Vaggeyakara came from Tanjore and settled there at Vizianagaram court by the invitation of the Pusapatis.

Vijayarama Gajapati (1826-1879), son of Narayana Gajapati, due to his interest towards Vedic education and Vaidika Dharma, established a Sanskrit college at Vizianagaram in 1860.

Poduri Venkataraju Kari, the writer of *Ramaleelavilasam*, and Sripada Venkatachala Kavi the writer of *Kousalyaparinayam* and *Ramakrishnopkhyanam* lived under the patronage of the Vijayarama Gajapati. Manda Kameswarakari dedicated his work Kurmapuranam to the same Gajapati. Durvasula Suryanarayan Somayaji his court musician composed a number of songs and music compositions in praising the achievements of the Pusapatis. Some Hindustani Musicians like Mohabat Khan, and Manvar Khan also adorned the court of Vijayaram Gajapati.

The period of Ananda Gajapati (1879-1897), who was described as 'Abhinava Andhra Bhoja', was considered as the golden period in the literary flourishment of the Vizianagaram Court. He was a perfect example for literary patronage and his period was brilliant epoch in the history of Telugu Literature.

Ananda Gajapati is described as 'a prince whose knowledge is of absorbing passion and whose appreciation, encouragement of letters, has attracted to his court, literary stalwarts of the period. [1]

The celebrated poets Tirupti Venkata Kavulu visited the Court of the Maharaja and praised him as 'a great literary giant' of eminence among maharajas who they visited in their tour. He could become such great not only because of his intellect and aptitude for poetry but also because of his eminent teachers both Indian and European, who instructed him Sanskrit grammar, kavyas and poetry. [1A]

Ananda Gajapati gave financial assistance to F. Max Muller for the publication of "Reg Veda Samhita". He is also stated to have written a number of 'Chatus' in Telugu and Sanskrit.

Manda Kameswara Kavi translated Tulasidas's Ramayana in the Telugu under the patronage of this Ananda Gajapati.

Mudumba Narsimha Charya, who belongs to the Vaishnava families at Simhachalam, was an important poet in his court. It is stated that he composed more than two hundred works on different aspects like yoga, Vedanta, Kavya and Sastras, both in Telugu and Sanskrit.

Peri Kasinadha Sastri another poet of the same period composed a number of works like *Gangastavam, Godavari Lahari, Pardhasaradhi Satakam, Srungararasamanjri,* and dramas like *Panchali Rakshna Natakamu* etc., in Prakrit and Telugu Languages. Kolluri Kamasastri was another poet who got appreciation by Ananda Gajapati. He has written a popular Sanskrit Kavya on the request of Ananda Gajapati praying the god Simhadrinatha with the title *Simhadrinatha Kara Sthavam*. He also translated the Sanskrit work of Kamalakar Bhattacharya into Telugu with the title Sudra *Kamalakaramu*.

Manda Lakshmi Kameswara Sastri (1857-1920), son Kameswara Kavi lived under the patronages both of Ananda Gajapati and Vijayaram Gajapati. He has written a number of works like Kalki Vijayamu, Sarvonnta Sangrahamu, Nilgiri Varnanamu, Simhagiriyatra Prakasika, George Sarvabhouma Prassti etc. It is also known that he made a treatise on Sarva Siddhaanta Chadrika at the request of Gurajada Venkata Appa Rao.[1B]

Narahari Gopalakrishnama Chetti, who closely associated with Ananda Gajapati in various games and sports like hunting, tennis, Gardi, and Chess was also a good writer. Aganampudi Radhotsvam, Anubhavarasika Satakam, Ganikamani Vilasam, Bhadharmahathyamu and Vijayarama Gajapatindra Charitramu etc., were written by him.

Pusapati zamindars encouraged Urdu Literature also. Munshi Muhaammad praised him for his munificence in his great Urdu and Persian work, *Firhugi Anandaraj*.

Thus, not only in the Visakhapatnam province, but in the entire North Coastal Andhra, the patronage and flourishment of literature has gone to its peak under the patronage of the Pasupati Chief; and their 'durbar'undoubtedly credits to be compared with the Bhuvanvijaya of the Hampi Vijayanagara Rulers.

Madugula Zamindari

Though belongs to border regions in between Andhra and Orissa on the hilly tracts in the Visakhapatnam province, the zamindars of Madugula extended their patronage to literature to the maximum extent. Majority of the zamindars patronaged poets and some of the zamindars were themselves masters of literature.

The details of the literature that was patronised until the period of Krishna Bhupati of this family were not known. Some of the traditional accounts like *Pusapati Rajula Purvottaram* referred to the patronage of Brahmin scholars and the grant of *agraharas* and *manyas* under Linga Bhupati of the early period.

Krishna Bhupati II (1853-1875) of the Zamindari of Madugula was a renowned scholar and good patron of poets. Literary critics appreciate his commitment towards literary patronize in comparison with Sri Krishna Devaraya of the great South Indian Kingdom of Vijayanagara.[1C] Owing to this scholarship in Sanskrit and Telegu, Krishna Bhupati was entitled as *Abhinava Krishna Devaraya.*[2] A number of great poets of the age adorned his court. Adidamu Bala Bhaskarudu, Sistu Krishna Murti Sastri, Allamaraju Subrahmanya Kavi, Allamaraju Ramakrishna Kavi, Indraganti Gopala Sastri, Peri Sarvesvara Sastri, Mantripragada Suryaprakasa Kavi, etc. were under the patronage of Krishna Bhupati II.

Adidam Bala Bhaskara Kavi (1802-1874)

Adidam Bala Bhaskara Kavi was the great grandson of the famous Adidam Sura Kavi.[3] A chatu verse of Mantripragada Prakasa Kavi, the court poet of Madugula, describes how Adidam Bala Bhaskara Kavi was honoured by Krishna Bhupati. It is stated that Krishna Bhupati honoured Bala Bhaskara Kavi by providing *Varshikam*, the annual grant. Though Bala Bhaskara Kavi was a great scholar and was hailed from a scholarly Adidam family, none of the great works composed by him, have not come to light. Only few '*Sataka Kavyas*' and '*Tharavalis*' were available. *Janaki Rama Sataka, Bhogalingeswara sataka, Sri Venkateswara Sataka, Simhasaila Nrisimha Sataka*, etc., were his compositions. *Sri Krishna Bhupathi Taravali* was the work describing the Krishna Bhupati of Madugula in 27 verses by using the names of 27 stars – Aswini, Bharani, Kritika, etc., in that, it was stated that Bala Bhaskara kavi composed that '*Taravali*' in dedication to Krishna Bhupati.[4]

Sistu Krishna Murti Sastri

Sistu Krishna Murti Sastri was another great scholar that was honoured by Krishna Bhupati. He was a great scholar both in Sanskrit and Telugu, and a good musician also. He was honoured by a number of zamindars of the then period; and was awarded with the epithet '*Abhinava Battumurti Nataka Dipamu, Pancha Tantramu, Vasucharitra Vyakhyanamu,* (commentary on *Vasucharitra*), *Viksharanya Mahathyamu, Venkatachala Mahatyamu, Sarvakamada Parinayamu, Srinithi Sastramu, Hanumad Satakam*, etc., were his Telugu works. *Asvasastramu, Kankana Bandhamu* (related to the story of Ramayana), *Nilasaila Nadiyamu* (A travelogue on Puri Jagannath), *Madanabhyudaya Yakshollasa vallavi Vallavollasa Bhanamulu, Harikarikalu* (a Sanskrit version to *Balavyakaranamu*), etc., were his Sanskrit works. In addition to these a number of his *chatu* verses, *Dandakas*, *Malikas*, *Sthotrams*, testify to his scholarship. Krishna Bhupati has awarded to him land grants in the Madugula estate. Being a learned scholar in music also, he praised his patron in *chatu* sloka thus:[5]

"Sri Krishna Bhupa Krityavasara girigari sarisameti vineyam brute tattata hitadhikata kadhiteti murajonu"

Commenting on this, Allamraju Subrahamanya Kavi, who also lived in the Madugala Court in his *Chatudhara Chamatkara Saram,* stated that the melodious music of Vina, narrates how the fame of Srikrishna Bhupati excels the fame of Lord Siva, and how it dominates the greatness of the goddess Saraswati. The same Krishnamurti Sastri was patronised by the Kakarlapudi Zamindars also. He was patronised by Kakarlapudi Ramachadra Raju, and his brother Jagannadha Raju, probably prior to his entry into the Madugula Court. His *Sarvakamada Parinyam* was dedicated to Jagannadha Raju.[6]

Though Sistu Krishnamurti was a great scholar, who lived under both the Zamindaris of Kakarlapudi and Bhupati, he seems to be a controversial scholar. He differs with a number of poets of his age like Pindiprolu Lachchanna, and Parvastu Chinnayya Suri. Changanti Venkata Krishnayya, the writer of the *Hymavati Parinayam* appreciated this Sistu Krishna Murti with all respects. Nidadavolu Venkata Rao noticed that this poet had a title *Abhinava Bhattumurthi.*[7]

Allamraju Subrahmanya Kavi (1831-1892)

Another great poet that adorned the Court of Krishna Bhupati at Madugula was Allamraju Subrahmanya Kavi. He originally belongs to Chebrolu near Pithapuram in the East Godavari [8], and he migrated to Madugula and enriched Krishna Bhupati's Court with his literature. He had a number of titles like *'Ubhaya Bhasha Kavithva Vilasitudu'*. In dedication to his patron Krishna Bhupati, he made a number of works like *Pratyakshara Slesha Padyavali*, and one sataka in Sisa metre, with a suffix

> *"Matsyakuladhipa Divyamanmadha Swarupa!!*
> *Paramagunadhama! Krishna Bhupati Lalama"!!*

In appreciation to his literary talent Krishna Bhupati arranged *Varshikam*, an annual grant to his life period.[9]

Allamraju Ramakrishna Kavi

Allamraju Ramakrishna Kavi, the step-brother of the Allamraju Subrahmanya Kavi was another great poet that was honoured by Krishna Bhupati. Ramakrishna Kavi composed a number of works like *Acharya Telugu Bhagavata, Adhyatma Ramayana, Kavichakora Chandrodaya, Gowtami Mahatyam, Droupadi Parinayam, Madalasa Parinayam, Vainateya Vijayam, Santana Vilasa, Satyabhama Vilasam, Sukavi-Jana Manoranjanam, Susobha Parinayam, Hanuma dvyakhyana.*[10]

In addition to those he had made a commentary by name *Ramakrishniyam* on *Andhra Sabdha Chintamani.*

Mantripragada Surya Prakasa Kavi (1808-1873)

Another famous poet that enjoyed the patronage of Madugula Krishna Bhupati was Mantripragada Surya Prakasa Kavi. He has written various books like *Sita Rama Charita, Krishna Arjuna Charitra* and *Bhimalinga Satakam. Sita Rama Charitha* is a *prabandha* with six *Asvasas*. *Krishnarjuna Charitra* was a *Dvyardhi Kavya,* a typical model of writing in which each stanza conveys two different puranic stories, *Subhadraparinayamu* and *Parijatapaharanamu*. *Bhimalinga Sataka* was a compilation of hundred stanzas, in *Kanda* metre with the suffix "*Bhimalinga! Kalusha Vibhanga*"!!

He praised the fame of Krishna Bhupati in comparison with the ocean of milk, with the goddess Saraswathi and with the sacred river Ganges as stated hereunder:[11]

> *"Krishna Bhupati Samkasam Krishna Bhupati Sannibham*
> *Krishna Bhupati nikasam Krishna Bhupati Sadyasah*
> *Krishnabhupati Sadyasah Madugula Samsthanadhipateh*
> *Sri Krishna Bhupalasya Kirtih"!*

Similarly, the poet appreciated the courage and valour of Krishna Bhupathi thus[12]:

> *"Vikramarjuna mukhah Krishna Bhupati tehitah*
> *Vikramanjuna mukhah Krishna bhupala tehitah*
> *Hey Krishna Bhupalah"*

Thus, a number of chatu verses in glorifying Krishna Bhupati were composed, by this poet.

Peri Sarveswara Sastri

Another poet that was honoured by the Madugula Zamindari was Peri Sarveswara Sastri. The land grants that were made by the Madugulu Zamindars at Pedanandipalli were enjoyed by the Peri family until recent past. Unfortunately none of the works that were composed by Sarveswara Sastri are available.

Indraganti Gopala Sastri

A great grammarian and scholar that lived under the patronage of the Madugula Zamindari was Indraganti Gopala Sastri. The writers of the famous grammar book *Koumudi,* Somanadha Sastri and Papayya Shastri learnt a number of treastises under this Gopala Sastri.[13]

Thopalli Venkata Rama Siddhanti was the court astronomer of Madugula. He has written a book by name *Manjari*, a commentary to a work *Tidhi Kalpavalli* composed by Rani Mahagni China Nrisimha Kavi.

Thus, a number of significant poets, popular writers, well-versed scholars, propounded grammarians, were honoured and patronised by the Madugula Zamindari. Some were given land grants whereas some others were satisfied with the arrangement of annual grants (Varshi Kamu). The critics and scholars on modern Telugu literature appreciate the great contribution that was made by the Madugula Zamindars to the Telugu and Sanskrit literatures and glorify that they stood as a model to the other later date zamindaris like at that of Pithapuram.

Madugula Zamindari carves a soft niche for itself in the Telugu literature of the Zamindari Period.

Another poet by name Renduri Anantha Dasu that belongs to Madugula has written a *Sataka* in *Utpalamala* and *Champakamala* metres with the suffix "Matsyapuradhinayaka" in praise of Lord Krishna, probably the god located there as 'Pardha Saradhi' (the driver of the chorait of Arjuna).

Kasimkota Zamindari

Kasimkota was one of the earliest Zamindaris, which was put to a number of political disturbances. As such, the literary patronage of the Zamindars of Kasimkota until the second half of nineteenth century has not come to the light of the day. From A.D. 1876 upto A.D.1931, a number of prominent scholars and poets enjoyed the patronage of the Kasimkora Zamindari.

Poets like Gandu Somanatha Sastri, Thopalli Venkata Rama Siddhanti; and great musicians like Tumurada Sangameswara Sastri, etc., have enjoyed the patronage of Kasimkota.[14]

Somanadha Sastri, a great scholar of Sanskrit and Telugu was an expert in grammar also. His only prose work entitled *Bhima Vikramam* is available.

The famous *Satavadhanis* of the Telugu country of the then times, Tirupati Venkata Kavulu in their tours to different royal courts, visited the court of Kasimkota, when Marrella Venkatachalam was the Zamindar. They described the Coronation ceremony of the Zamindar that was held in his flower garden 'Anand Bagh' and praised his literary patronage. In their *Nanaraja Sandarsanam,* they have written a number of stanzas in appreciation to the Zamindar Marrella Venkatachalam of Kasimkota.[15]

Kakarlapudi Zamindars

As referred to earlier the estates of Ankapalli, Satyavaram, Melipaka, Doddigallu etc., comes under the Zamindari of the

Kakarlapudi family. Their courage and valour in the Battle of Bobbili was highly appreciated in *Rangaraya Charitam.*[16] They played a significant role in the contemporary period in safeguarding the interests of their zamindari by protesting the joint forces of the Pusapatis and the British as already discussed earlier.

In the patronage of literature also the Kakarlapudi Zamindars, proved themselves that they were second to none. They patronised poets and scholars; and some of the zamindars were themselves poets. Ramabhadra Payak Rao, the brother of Payak Rao I, is stated to have composed a number of works like *Padmini Parinayam, Nilagirinatha satakam, Suprasada Mahatmayam, Navalekhini Lekhyamu,* etc., besides a number of *Chatu* verses.[17] Rekapalli Somappa, the court poet of Gopala Payak Rao described the scholarship as well as the details of the writings of Ramabhadra Payak Rao in the introduction to his work *Rukmavati Parinayam.*[18] By that it is evident that Ramabhadhara Payak Rao is a good poet in the Kakarlapudi Family.

Sanampudi Timmakavi, Velivela Gouthama Raju were the court poets under Gopala Payak Rao. Except their references in the contemporary *Chatu* verses, none of their works are available. Gopala Payaka Rao is stated to have honoured Sanampudi Timma Kavi by granting an *agrahara* by name Dosalapadu to him. After him, Rekapalli Somappa whose poetry was well appreciated by the scholars, and who is stated to have in a position to check the great poets like Adidam Surakavi, was made the Court-Poet of the Kakarlapudis.[19]

Somappa has made a *Sringara Prabandha* by name *Rukamavati Parinayam* which consists of five *asvasas*, in dedication to his patron Gopala Payak Rao. It is a romantic love story between Pradyumna, the son of Lord Krishna and Rukmini, and Rukmavati the daughter of Rukmi, the brother of Rukmini. The poet described his patron as a strong devotee of Lord Sri Krishna. *Visakha Zilla Vrithanta Sangraham* refers to another work by name *Pardhymnabhyudayam* as the work of Somappa. But scholars like Tumati Donappa, basing upon the proximity of the narration opined that this is another name to *Rukmavathi Parinayam.*[20]

As referred to earlier Rambhadra Payak Rao, son of Gopala Payak Rao was also a patron of letters. Basing upon the internal evidences of a work by name *Upmaka Venkateswara Satakamu*, written by Vaidarasu Appayya Kavi, it is known that he lived under his patronage. In that *Sataka* he described the event of marriage of Lord Venkateswara and Alivelumaga, which Lord's temple is located at Upmaka in the zamindari of his patron. This Sataka was composed in sisa metre, with the suffix "Vibudha Lokesa! Upmaka Venkatesa!!"[21]

It is known that he made another *sataka* in the same above sisa metre, with the suffix "Bhalira Karivelpa! Pasidi Valuva Dalpa!!" The philosophical interpretation of the romantic love between Radha and Krishna is described in this work.

In some of the *satakas* of the period, like the *Simhadri Narasimha Satakamu* written by Gogulapati Kurmantha Kavi, the attacks on the piligrim centres of the Hindus by the Muslims, the Marathas and the Pindaris were described.[22] They have given a graphical picture on the plight of the people on such occasions. Those satakas give us the picture of the fate suffered by the temples of the vicinity like Varaha Lakshmi Narsimha temple at Simhachalam, Kodanda Rama temple at Potnuru, Gopalaswami temple at Bhimasingi, Janardhana temple at Jami, and Kesavaswami temple at Chodavaram, all belong to the Visakhapatnam province.[23]

One poet Nallini Narasimha Charyulu, who has written *Padmini Parinayam* in four *asvasas,* is stated to have dedicated to his patron Gopala Raju of the Kakarlapudi Zamindari whose details are not known. But as stated already, Telugu literary critics like Arudra consider that it was written by Gopala Raju.

Sringavarapu Kota (Kasipuram) Zamindars

Sringavarapukota Zamindari otherwise known as Kasipuram Zamindari was one of the hill Zamindaris under the Mukhi family. In the Visakhapatnam province they played their due role in balancing the relations between the tribal Zamindars and the Pusapatis of Vizianagaram. *Padmanabha Yuddham* describes that Mukhi Kasipati Raju of this family assisted Pusapati Peda Vijayarama Gajapati in the Battle of Bobbili.[24] As discussed earlier, in course of time this zamindari merged with the Pusapati zamindari of Vizianagaram. After the Battle of Padmanabham the authority over the estate rotates in between the

English Company and the Pusapatis; and the successors of the Mukhi family were paid nominal monitary compensation. The last known Mukhi Chief Virabhadra Raju revolted to regain power, for which act he was imprisoned at fort Gutti where he died.

Amidst of their political disturbances, the Mukhi Zamindars of Sringavarapu Kota have honoured and patronaged some of the poets and scholars. Peri Sarvesa Makhi of Viravalli on the banks of river Godavari was welcomed to adorn the court of the Mukhis. It is stated that he received five land grants from their patrons. Sarversa Makhis son Jagannadha Makhi is known as an expert in Vedic lore as well as in Dhanurveda (archillary).

Adidam Sura Kavi, the famous poet of the age, was the contemporary of Raja Bhupala Raju of the Mukhi Zamindari; and he described the rivalry of Raja Gopala Raju with the Pusapatis in some *Chatu* stanzas.[25]

Ponugupati Venkata Mantri (1720-1780), the diwan of this Mukhi Family was also much interested on literature. Appreciating the good qualities of Ponugupati Venkata Mantri there are a number of *Chatu* verses stated by Adidam Sura Kavi.

Another diwan of the Zamindari Patrunimahanti Krishna Mahanti Patnayak was also a good appreciator of literature. Andaluri Sarabha Kavi dedicated his poetic work *Mukti Chintamani* to this Patnayak.

Gode Zamindars

Gode Zamindari family which had its authority over Share Mohammadpuram, Visakhapatnam and Anakapalli estates made a significant contribution for the flourishment and promotion of literature. They were great patrons of poets and scholars; and some of them were themselves good writers. Their intimate relations with British officers in the later period brought a tremendous change in their approach and outlook. They stood as a bridge between traditional and modern cultures. On one side they patronised Telugu and Sanskrit literatures in the traditional patron and on another side some of them were influenced by Western thought and concept, mastered different sciences with Western approaches, made experiments and published their results in reputed international journals of the then times. Regular publication activity, procurement of ancient manuscripts, their preservation in their libraries, patronage of poets and scholars, establishment of schools and colleges, etc., are the chief qualities of the Gode family in promoting education and literary activity in the Visakhapatnam province. Next to the Pusapati Zamindari of Vizianagaram, it is Gode Zamindars that played a significant role in the promotion of education and in the patronage of literature. One more notable feature of the Gode family is the literary critics like Kandukuri Veeresalingam observed that after Tarigonda Vengamamba until the Gode family there were no lady writers that enriched Telugu literature.[26] Madiney Subhadramma, daughter of Gode Pedda Jagga Rao and China Janakamma, the wife of Gode Narayana Gajapati Rao composed a number of works.

A number of poets and scholars like Kakaraparti Tirupati Patra Kavi, Krishna Kavi, Buchchi Patra Kavi, Akkineypalli Narsimha Kavi, Erramilli Perraju Kavi, Nadiminti Sarvamangalesa Sastri, Rani Mahagni Chinna Narsimha Kavi, Paravastu Srinivasa Jagannadha Swami, Paravastu Venkata Ranganadha Swami, Gorty Venkata Sastri, Kakaraparti Sitarama Swami, etc., were the poets that enjoyed the patronage of the Gode Zamindars.[27] Besides these, a number of great poets of the then times visited the court of these Zamindars, and were duly honoured.

Gode Pedda Jagga Rao, the founder of the Gode family was popular for the establishment of *Sapta Santanas*, (Seven great deeds,) as per ancient Hindu customs.[28] To get his support in suppressing the local revolts and in controlling some of the Zamindars like Mailavaram, the English East India Company honoured him by providing him a number of royal privileges, as was described in *Satyavati Parinayam.*[29] It states the honours like 'Jodu Mashallu', 'Shaheba palaki', etc., besides 'Vetrahastas' with gold and silver sticks and a number of significant titles. Kakarparti Tirupati Patrakavi, who lived under his patronage, wrote a book by name *Satyabhama-Krishna Samvadam*, a *Sringaraprabandha* in three asvasas in dedication to his patron. In the introduction to his work he described and appreciated the various achievements of Pedda Jaggarayudu. His interest in literacy appreciation, Vijayarama Gajapati's honour and respect towards him, his installation of *Sapta Santanas*, his construction of choultries at pilgrim centres like Banaras, are referred to in that work.[30] It is also stated that Pedda Jagga Rao appreciated his poetry in comparison with the writings of Nandi Timmanna, Ramabhadara Kavi, Allsani Peddana, and Pingali Surana. His habit of discoursing with poets and scholars in his 'darbar' was described thus: *Hridyana Vidya Gadya Padya Pathana lasitha Vadana.* He has granted two agraharas in the name of his parents, Subhadrapuram, and Suryanarayana Puram to the Kakaraparti poets.[31]

More than five generations of the Kakaraparti family that belongs to Tirupati Patra Kavi, were under the patronage of the Gode Zamindars. With the encouragement and the support received by Godes, they enriched Telugu literature with their significant contributions.[32] Kakaraparti Krishna Kavi, the son of Tirupati Patra Kavi composed works like *Sasirekha Parinayam, Mukhalingeswara Kshetra Mahathyam* and *Mukha Lingeswara Taravali. Sasirekha Parinayam* is a sringaraprabandha of three asvasas, the theme of which is derived from the epic story of *Mahabharata. Mukhalingeswara Kshetra Mahathyam* is a devotional Kshetramahathyam in praise of the Lord Mukhalingeswara at Sri Mukhalingam which is an ancient Siva *Kshetra* adjacent to the Zamindari of the Godes. *Mukhalingeswara Taravali* is a *Nakshatra Malika*, a poetic work of 27 Stanzas in token of the 27 stars, all ends with the suffix Sri Mukhalinga. In the introduction to *Mukhalingeswara Kshetra Mahatyam*, Krishna Kavi referred to the scholarship, religious devotion the various honours received by his father by Gode Pedda Jagga Rao. He dedicated that work to Lord Mukhalingeswara.

Buchchipatra Kavi, the son of Kakaraparti Krishna Kavi is also a good poet and composed a *Prabandha* by name *Satyavati Parinayam*. Venkata Sastri, the cousin of Buchchipatra Kavi, and Sitarama Sastri, the grandson of Buchchipatra Kavi were the poets who lived under the patronage of the Gode Zamindars of the later period. Kakaraparti Nrisimha Kavi the writer of *Sarangadhara Yakshagana* also belongs to the same Kakaraparti family that enjoyed Gode patronage.

Gode Surya Prakasa Rao, the son of Pedda Jagga Rao is also much interested in literature and patronised scholars Paravastu Srinivasacharyulu, a great scholar not only in Telugu and Sanskrit but also in English. He has made a critical study on various works on architecture and botanical science that were published in European countries. Gode Surya Prakasa Rao requested Srinivasacharyulu to prepare a standard dictionary of Sanskrit to Telugu in Western model. Paravastu Srinivasacharyulu could not complete that work entitled *Sarvasabdha Sambodhini* during his life period and the same was completed later by his sons Venkata Rangacharylu and Ramanujacharyulu at the patronage of Janakamma, the wife of Surya Prakasa Rao after his death. Gode Surya Prakasa Rao was the recipient of several poetical works and prominent among them was *Oghavati Parinayam* by Akkinepalli Nrisimha Kavi. *Oghavati Parinayam* is an interesting prabandha written in four asvasas originally taken from the *Anusasanikaparva* of *Mahabharata.*[33]

The marriage of Oghavati, who born in Solar dynasty of Ayodhaya, selected her grandfather Sudarsana to marry in her *svayamvara* (the function arranged to select the bridegroom by the bride). As that type of marriage of grand daughter with grand father was against to Dharma, later she herself turned as a scared river and that tragic story was described in that work *Oghavati Parinayam*. Basing upon the indication of the *Saka* year (1739) stated in this work, this was dedicated to Gode Surya Prakasa Rao by Akkinepalli Nrisimha Kavi in A.D. 1817.[34] As this was written in dedication to a Gode Zamindar in the introduction he elaborately discussed the family history as well as the glory of the Gode Zamindars in more than two hundred stanzas in the introduction to his work.[35]

The same poet has written some more works like *Vallamamba Parinayam, Sukumari Parinayam* and *Adilakshmi Vilasam*. *Vallamamba Parinayam* is the story of marriage of Vinayaka with Vallamamba that was written in three *asvasas*. This was dedicated to Pulipaka Ramayya. Another work on the similar marriage story of Narada with Sukumari, the daughter of Srinjaya, the king of Ayodhya, by name *Sukumari Parinayam* was also composed by him.[36]

In addition to the works on such marriage themes, Akkinepalli Narasimham has written a *kavya* by name *Adilakshmi Vilasam*. He has narrated the popular story of *Akkala Katha* related to Adilakshmi and Kamavalli, which was described in the medieval Telugu works like *Kridabhiramam*. How Adilakshmi fell in love with Vishnu in the incarnation of Krishna, born as Rukmini and how she married him is the story in this work. At the request of Koppanati Krishnayya, he made this work and dedicated to Lord Narasimha Swami at Antarvedi. Literary critics noticed that this poet made the theme, a simple popular song of the ladies, as much difficult in this work. C.P. Brown commented that this work is waste, as it failed in delivering that simple story as it was composed in a so deep unwanted scholarship witch is not easy to understand by all.[37]

In his words "this poem is so obscured with pedentry that it is quite useless."

Another great poet and scholar that was patronised by Gode Surya Prakasa Rao, and was appreciated by a number of contemporary poets is Erramilli Perraju Kavi. At the request of Janakamma, the wife of Surya Prakasa Rao, he has elaborated the orginal work *Mallari Charitra* that was written by Maringanti Venkatacharyulu.[38]

Mallari Charitra, a dvipada *Kavya* is the *purana* of Malaharesvara Swami, the tutelary deity of the Gode Zamindars. It is a regular habit to worship the statue of Malaharesvara on all ceremonial occasions of the Gode family. It is believed that the Gode family otherwise known as *Karnakulinulu*, acquired name and fame by their worship of Malaharesvara, popularly known as Mallari Deva. The patron of worship of Mallari Deva and other details are elaborately described in the introduction of *Oghavati Parinayam* of Akkinepalli Nrisimha Kavi. Maringanti Venkatacharyulu has written the same story with the title *Mallari Charitra*, in a dviapada form. As it is a work on their family deity Mallarideva, as well as the family history of Godes, Gode Janakamma, not satisfied with the brief composition made by Maringanti Venkatacharyulu earlier, requested Erramilli Perraju to write it elaborately. To please his patron, Perraju added a number of *Manjari* dvipadas to the original and made *Mallari Charitra* in four *asvasas*. It is stated that this story had its origin in *Skandapurana*; and described that in Puranic days Giri Raju worshipped Mallari and acquired name, fame and prosperity. He is stated to have founded the Gode lineage. Such a great history of the Gode family was elaborately written by this poet at the request of Janakamma, wife of Gode Surya Prakasa Rao. This is an unpublished work and its manuscript copy is found in the Oriental Manuscripts Library at Chennai.[39] The date of the composition of that work is stated in a chronogram in the Saka year *Gaganebha-Nagabhumi*, i.e., Saka year 1780, which is euivalent to A. D. 1858.

In this context special mention should be made of Madiney Subhadramma (1781-1840), the daughter of Pedda Jagga Rao, a poetess of rare eminence in the Gode family. Gode Jagga Rao, her father provided all facilities for her education in a period when women's education was not only neglected but also protested by the society. She married her aunt's son Madiney Suranna and get educated under the guidance of the scholarly Parvastu family. Subhadramma evinced enormous interest in Telugu poetry and acquired the reputation of a poetess of great prowess. It seems that she have composed a number of works out of which only some are available. A number of *Sataka* works with suffixes, Krishna, Kesava, Kodanda Rama, Raghunayaka, Raghava Rama, Venkatesa, Sri Rangesvara, Sri Hari Ramesa, Simhagiri Simhachala-adhisvara, and *Dandakas* like Sri Rama Dandakam are her works that were available. In all her compositions she propounded Vaishnava Bhakti, morality and good human qualities. Her poetic talents were well acknowledged by a number of literary critics like Kandukuri Veeresalingam,[40] Vanguri Subba Rao,[41] Utukuri Lakshmi Kantamma,[42] Thumati Donappa[43] and Arudra.[44]

Thus, Subhadramma, probably due to her interaction with all the literary activities of her father's court turned as a poetess and composed many works out of which only twelve works are available and they were published during the period of Gode Narayana Gajapati Rao.

The following are the details after published works[45].

Krishna Satakam:

Normally a Sataka consists of one hundred or above one hundred stangas

This work consists of 95 stanzas in *Kanda* metre with a suffix "Krishna"!

Kesava Satakam:

It consists of one hundred and sixty stanzas in *Utpalamala* and *Champakamala* metres with suffix "Kesava"!

Kodanda Rama Satakam:

This work consists of 19 stanzas in *sisa* metre. It is a work made in dedication to the Lord Kodanda Rama, to whom a temple was constructed by her father Gode Jagga Rao at Visakhapatnam. In the suffix (*makuta*) of each stanza Lord Kodanda Rama was praised thus[46]:

> *"Charu Vaisakha Puradhama*
> *Jaggaraya Hridayabdisoma Kodanda Rama"*

Janaki hridayesvara Satakam

Ashtakam means a composition of eight stanzas on a particular theme. But in this poem only one stanza, praising Lord Rama with a suffix *Janaki hridayesvara* or *Janaki Paramesvara* in *Matta Kokila* metre is available[47].

> *"Meluga bratimalaga jalamelera vetajalura*
> *Jali nondagalenura ninu sannutimpagajalara*
> *Yela nee dayaradura nanu nelara vagabapara*
> *Jalamela viskahapatana janaki parmesvara"!!*

Rangesvara Satakam:

This *Satakam* consists of four stanzas in *Sardhula* metre with the suffix "*Rangesvara*"!

Raghunayaka Satakam:

This work consists of 95 stanzas in *Utpalamala* and *Champakamala metres* with suffix *'Raghunayaka Dinaposhaka!'*

Raghava Rama Satakam:

This consists of 93 stanzas in *Kanda* metre with suffix *"Raghava Rama"!*

Venkatesa Satakam:

This work consists of only 12 stanzas in *sisa* metre with suffix "*Venkatesa*".

Sri Rama Dandakam:

Dandakam is a type of writing come out of an emotion with a deep sense of feelings of sringara, roudra and Bhakti.

This *Sri Rama Dandakam* is a brief narration of entire story of *Ramayana*, with a deep sense of emotion.

Simhagiri satakam:

In this *Sataka* only nine stanzas in *sisa* metre were available.

Simhachaladhisvara Satakam:

In this *Sataka* which was written in praise of Simhachaladhisvara, only four stanzas in *Sardhula* metre were available.

Hari Ramesa Padyalu:

In this, only five stanzas in *Sisa* metre with suffix "*Hari Ramesa!*" are available.

Besides the above works, Madiney Subhadramma seems to have composed some more works, as some verses with suffixes like "*Dharmarakshana!*", "*Daithyanasana!*", "*Parmesvara!*", "*Kuranganabhama!*" and *Nitimuthema* were available.[48]

As stated earlier, Madiney Subhadramma in her *satakas* has written some stanzas in *Mattakokila metre*. The literary critics noticed the style of an *ashtaka* in her writing. Such stanzas ends with the suffix "Visakhapattana Janaki Paramesvara."

The devotion towards God, scholarship in narration, respect towards elders and scholars, are found throughout her works. She was appreciated by her contemporary scholars as "*Ayata Vidya Samagra*" and "*Andhra Girvanabhasha Parignana Prasasti*". In the opinion of some scholars her poetry excels the composition of Tarigonda Vengamamba.[49]

Some writers like Angara Surya Rao, by mistake considered the work *Satyavati Parinayamu,* as written by Subhadramma.[50] But as stated earlier that work was initiated by Kakaraparthi Buchchipatra kavi in dedication to Gode Suryanarayana Rao. But due to his sudden death it became incomplete and Venkata Sastri and Sitarama Sastri later completed that, and dedicated to Gode Narayana Gajapati Rao.

Some of the understated stanzas give us a clue about the existence of some more writers under the patronage of Gode Surya Prakasa Rao.

Recollecting the lavish experiences done for the construction of a number of buildings adjacent to Upputeru in Visakhapatnam by Surya Pradasa Rao, a poet Nadiminty Sarvamangaleswara Sastri is said to have stated thus:[51]

> *"Karuna matha dharunam silpakanam tadhaiva cha*
> *Gode Narayana dravya mayyo ayyo vridha vridha"*

Another prominent personality that showed much interest in different fields of knowledge, done researches in modern approach and perception, encouraged writers and poets for the composition of works which are useful for the society, is Gode China Venkata Jagga Rao. In the history of the aristocracy of the Andhras, he is the first scientist that contributed much to astronomy and agricultural science.[52] He not only published a number of research papers on astronomy in reputed journals, but also patronised a number of writers and scholars.

To teach people, the process of time, '*Kalagati Sighrasphurti bodhimpaga*' he established an astronomical observatory at Visakhapatnam. The results of his researches like that on the study of planet *Bruhaspati*, on the passion and purpose of zero etc., in the popular English magazines of the day. Owing to his deep interest on such matters, he regularly used to visit the 'Magnetic Observatory' at Chennai.

From A.D.1833 onwards, he served as a patron to 'Hindu Literary Society at Madras' and helped to a number of poets and scholars. A writer of eminence, well-versed in *Kavyas* who can compose different varieties of poetry in '*Chitra*' and '*bandha*' models, is Kola Seshachalam; and he get patronised under Venkata Jagga Rao.

Kola Seshachalam, who lived in and around A.D. 1846, served the Company Government as a clerk in the office of the Auditor-General, at Fort St. George in Madras. As a part of his job, he stayed at Nilagiri from May, 1846 to January, 1847, i.e., for a period of seven months. His activities, observations and experiences during that stay of seven months at Nilagiri were recorded in his diary. After one decade, it is in 1858 A.D., he composed a prosedy by utilising that material in three chapters by name *Nilagiri Yatra*. He dedicated that work to Gode China Venkata Jagga Rao.[53] In the opinion of the literary critics,

Seshachalam made this work unnecessarily in a tough Telugu language which is not understandable even to the learned men; and probably due to that it has not come to print until 1963.

Nilagiri Yatra, though composed in tough Telugu language, it is a unique work in giving more information on some important aspects. It vividly describes the climate on Nilagiri hill ranges and how that soil and environs are suitable to raise some Western crops like radish, beetroot, noolkol, turnips, carrot, cauliflower, leave maroya, raspberry, mulberry, strawberry, hillgoose berry, peaches, pears, apple, etc. The introduction of such crops at Nilagiri hill ranges is attested to, in another work *Nilagiri Charitramu* written by Bethapudi Sundara Rayudu, who worked at that place during the period of C.P. Brown.[54]

Interestingly, it is noticed that under this Gode Venkata Jagga Rao, the first Telugu newspaper "Vrittantini" was started.[55]

A great scholar, a great patron of letters, founder of various educational institutions, libraries and charitable organisations, a publisher of numerous literary works, was Maharaja Sir, C.I.E., K.C.I.E., Gode Narayana Bahadur (1828-1903). He started his academic career under a learned scholar of the period Paravastu Srinivasacharya; and later studied English education at Calcutta. He served as the member of Academic Senate of Madras University. Owing to his interests towards culture, education, literature and social reforms he became very close to a number of contemporary aristocrat families like the Rajas of Venkatagiri as well as the champions of Brahmo Samaj like Devendranath Tagore and Kesavachandra Sen. His visit to Venkatagiri to grace the coronation ceremony of the Raja of Venkatagiri is described in *Radhakrishna- Samvadhamu.*[56]

As stated earlier, *Satyavati Parinayamu* originally started by Kakaraparti Buchchipatra Kavi and completed by Venkata Sastri and Sitarama Sastri was given in dedication to this Narayana Gajapati. It is a *prabandha kavya* with 18 descriptions (ashtadasa varnanas) and deals with the marriage of Santanu and Satyavati.

Paravasthu Srinivasa Jagannadha Swami, one of his court poets has written on the request of Narayana Gajapati, a commentary of Upanishads entitled *Bhagavad Vishyopanishattulu*. The same scholar has also made in Telugu another philosophical work *Vaidika matavali*, the essence of all the important aspects of Nyaya, Vaiseshika, Yoga and Sankhya aspects. Interestingly his patron Narayana Gajapati has written the 'foreword' to that work. It indicates the keen interest of Narayana Gajapati towards the Hindu Dharma.

Another court-poet Gorty Venkata Sastri has written on the request of Narayana Gajapati, a work entitled "*Satprabhu Padyamala*", and with a suffix "Satprabhu!!" addressing to his patron.[57]

Besides encouraging poets and scholars, Narayana Gajapati Rao initiated for the collection and publication of almost all the works either written or patronised earlier under the Gode Zamindars.

The following is the list of the important works published by Narayana Gajapati Rao.

Table - 6.5

Sl. No.	*Name of the Work*	*Name of the Poet*
1.	*Satyabhama-Krishna Samvadamu*	Kakaraparti Tirupati Patra Kavi
2.	*Sasirekha Parinayam*	Kakarparti Krishna Kavi
3.	*Mukhalingesvara Taravali*	Kakaraparti Krishna Kavi
4.	*Mukhalingesvara Kshetramahatyamu*	Kakaraparti Krishna Kavi
5.	*Oghavati Parinayam*	Akkinepalli Nrisimha Kavi
6.	*Satyavati Parinayam*	Kakaraparti Buchchipatra Kavi
7.	More than dozen works of Subhadramma listed earlier	Madiney Subhadramma
8.	*Char Darvishu* (Naluguru Phakirula Charitramu)	Erramilli Mallikarjuna Kavi
9.	*Sarva Sabda Sambodhini*	Paravastu Srinivasa-charyulu
10.	*Gadyatmaka Vishnupuranamu*	Nori Gurilinga Sastrulu

Almost all the prominent poets of the then times like Tirupati Venkata Kavulu,[58] Chilakamarti Lakshmi Narasimham[59] and Tumurada Sangameswara Sastri, etc., were welcomed and honoured at the Darbar of the Gode Zamindars of Visakhapatnam during the period of Narayana Gajapati Rao.

Besides the promotion and patronage of sciences and literature, the said zamindar has shown keen interest on music also. Srirangam Suryanarayana Sarma adorned his court and composed a work *Sri Bhagavath Gita Sara Sankirtana*, the essence of *Bhagavath Gita*.

China Janakamma, the lady of Narayana Gajapati Rao was also a poetess and patron of scholars. She has composed, probably in a state of sorrow after the death of her husband, a devotional work named *Bhagavad Prardhana*. At the request of this lady zamindar, Kakaraparti Sitarama Kavi has written a *Sataka* on Lord Satyanarayana Murti of Annavaram with a suffix 'Satya!!'

One Gode Jagannadha Rao, whose relations with the main Gode family was not known, appeared in some of the stanzas which contain the suffix "*Jnanabhogi Gode Jagannadha Yogi.*" Though the position of him in the Gode family and his period is not known, one poet Nimusha Kavi Venkatesam roughly of A.D. 1850, composed a *sataka* addressing to that Gode Jagannadha Yogi.[60] Nidadavolu Venkata Rao identified that Jagannadha Yogi, who was described as 'Jnana Bhogi', as a brother of Gode Narayana Gajapati Rao.[61] No doubt Narayana Gajapati Rao had a step-brother Gode China Venkata Jagga Rao, the well-known scientist in the family. But to identify him as Jagannadha Yogi seems to be not correct as it is not supported by any of the evidences. Jagannadha Yogi of the Gode family belongs to the same decade chronologically; but his relations with the main family, is not known.

Sitabai, the Rani Saheba of Wadhwan, the eldest daughter of Gode Narayana Gajapati Rao is also a good scholar and patronised writers and poets. She lost her husband Raja Thagore Saheb, returned to Visakhapatnam, settled there and spent the next of her life in literary activity and in performing neighous works and philanthropy. As she seems to be a good devotee of Lord Venkateswara of Upamaka, she is much interested in the translation of the Sanskrit verses *'Samvada Traya'* which were used to chant on the occasion of the *Kalyanotsava* ceremony of Lord Venkateswara Swami of Upamaka. *Chora Samvadamu, Lakshmi Varana Samvadamu*, and *Lakshmi Narayana Samvadamu* are known as *Samvadatraya* in Vaishnavitc literaturc. Paravastu Venkata Ranganatha Swami has written *Chora Samvadamu* and Paravastu Lakshmi Narasimha Swami has written *Lakshmi Varana Samvadamu* and *Lakshmi Narayana Samvadamu*. These three *Samvadas* were written and published as per the intention and encouragement of the Rani Saheba Sitabai.

Another important book that was written under the patronage of the above Rani Saheba is *Upamaka Kshetra Mahatyam*. This is originally a story of five *asvasas* in the *Garudachala Mahatyam* which is originally drawn from *Brahma Vaivarta Purana*. The Court-Poets of Sita Bai, Paravastu Venkata Ranganatha Swami and Kakaraparti Sitarama Swami translated it with a simple commentary.

Gode China Venkata Jagga Rao's daughter Achchayamma married Ankitam Venkata Narasinga Rao, who came and settled in Visakhapatnam. Achchayamma became the Zamindar of Embaram and Sher Mohammadpuram, after the death of her father. She is also much interested in the promotion of education and literature. After her death, in token of her interest towards the promotion of education, in A.D. 1892, one lakh and fifteen thousand rupees (1,15,000) were given for the establishment of a college in her name, and that is the present Mrs A.V.N. College in Visakhapatnam.

Later, the Ankitam Venkata Jagga Rao Bahadur, F.R.A.S., F.R. Met. Soc., F.A.S., F.R.C.I., succeeded to the ancestral seat and continued the early traditions of the Zamindari. *Andhrabhyudayam* describes his interest towards astronomy[62], astrology and sciences. He has brought a number of scientists and appointed them in his observatory. He patronised Rani Mahagni-Chinna Nrisimha Kavi who has written *Tidhikalpavalli*, a work on Jyotisha, in dedication to his patron. Thopalli Venkata Rama Siddhanti, the court-astrologist of Kasimkota zamindari has written a commentary to *Tidhikalpavalli* with the title *Manjari*. A work *Daivajna Sarvabhouma Vijayamu* written by Janamanchi Seshadri Sarma, which describes the life and achievements of Rani Mahagni Chinna Nrisimha Kavi, refers to the importance of *Tidhikalavalli* and its dedication to Ankitam Venkata Jagga Rao.[63] It is also stated that with the help of eminent scholars, he has compiled a book on *Mantra Sastra* entitled *Deviastangahridayam* describing the powers of Devi-worship. He also published a number of books like *Drigganita-panchangam*. It is stated that due to his keen interest on 'Mantra Sastra', he followed and practised Tantricism which seems to have become the cause of his death.[64] It is interesting to note that it is in the same decades that C.P. Brown and some of the Professors like Wilson of Oxford University showed much interest on tantricism and on Sakteyam; and collected a number of authentic books on that subject in India.

Thus, the Gode Zamindars and their ladies contributed much to literature by their liberal patronage to scholars and poets, as well as by their writings. That legacy was continued later by the liberal patronages of Vairicharla, Kurupam, Jaipur, Ankitam and other families who connected themselves with this family as well as this province.

It is interesting to note that on one side these zamindars patronised Kavyas, Prabandhas and other bhakti literature and on another side they showed much interest on Western education, Western ideology and Western thought. It is interesting to notice that from the same zamindari courts, where the traditional literature flourished, the modern Telugu literature in colloqual like *Mutyala Saralu,* and Telugu popular dramas like *Kanya Sulkam,* also originated.

This occurrence was probably due to a number of socio-economic as well as religio-cultural changes in the society. Either due to the propularity as well as due to the propagation towards the Western education, or other economic motivations, such as seeking of employment either in the company or governmet services, at least some sections in the society came under the influence of Western ideology and Western systems, and consisted of liberal views. On another side either due to the legacy of the Bakti movement of being influenced by the trends from Bengal, or due to the inherent interests on their own religion and traditional culture, the society wants to revive its past glory. Amidst of such ideological struggle, literature of this period turned into different directions. With the advent of the Christianity into this land, to propagate their religion they have also taken literature as the vehicle, and in counter to it, from the side of the Hindu faith, voluminous literature was produced throughout the land. To gain support from the local public or due to their personal faiths those local chief also became instrumental in encouraging such literatures. Due the demand of the times, reformist literature also flourished during these countries. As a result, literature of all typcs sccms to have flourished during this period. Editing the inscriptions of historical importance and editing some of the important books of significance like *"History of Anantapur Kings"* by Gurajada Appa Rao, testifies to the keen interest of at least some of the zamindars of this province on history.[65]

Adibatla Narayana Das (1864-1945), was a multifaceted personality lived under the patronage of the Pusapati family. He was popularly known as 'Harikath Pitamaha'. A number of Harikathas were composed by him. His autobiography *Na Eruka* gives a detailed description of the life and ideology of Narayana Das.

It is also interesting to note that in no period in the history of the literature of the country, except during this period, such a number of dictionaries came to the light. Of course, it may be due to the expansion of knowledge from one area to another, and also due to the entry of Europeans into this land.

Enugula Viraswammayya (1780 – 1836), the head-interpretor in the Supreme Court during the Company period, is a good scholar in Telugu, Tamil, English and Sanskrit. He has commendable knowledge on *Sriti, Smriti, Puranas,* and on the commentaries on the *Dharmasastras*. His *Kasiyatra Charitra* is highly useful to understand the socio-economic history of that period.[66] He visited Visakhapatnam, Kasimkota, Ellamachili, Dimili, Nakkapalli, Payakrao Peta and other areas in the Visakhapatnam province and collected and recorded valuable information about the society, economy, agriculture and other aspects of this province.

Pakki Venkata Narasayya, who served as a Telugu Pandit in a Christian School at Visakhapatnam has written two important *satakas* - *Kumari Satakam* and *Narayana Satakam*. *Kumari Satakam* is very popular and is byhearted by all, as it highlights the morals advocated by Hindu religion. In the same period Pusapati Virapa Raju of the Visakhapatnam province has written a *sataka* in *kanda* metre with the suffix "Chiruta Vajiru."[67]

It is during this period, in the Visakhapatnam province, probably due to the encouragement that was given to the poets and scholars we come across the works of some poets. But their connections to the Zamindari courts, or the favours they have received by the zamindari families, are not known.

Another important scholarly family that lived during the period of the Gode zamindari in Visakhapatnam province is the Kallakuri family.[68] The successive five generations of this family are known as poets. Kallakuri Nagayya has written *Krishnarjuna Samvadam*; his son Lakshmipati has written *Bhadra Kalyanam*; Kallakuri Perayya of this family has written *Rasavinodam* his grandson Gowrikantam (A.D. 1815) has written a Sringara Prabhanda named *Dharmanandana Vilasam*, in dedication to Velicheti Guru Rayudu who served under Pusapati Narayana Gajapati.

Another poet that lived at Enuguvalasa in the province of Visakhapatnam is Poduri Venkata Raju who lived around A.D. 1848. He has written a work of three *asvasas* named *Ramaleela Vilasam*, which describes the history of the Pusapatis.

Dittakavi Narayana Kavi, son of Papa Raju who received honours in a number of zamindari courts of this province during this period has written an important, work *Rangaraya -Charitramu*. This is a work of three *asvasas* which describes the Battle of Bobbili. In this work he has elaborately narrated how a number of zamindars of this province like Kakarlapudis supported the Bobbili rulers against the French, where as the Pusapatis and their allies supported the French. He has used occasionally a number of English and French words in the narration of the story.[69]

Whereas Ditta Kavi Narayana Kavi has written a work by name *Rangaraya Charitra*, describing the valour and courage of Bobbili Chiefs which ends in tragedy; Chatrati Lakshmi Narasu Kavi has written the tragic story of the Pusapatis at the Battle of Padmanabham with title '*Padmanabha Yuddham*'. Like Dittakavi Narayana Kavi[70], Lakshmi Narasu Kavi also used Urdu, Persian and English words, in narrating the events. These two works, describes the tragic end of two powerful zamindars of this province during this period, in the hands of the French and the English Companies respectively.

The same Chatrati Lakshmi Narasu Kavi has also written a number of works like *Isvariparinayam*, *Viseshandhram* and *Kodanda Rama Satakam*. In the *Kodanda Rama Satakam*, only 13 stanzas are available. It is understood that Lakshmi Narasu Kavi aimed those stanzas, to reveal the tyranical rule and attrocities during the Diwangiri of Sitarama Raju, in the contemporary Pusapati zamindari.[71]

Inspite of the extensive patronage towards literature by the zamindars during this period, it seems that some of the poets are not thoroughly satisfied with that. Pantula Brahmma Devayya, who lived in the Court of Urlam zamindars, refers to the deteriorating patronage of the zamindars of the Visakhapatnam District towards literature, thus:[72]

> *"Ranan minchu visakhapattanapu zillalo zamindarula*
> *Kshinoudaryamunan rasajna gunasri dadrusul gami*
> *Dakkanai yunduta jeta .... "*

Another great poet that hailed from the family of the estatedars who lived in the same period, in the same province is Bhagavatula Krishnayya. Just like Tarigonda Vengamamba, by adopting the style of the *Yakshaganas* in *Kanda* metre, he has written some hundreds of stanzas for the promotion of the subject matter of philosophy and on the practices of Yoga.[73] He was a very generous Estatedar of Dimili near Elamanchili in the Visakhapatnam District. In A.D.1830, when Enugula Viraswamayya was touring in the Visakhapatnam province, he enjoyed the hospitality of this estatedar of Dimili, and acknowledged him in his *Kasiyatra Charitra* in glorifying terms.[74]

In 302 *kandardha* stanzas, in a very simple language, he described the doctrine of *Achalamata*. He has stated that he toured in different countries and has written a number of works. But except '*Achalamata*' the details of his other works are not known. Birudu Raju Rama Raju opines that the stanzas of this poet are very popular in theTelangana province,[75] but his connections with the Telangana area are otherwise unknown.

In the introductory portion to his work, Krishnayya expresses his love and respect towards Telugu and appeals to all not to discriminate any work simply because of its composition in Telugu.[76]

Vaddiparti Konama Raju (1754-1834), a native of Sarvasiddhi has written a number of works which are very useful to understand the contemporary socio-economic as well as religio-cultural systems. *Jamabandi-Dandakam, Committee Uttaram, Venkateswaropakhyanam,*

Revatiparinayam, Sri Maha Lakshmi Parinayam, Janaki Rama Satakam etc., are his works. *Sri Maha Lakshmi Parinayam* is a *Sringarakavya* in five *asvasas* that was appreciated by the scholars. The problems faced by the village 'karanams' during the Company period, the information about the 'Mirasidars' and the details on Inamlands, are clearly stated in *Jamabandi Dandakam* and *Committee Uttaram*[77]. The problems at the time of Jamabandi, and the difficulties of the village revenue officers, like the karanams were vividly described in lengthy stanzas, written in Sisa metre with the suffix "*Vinuta Gowrisa Upamaka Venkatesa*!" The personal Court disputes and other related problems of the poet on his landed property etc., were also referred to in his *Janaki Rama Satakam*.

In addition to the above, he has composed a number of works on the contemporary events. By the internal evidences of such works it is understood that he served as the 'karanam' of the village Sarvasiddhi near Upamaka, the ancient village in the Visakhapatnam area.

Besides Telugu and Sanskrit Kavyas and other literary styles, Visakhapatnam is also credited with the Christian publication activity.[78] For the first time, the translation of the Bible into Telugu started at Visakhapatnam. By A.D. 1810, Mattai, Mark and Luka Suvarthas were translated and published in 319 pages with the Telugu titles:[79]

> *"Devuni Yokka Samastamaina Vakyamu",*
> *"Suviseshamu Mammunu Rakshinche Karta Ayina*
> *Yesu Krishtu Yokka Subha Samacharamu!"*

During 1804, 'London Missionary Society' deputed two missionaries, George Crane and Augustus - Dingragus to propagate Christianity. They came and settled at Visakhapatnam in 1805, and served in the religious activities of the soldiers in the Fort. One Brahmin by name Subba Rao, who turned as a Christian, renamed as Ananda Rao, who is much interested in translating Bible into Telugu, joined them.[80] As stated the above three Suvartas; Mattai, Mark and Luka were translated by 1810, and by 1818. The entire Bible was translated in 800 pages, and published by 'Baptist and Foreign Bible Society' with the Telugu title "*Iswaruni Annimatalu* ididamanu pustakamu". All the Telugu translations of the Bible, that have taken place in the succeeding periods have based upon this work. By 1840, one printing press - 'Mission Press' was established at Visakhapatnam for the Christian Missionary publications.[81] In between A.D. 1856 and 1866, one more press, 'London Mission Press' was established at Visakhapatnam.

Besides the patronage of zamindars and nobles, some of the traders and business people encouraged poets. An overseas trader by name Magatapalli Kamayya Setti, has patronaged a poet by name Pachchametta Papayya. That Papayya has written a *sataka* in *Kanda* metre with a suffix "Magatapalli Kamaya Chandra!!" and dedicated it to his Patron.[82] In addition to that he has written another *sataka* in *Utpalamala* metre with the suffix "Mahishasuramardhani Siva", and a *dandaka* by name *Hanumad dandaka*. Literary critics noticed that this poet followed the literary style of Adidam Sura Kavi and Nadiminti Rama Jogi Kavi. In some of his stanzas, he denies that even a he-buffalo is better than a ruler who is not helpful to his followers, as it tills the land and yields produce to its owners.

Mrityunjaya Nissanka who belongs to the family of Sangamvalasa zamindars is an accomplished scholar, and a great poet. He made commentaries on the three works of Kalidasa, *Abhijnana Sakunthalam*, *Vikramorvasiyam* and *Malavikagni Mitram*. His book of morals, known as *Nithi Sastra Sangraham*, has become a popular one, and is highly spoken of by the educated classes. He has also published some works like *Sri Samba Satakam*, *Gowri Vivaham*, *Rajasekhara Vilasam*, *Sri Suryanarayana Charitam*, *Dasavatara Natakam* and *Parijatam* in Telugu. He is also the author of a book which contains the Code of Laws which is intended to help the zamindars.[83] He composed some verses in praise of the Queen Victoria's Majesty and presented them to her. Pleased with the literary contribution of the Zamindar, King Edward VII, the then president of the Royal Asiatic Society appointed him as the member of that body.[84]

Being benefitted by the East India Company, some of the Telugu poets of the day appreciated and praised the Company Rule in their Chatuverses.[85]

Mohamahopadhyaya Sriman Paravastu Venkata Rangacharyulu was another famous scholar that was patronised by Vatsavai Zamindars, who belonged to the north of river Tandava near Payakarao peta.

The Vatsavai Zamindars who are adjacent to the Kakarlapudi's, established a press with a large establishment for the printing of medical books.[86]

William Brown (1783-1837) who served in different capacities at Visakhapatnam, Vizianagaram and Kasimkota translated with the help of Telugu Scholars a Telugu grammar book into English in 1817.[87]

Learning of European languages among the local people, particularly Christian converts, is encouraged by the Colonial agencies. They were given priorities in selecting as dubasis.[88] It is stated that as early as in the end of sixteenth century itself, the Portugese Emperor ordered his officers in India to select those Christian converts who learnt Portuguese language, as dubasis in India.[89]

Thus, as discussed earlier, the period under study witnessed a number of changes and new trends in the field of literature. The zamindars as well as their family members, enriched and patronaged literature, either due to their inherent interests or as it became a symbol of social status of the aristocracy in that period. As per the ancient Indian tradition, they followed the earlier concept of 'Sapta Santanas',[90] and supported poets and writers by taking their literary compositions as 'kritis'. In return to that they have granted inam lands, agraharas and 'Varshikam' (annual payment of money) to them. As referred to already, those poets who enjoyed patronage made works describing the family history of the patron, and also composed them in accordance with their interests on either 'rakti' or bhakti. An analysis of the works of that period gives a clue on the different types of works of that period.[91] A number of new temples either constructed by those families, or those continued under their patronage were described and glorifies in the writings. Efforts were made in some works to trace the history and antiquity of those chiefs or zamindars to connect them with either legendary or historical personalities. Majority of the works were made in dedication either to their tutelary deities or to their patrons. Literary critics like Gurajada Sriramamurthy, Arudra, Donappa and others elaborately and critically analysed the works of this period.[92] The voluminous literature that was produced during this period in this part of the country clearly indicates the keen interest of the zamindars in patronaging the poets and scholars. It also hints to the increase in the literacy rate in the contemporary society.

The period under study witnessed the growth of literature in multidimensions. Works of all kinds viz., bhakti, Vedanta, tantric, philosophical, sthalapuranas, grammar, rhetoric, puranic stories, histories and achievements of the patrons, works on sringara, ethical and moral stories etc., were composed during this period.

As the society of the period was disturbed by alien races and religions, to revive the prestige and honour of its native religion, the concept of bhakti was revived and it was reflected in the medium of literature. It resulted in the composition of a number of bhakti works on Saiva, Vaishnava, Sakti, Hanuman cult etc. Interestingly works on Vaishnava sampradaya like *samvadatraya* and stories on alvars appeared frequently during this period. In-depth theological discussions on Vedic works were also noticed during this period. *Rigvea Samhita, Bhagavath Vishayopanishattulu, Achalamata, Vaidika Matavali*, etc., belonged to that category.

Prabandha style of kavyas which were very common and popular in medieval centuries of Andhradesa still gained ground in the havelies and places of the zamindars. Almost the marriages of all the puranic ladies were composed in prabantha style with eighteen types of descriptions. *Adhlakshmi prinayam, Rukmini parinayam, Eswari parinayam, Usha parinayam* etc., were of that type.

In general, those zamindars represent the local power and hence the important centres in that locality were necessarily glorified; and as a result a number of puranas or histories on local temples came to light. *Upmaka Kshetra Mahatyam, Nilasaila Nadiyam, Mukhalingeswara Kshetramahatyam, Aganampudi Rathotsvam, Kurma puranam*, etc., were of that type.

Some of the social practices like polygamy, concubinage etc., which were followed in the early centuries continued during this period also. The sensuousness or the licentiousness that found in all sections of society was also not a new phenomenon.[93] Some of the poets followed the foot-prints of the early centuries and moulded their works and identified srinagara, the supreme among all the feelings with the crude, erotic sentiment associated with physical action. Some of the poets of the period went to the extent of identifying their kavyas as courtesans with all their knowledge and experience of sexual play. They viewed the society in such an order and projected the same in their creations. In such works though names and places changed, the subject and context were almost the same. Even the pativratas and sacred ladies were also not spared. *Simantini Charitramu, Sundarimani Satakamu, Ganikamani Vilasamu, Sringara Rasamanjary, Madana bhyudayam* etc., were of the works of such category. Adilakshmi, Rukmini, Satyabhama, Satyavati etc., puranic ladies were not spared.

Polygamy and concubinage, the outcome of the male domination in the society, seems to have gone to its peak by that time. Some literary works describe how people sold and lost their properties to satisfy such of their desires. There were various descriptions about the exploitation and sexual assault of ladies on the occasions like chariot festivals. It is stated that a number of ladies were cheated, sold and were taken on the ships to other countries like that of the Dutch.[94]

Thus, some of the poets made their efforts in writing such works to satisfy the desires of the people. As a legacy of prabandha literature, there is no scope to imagine the literature of the period to be otherwise. The trade and cultural relations of Andhradesa with the rest of the world should also be taken into consideration in this context.

Another type of literature that was enriched during this period was historical works. This includes the narrations of important incidents like those of the battles, the euologies and the family histories. To bring significance and sanctity to the family histories of some of the zamindars like the Pusapatis who traced their origin from *Skandapurana*, which was composed in far late centuries, and with full of fabrication. *Vijayarama Gajapatindra Charitramu, Kshatriya gotra Sisamalika, Srikrishna Bhupati Taravali, Rachirajusismalika* etc., were that type. Though Telugu poets never prefer the kavyas of *Vishadanta* (tragic ending), interestingly this period witnessed the works like *Padmanabha Yuddham* and *Rangaraya Charitam* which narrated the tragic end of the Pusapatis of Vizianagaram and Raos of Bobbili.

The patronage of the poets by the zamindars resulted in the production of treatises on grammar as well as rhetorical works like *Sukvijanamanoramjanam, Nava lekhni Lekhyam, Andhra Chandrolokam* and *Andhra Namasesham.*

To exhibit their creative skill, some of the poets of the period had chosen a typical model of writing called 'Dvyaradhi' and 'Tryardhi' kavyas in which each stanza conveys two or three different meanings of puranic stories. *Krishnarjuna Charitra* and a number of others were of that type.

The works like *Jamabandi Dandakam* and *Committee Uttaram* etc., clearly describe the problems and sufferance faced by the Village Revenue Officers and others at the time of zamabandi. Some interesting information about the mirasidars and tyots was also narrated in such works. Some of the problems related to the lands and properties, personal courts disputes etc., generally faced by the common people were described in works like *Janikirama Satakam*.

As referred to already Visakhapatnam province is credited with the Christian publication activity like the translations of Suvartas of Mattai, Mark and Luka. Bible was also translated into Telugu with the title: 'Iswaruni Annimatalu, idi damanu pustakamu'. It is interesting to note that all the Telugu translations of the Bible of the later period based upon that work.

C.P. Brown collected a number of manuscripts at places like Kadapa, Nellore, Chittoor, Machilipatnam, Kurnool, Kakinada Rajahmundry, Draksharama, etc.[95] It is strange to notice that not even a single manuscript was collected from any place in the Visakhapatnam province, inspite of the tremendous contribution to literature continuously in this area.

References

1. Venta Appa Rao, Gurajada, *Kanya Sulkam*, 1897, (Ed). P. Eswara Rao, Visaladra Publishing House, Hyderabad.

1A. *J.A.H.R.S.* Vol. XXVII (1962-63), p. 9.

1B. Donappa, T. *Andhra Samstanamulu-Sahitya Poshanamu*, p. 291.

1C. Anjanikumari, B., "*Madugula Zamindari, an Off-shoot of the Jeypore of Orissa*" article published in *Cultural Heritage of Orissa*, Berhampur, 2011, p. 13.

2. *Ibid.*

3. Adidam Surakavi was a famous poet that lived under the patronage of the rulers of Chipurupalli. He visited a number of Royal Courts, acquired name and fame, and became popular as a poet of 'Tittu kavita' (curse poems).

Veturi Prabhakara Sastri in his *Chatupadya Manimanjari* (p.172) and a number of others referred to a number of his stanzas (*chatus*).

4. Donappa, T., *Op.Cit,* p. 325.
5. *Ibid,* p. 327.
6. *Ibid.*
7. *Andhra Kavi Sapta Sati,* p. 40.
8. Chebrolu seems to be the original home of the Allam Raju families. Even now a number of families of that surname are there at Chebrolu, in East Godavari District.
9. *Andhra Chmpu Bharatamu,* Asvasa I, Stanza – 33.
10. Donappa, T., *Op. Cit.,* p. 328.
11. *Ibid,* p. 329.
12. *Ibid,* p. 329.
13. Subba Rao, Vanguri, *Andhra Vajnmaya Charitramu,* p. 110.
14. *Trilinga,* 1931, Feb. 2, p. 14.
15. Tirupati Venkata Kavulu, *Nanaraja Sandarsanamu,* p. 201.
16. Narayana Kavi, Ditta kavi, *Rangaraya Charitramu,* Asvasa I Stanza, 152.
17. Somappakavi, Rekapalli, *Rukmavati Parinayamu, Asvasa I, Stanza,* 62.
18. *Ibid,* Stanza 63.
19. Donappa, T., *Op. Cit.,* p. 555.
20. *Ibid.*
21. Subba Rao, Vanguri, *Satakakavula Charitra,* 1957, pp. 335-340.
22. Kurmanadha Kavi, Gogulapti, *Simhadri Narasimha Satakam,* Stanza. 28.
23. Arudra, *Samagra Andhra Sahityam,* Vol. III, p. 470.
24. Narayana kavi, Ditta Kavi, *Op. Cit.,* Asvasa I, Stanza – 160.
25. "*Vijayarama Mahaaraja Virundelu Pattamulikinche Raja Bhupala Raju*" Cited by Donappa. T., *Op. Cit.,* p. 525.
26. Veeresalingam, Kandukuri, *Andhra Kavula Charitramu,* Vol.III, p. 95.
27. Donappa, T., *Op. Cit.,* p. 138.
28. *Kalpalatha,* 1921, February, p. 29.
29. Buchchipatrakavi, Kakaraparti, *Satyavati Parinayam,* p. 10.
30. *Ibid.*
31. *Ibid.*
32. Donappa, T., *Op.Cit.* p. 140.
33. Nrisimha Kavi, Akkinepalli, *Oghavati Parinayam,* Asvasa – I, Stanza – 199.
34. The date of the composition of *Oghavati Parinayam* is stated in the introduction as: *Salivahana Sakamuna Bingala Sanjya Samvastyaramuna*

Dagu Kartikkamuna Sukla Pakshamuna......... " by calculating the date with the help of *Indian Ephimaries* of Swami Kannupillai, the date is correctly calculated as A.D. 1817.

35. Nrisimha kavi, Akkinepalli, *Op. Cit.,* Asvasa I, Stanza - 29.
36. Arudra, *Op. Cit.,* Vol. III, p. 347.
37. *Ibid.*
38. Donappa, T., *Op. Cit.,* p. 143.
39. Madras Oriental Manuscript Library R.No. 338 (b).
40. Veeresalingam, Kandukuri, *Op. Cit.,* Vol. III, p. 312.
41. Subba Rao, Vanguri, *Op. Cit.,* p. 314.
42. Lakshmikantamma, Utukuri, *Andhra Kaviytrulu,* p. 71.
43. Donappa, T., *Op. Cit.,* p. 349.
44. Arudra, *Op. Cit.,* p. 335.
45. Anjani Kumari, Badarala, *Contribution of the Gode zamindars in the fields of Agriculture, Economy and Cultural in Vizagapatam District. Unpublished M. Phi Dissertation.*
46. *Andhra Patrika Hevalambi, Ugadi Sanchika,* 1957, p. 134.
47. Lakshmi Kantam, Utukuri, *Op. Cit.,* p. 71.
48. *Ibid.*
49. Donappa, T., *Op. Cit.,* p. 149.
50. Surya Rao, Angara, *Rendu Satabdala Visakhanagara Charitra,* p. 53.
51. Donappa, T., *Op. Cit.,* p. 144 Foot notes.
52. Suryanarayana, Kolluru, *"A Study on the Contribution of Telugu Literature to Agricultural Science.* Paper presented in the National Seminar Organised by Ministry of Culture, New Delhi in Visakhapatnam in 1998.
53. *Ibid.*
54. Arudra, *Op. Cit.,* p. 242.
55. Surya Rao, Angara, *Op. Cit.,* p. 53.
56. *Radha Krishna Samvadamu,* Asvasa, II, p. 181.
57. Donappa, T., *Op. Cit.,* p. 147.
58. Tirupati Venkata Kavulu, *Op. Cit.,* p. 14.
59. Lakshmi Narasimham, Chilakamarti, *Sviya Charitram,* p. 148.
60. *Andhra Kavi Saptasati,* p. 259.
61. *Telugu Vijnanasarvasvamu,* Vol. III, p. 1171.
62. *Andhra bhyudayamu,* Vol. III, Stanza 13, it states like this, "Katte nakshitra sala na pattanamuna".
63. "Dai vajya *Sarvabhouma Vijayamu*" Stanza. 229.
64. Varma, G.R., *Gudi Gumpha,* p. 70.

65. Satyanarayana, K., *Gurajada Appa Rao – A study* (unpublished Thesis submitted to Andhra University, p. 160.)
66. Arudra, *Op. Cit.*, p. 55.
67. *Ibid,* p. 512.
68. *Ibid,* p. 418.
69. Narayana Kavi, Dittakavi, *Op. Cit.*, Asvasa – III, pp. 79-80.
70. Lakshmi Narasu Kavi, Chatrati, *Padmanabha Yuddham,* p. 63.
71. *Proceedings of South Indian History Congress,* Vol. XVIII, 1998, p. 314.
72. Arudra, *Op. Cit.*, p. 415.
73. *Ibid*, p. 548.
74. Viraswamayya, Enugula, *Kasiyatra Charitra,* p. 334.
75. Ramaraju, B., *Telugu Janapada Geya Vanjamayam*, p. 372.
76. "*Idi Yandhra Kavitvambani*
    Madi royandagadu, dini marma marayudi"
    Cited by Bhagavatula Krishnayya, *Kandardham;* No. 14.
77. Arudra, *Op. Cit.*, p. 330.
78. *Ibid,* p. 590.
79. *Ibid,* p. 587.
80. *Ibid,* p. 584.
81. *Ibid,* p. 590.
82. *Ibid,* p. 332.
83. Vadivelu, A., *The Aristocracy of Southern India,* Vol. II, p. 225.
84. *Ibid,* p. 226.
85. Pichchaya Sastri Dipala (Ed.), *Chatupadya Ratnakaramu*, p. 290.
86. Arudra, *Op. Cit.*, p. 226.
87. *Ibid,* p. 18.
88. *Ibid,* p. 3.
89. Donappa, T., *Bhasha Charitraka Vyasavali*, p. 236.
90. Varma, G.R., *Op.Cit,* p. 92.
91. Arudra, *Op.Cit,* Vol. III, p. 365.
92. Donappa. T., *Op.Cit,* p. 310.
93. Social Evils in Andhra desa: 17th and 18th centuries A.D, Hyd, 1999, p. 38.
94. *Ibid.*
95. Donappa, T., *Bhasha Charitraka Vyasavali*, p. 115.

Conclusion

From the historical periods, Visakhapatnam Province shows its unique nature and significance in many respects. It became a centre of political activity and turned as a buffer zone between different political powers and cultural influences in different centuries. At the time of the advent of Muslims as well as the Colonial agencies, it came into authority of the local chiefs and zamindars that dominated administratively and strengthened themselves. Following the medieval character of the kingship, some of the zamindari families traced their origin from the earliest centuries, and tried to connect themselves with historical and Puranic personalities. They received land fiefs in different periods and different circumstances from the Sultans of Golkonda, Chiefs of Orissa, and from the European Company Governments. The zamindars like Kakarlapudis of Anakapalli and Pusapatis of Vizianagaram were established under the Sultans of Golkonda. The Bhupati families of Madugula, Golugonda and Gudem were established under sub-ordination to the Orissan powers and the rest of the zamindars like the Godes originated under the East India Company.

This zamindari period is a transition of polity which is essentially medieval in character to what may be called a modern polity. When the Nizam was not in a position to control the affairs effectively, these local authorities tried for the support of either the French or the English. The French were the first to gain political ascendancy, but later the English due to their various resources ousted the French and established themselves in power over this province.

The zamindars in general and of this province in particulars wished to deal with the Company in the same manner as they dealt with the Nizam earlier. But the limited resources of the zamindars were not enough to control the Company. The Company put down with a high hand all the rebellious zamindars. With the introduction of new administrative policies for agency and plains, to the maximum extent administration was systematized and modernised under the British system.

The micro-level political analysis of the Visakhapatnam province during the troubled period between fading away of the Muslim power and the establishment of British power, testifies the political dynamics of the British diplomacy. Evidently this was the significant region to put up resistance to the expansion and consolidation of the British authority both from the petty tribal chiefs as well as the zamindars. Several efforts were done by the Kakarlapudi Payak Raos, the Bhupatis of Golugonda and Gudem, and lastly by the Pusapatis of Vizianagaram to check the authority of the English.

During this period the Company introduced Permanent Settlement during the years 1802-03 to remove "all the generated evils of unsettled principles of revenue administration" to "reform and establish it on a firm and efficient footing not less to the advantage of the people than to the security of the revenue"; suppressing "rebellion and insubordination" which was conspicuous, by 'annihating' the troops of the zamindars and bringing them to subjection, and 'acknowledge' and submit to the principle, that as they must be indebted to the beneficience and wisdom of the English Government for every advantage they were to receive so in like manner, they must feel indebted solely to its protection, for the continuance and enjoyment of them.

Throughout this period, the zamindars, chafing at their reduction as mere landholders and aided by wild and unhealthy country, kept the district in continual ferment with their recalcitrance and feuds. The disturbances, which entirety resulted from their own feuds, impoverished them and made them defaulters. Such estates of the zamindars were auctioned by the English and were purchased by different families.

The modernisation process that was commenced during the Nineteenth Century, coupled with the introduction of English language and education and compulsions of the administrative needs of the colonial rulers, posed a serious threat to the traditional learning and indigenous professions based on that. The impact of this could be seen in the slow but steady shift of interest of these sections of society towards learning of English language and education. As such this region was first to react favourably to the impact of Western culture and ideas. Some of the zamindari families like that of the Godes had the benefit of Western Civilisation to a remarkable extent and also privilege of moving freely in European Society.

This period witnessed the thorough suppression of the anti-British tendency of the zamindars, muttadars, and estatedars and Pro-British attitude is encouraged and honoured by giving various honours and titles. The internal rivalries between the zamindars and their vested interests became an advantage to the British power. They left no opportunity to interfere into the matters of the zamindaris like the struggles of succession and to act accordingly. They divided the muttas, zamindaris and districts to safeguard their interests, and no uniform measure was taken to deal with such matters. Except on few occasions the English Government never thought it essential to enquire into the grievances of the zamindars. The revenue innovations of Madras Government also caused economic distress among majority of the aristocratic families and produced in them a feeling of general aversion towards British Rule. The growing discontent among the zamindars became more intensified when their lands were threatened to be taken away from them, even for delay in the payment of tribute. This attitude of the government struck a blow at the hereditary basis of their estates and their authority. Some anti-governmental revolts broke out in some of the zamindaris in different parts of this vicinity. They continued an open fight, did not disband armed personnel nor remit the revenue as directed by the District Collectors. The zamindari families at places like Anakapalli, Kasipuram and Golugonda belongs to such group.

In the case of the Gode zamindari who exercised their authority from river Nagavali to river Tandava, either due to their inclination towards Western thought and idealogy, or due to their zamindari interests supported the British throughout their career. Thus, we can see the pro, as well as the anti-British tendencies among the zamindars of this province.

From the second half of the nineteenth century, there was a radical transformation in the nature, attitude and thinking of the feudal lords and zamindars. Coming under the influence of British education, British administration and modern thought, many of them began to cultivate a sense of responsibility of the society and of the people. They began to involve themselves in public activities and to encourage public organisations. Their liberal policies and constructive role in the domain of social, educational, cultural and economic activities won the appreciation and approbation of the people. It is known that majority of zamindars of the region are learned men and enlightened scholars. The liberal Western ideas and Western education succeeded in moulding the values and attitudes of at least some of the zamindars of this province.

Another important factor in the zamindaris of this province is the successful regimes of the lady zamindars. Some of the ladies like China Janakamma, Rajendramani Devi and Sita Patta Mahadevi contributed much through their services and won the hearts of the people.

Some old forts at places like Anakapalli were ruined and some new forts were constructed at places like Visakhapatnam and Madugula. A number of bunglows, choultries, guest houses and temples were constructed during the zamindari regime in this province. The gardens rised by the Gode family at Anakapalli were appreciated by the European officers. The keen interest and scientific knowledge of the zamindars like the Godes made them to establish an astronomical observatory and the introduction of new sugarcane varieties in the Anakapalli areas.

Their modern approaches and outlook nowhere deviated them from their traditional systems. On one side their regime reflects the ideology of ancient feudalistic tendencies and the earlier practices like child marriage, Kanyasulka, Polygamy, Devadasi system, concubinage etc., were allowed to continue. They made a number of grants to temples and scholars. They made contributions to a number of institutions within and outside their province. They have constructed a number of schools, colleges and hospitals for the benefit of the public.

They are very much interested in the patronage of literature and some of the zamindars and their family members are poets themselves.

In fact, the patronage of literature under this period is in no way less than that of any period in the history of literature of the land. The literature that was composed and patronised under the zamindars of the Visakhapatnam region had its own significance. Some of the zamindars are much interested in scientific discovery and published those results in well reputed national and international journals. Ladies in zamindari families like Madiney Subhadramma, Gode China Janakamma etc., had written different types of devotional and philosophical writings. Their poetic talents were well attested to by a number of literary critics. A number of well versed scholars and great poets of the age enjoyed their patronage and enriched literature in multi-directions both in Telugu and Sanskrit.

Besides Telugu and Sanskrit *kavyas* and other literary styles, Visakhapatnam is credited with the Christian publication activity. For the first time the translation of Bible into Telugu started at Visakhapatnam.

The contribution of the zamindars to the history and culture of the Visakhapatnam region is undoubtedly a significant factor.

Bibliography

I. English

(i) Primary sources

Administration Report of the Government of Madras, 1875-76, Part II.

Administration Report of the Madras Presidency, 1896-97.

A Short Account of the Madras Presidency, Gantz Brothers, 1861.

A Statistical Atlas of the Madras Presidency revised and brought upto the end of Fasli 1340, Government Press, Madras, 1936.

A Statistical Atlas of the Madras Province revised and brought upto the end of Fasli 1350, Government Press, Madras, 1949.

Bridwood, George, *Report on the Old Records of the Indian Office,* London and Calcutta, 1891.

Carmichael, D.F., *A Manual of the District of Vizagapatam in the Presidency of Madras,* Madras, 1869.

Forrest, G.W., *Bengal and Madras papers, 3 Vols. Imperial Records*, Calcutta, 1928

Francis, W., *Vizagapatnam District Gazetteer*, New Delhi, 1992.

Firminger, Walter. F., (Ed.), '*The Fifth Report from the Select Committee on the Affairs of the East India Company*', Vol. II.

Gazetteer of India, History and Culture, Vol. II, Publications Division, New Delhi, 2003.

Grant Duff, M.E., *General Survey of the Madras Presidency,* Ooctacamund, 1884.

Heming Way, F. R., *Madras District Gazetteers, Godavari District,* Government Press, Madras 1915.

Hunter, W.W., *'The Imperial Gazetteer of India'*, London, 1886, Oxford, 1908.

Imperial Gazetteer of India, Provincial Series, Madras I, Calcutta, 1908.

Lemon, *Ganjam District Manual*, Madras 1918.

Maciver, L., *'Report of the census of the Madras Presidency'*, 1881.

Maclean, C. D., *'Manual of the Administration of the Madras Presidency'*, 3 Vol, New Delhi, 1885.

Madras Administration Report, 1860-61.

Madras Census Report, 1871.

Madras Census Report, 1891.

Maltby, T. J., *'The Ganjam District Manual'*, Madras, 1882.

Morgan Williams, *Factory Consultations; Vizagapatam Factory*, Vols. 3681-3689.

Morris, H., *A Descriptive and Historical Account of the Godavari District in the Madras Presidency*, London, 1878.

Prakasam, T., *Estates Land Committee Report*, Madras, 1938, p. 41.

Raghava Iyengar, S.S., *Memorandum on the progress of the Madras Presidency during the last forty years of British Administration,* Madras, 1893.

Ramesan, N, *Andhra Pradesh District Gazetteers*, Srikakulam, Visakhapatnam, East Godavari, West Godavari, Hyderabad, 1979.

Report of Board of Revenue of Vizagapatnam, Madras, 1811.

Report of the Collector of Vizagapatam submitted to the Famine Commission, 1880.

Report of the Famine Commission, 1898.

Report of the Administration of the Madras Presidency during the year 1867-68, Government Press, Madras, 1869.

Report on the Administration of the Madras Presidency during the year 1870-71, Government Press, Madras, 1872.

Russell, G. E., *Reports on the Disturbances in Parlakimidy, Vizagapatam and Goomsoor in 1832-1836*, Madras 1856, (2 Vols).

Sastri, V.L. (Ed.), *Encyclopedia of the Madras Presidency and the Adjacent States*, Madras, 1920.

Report of the zamindari enquiry Committee, 1939, Madras.

ENGLISH

(ii) Secondary Sources

Aitchison, C.W., *Account of the War in India Treaties, Engagements and Sanad,* Calcutta 1909 (9 Vols).

Ambirajan, *Classical Political Economy and British Policy in India*, New Delhi, 1978.

Anjaneyulu, M.S.R., *Vizagapatam District 1769-1834*, Visakhapatnam, 1982.

Auber, Peter, *'The Rise and Progress of British power in India'*, London, 1837.

Baden-Powell, B.H., *Land Revenue in British India,* Oxford, 1894.

Balanagamani, T., Cultural Surge during the Gajapati's Rule (1850-1995 A.D)-A study of the Cultural Achievements of the Pusapatis of Vizianagaram (unpublished thesis submitted to Andhra University).

Baliga, B.S. Studies in Madras Administration, Madras, Government of Madras, 2 Vols. 1960.

Batta, V.V., *Aspects of Economic Change and Policy in India 1800-1960.*

Beagle Hole, T. H., *Thomas Munro and the Development of the Administrative Policy in Madras, 1792-1818,* Cambridge, 1966.

Bearce, George, *British Attitudes towards India 1784-1858,* Oxford, 1961.

Bilgrami and Will Mott, *Historical and Descriptive sketch of his Highness: the Nizam's Dominions*, Bombay, 1884.

Briggs, H.G. *The Nizam, 'His history and Relations with the British Government'*, London, 1861.

Cambridge, R., *Account of the War in India*, London, 1761.

Chaudhari, K.N., '*The Economic Development of Indian under the East India Company' (1814-1858)*, London, 1971.

Chaudhari, S.B., *Civil Disturbances during British Rule in India 1765-1857*, Calcutta, 1955.

Chesney, George, *Indian polity*, London, 1870.

Das, A.C., '*The Indian Ryot, Land Tax, Permanent Settlement and the Famine'*, Howrah, 1881.

Deo, Kumar Bidyadhar, Nandapur, (A Forsaken Kingdom) Jeypore, 1938.

Dhires Batta Charya, '*A Consice History of the Indian Economy'*, 1750-1950.

Dod Well, H., *Ananda Ranga Pillai's Dairy*, Vol. XII, Madras, 1920.

_____., *Dupliex and Clive*, London, 1920.

_____., '*The Cambridge History of India'*, Vol. VI.

_____., '*The Indian Empire 1858-1918 with Chapters on the Development of Administration'*, 1818-1858.

Dutt, R.C., *Economic History of British India*, Delhi, 1908.

_____., '*Famines and Land Assessment in India'*, (Reprint), Delhi, 1985.

Fathima Kutty Kapil, British Administration in the Northern part of Vizagapatam District-1794-1898.: A historical survey.

Forde, Col. Lionel, *Lord Clive's Right Hand Man, Col. Francis Forde,* London, 1910.

Forrest, George, '*The Life of Lord Clive'*, London 1918.

Fryken Berg, Robert Eric, *Guntur District, 1788-1848*, Oxford, 1965.

Georg Berkemer, *Little Kingdoms in Kalinga, Ideologies, Legitimation and Politik regionaler Eliten* 1993, (German) published by F. Steiner in Stuttgart, reviewed by Burkhard Schnepel in *the Journal of the Economic and Social History of the Orient* (1986).

George Watts, *India: Geographical, Statistical and Historical*, London, 1858.

Gleig, G.R., *History of the British Empire in India,* 4 Vols, London, 1841.

Gopal, Sarvepalli, '*The Permanent Settlement in Bengal and its Results',* London, 1949.

Gribble, J.D.B., '*A History of the Deccan',* London, 1924, (2 Vols).

Gupta, Sulekha Chandra, *Agrarian Relations and Early British Rule in India*, Bombay, 1963.

Habib, Irfan, '*The Agrarian system of Mughal India',* (1556-1707) Bombay, 1963.

Holling Berry, W., '*The History of Nizam Alikhan'*, Calcutta, 1805.

Hume, A.O., *Agricultural Reform in India*, London 1879.

Iyengar, S.K., '*Historical Inscriptions of South India 1728-1805*, Madras', 1950.

Kaye, John. W., *The Administration of the East India Company: A History of Indian Progress,* London, 1853.

Kesavanarayana, B., *Political and Social Factors in Andhra*, Vijayawada, 1976.

Lucy, S., *East India Company in 18th century Politics*, 1952.

Mangamma, J., *Alluri Sitarama Raju*, Hyderabad, 1983.

Majumdar, R.C., *History of the Freedom Movement in India*, Calcutta, 1962.

Malaviya Madan Mohan, *Economic Decline in India*, Madras, 1918.

Malcolm, John, *Life of Lord Clive*, 3 Vols, London, 1836.

Malleson, G.B., *History of the French in India*, London 1983.

————, *The Decisive Battles of India, (1746-1840)* London, 1914.

Martineau, A, *Bussy in the Deccan Being extracts from Bussy and French India*, Translated by A. Cammiade, Pondicherry, 1941.

Mill, James, '*The History of British India London'*, 1840.

Misra, B.B., '*The Administrative History of India' (1834-1947)*, London, 1911.

More Land, W.H. (Ed.), *Relations of Golconda in the early Seventeenth century*, London, 1931.

Mudaliar, Gnana, Sundara, P.K., *Note on the Permanent settlement*, Madras, 1940.

Muir, Ramsay, *'The Making of British India' (1765-1858)* London, 1915.

Mukharjee, Nilamani, '*The Ryotwari System in Madras*', Calcutta, 1965.

Nagamamba, E., History of Pusapati Family (unpublished thesis submitted to Andhra University).

Narla, V.R., *Veeresalingam*, New Delhi, 1968.

Nicholas Dirks, *The Hollow Crown*, the ethnohistory of an Indian Kingdom (1987), reviewed by David Ludden in *the Journal of Interdiciplinary History* (1989).

Ohn Greenfield Leonard, *Kandukuri Veeresalingam (1848-1919)*, Hyderabad, 1991.

Orme, Robert, *History of the Military Transactions of the British Nation in Industan,* 3 vols, Madras, 1861 and 1862.

Powell Baden, *The Land Systems of British India*, 3 vols, Oxford 1892.

Raghunadha Rao, P., *History of Moderm Andhra*, New Delhi, 1980.

Rama Chandra Reddi., Tribal revolts in Vizagapatnam and East Godavari Districts, 1857-1917. (Unpublished thesis submitted to Andhra University)

Ramadas, V., *'The Madras Estate Land Act 1908'*, Madras, 1915.

Ramakrishna, V., *Social Reform in Andhra 1848-1919*, New Delhi, 1983.

Ramalakshmi, C., *'The Northeren Circars under the East India Company'* (1766-1857).

Ramana Rao, A.V., *Economic Development of Andhra Pradesh*, Bombay, 1958.

Ranga Rao, S., *Account of the Bobbili Zamindary*, Madras, 1907.

Ray, P.C., *Indian Famines-Their Causes and Remedies*, Calcutta, 1901.

Reddi, M.P.R., *Peasant and State in Modern Andhra History*, Vijayawada, 1986.

Reddi, V.M and Raghunadha Rao, *Andhra under British Rule*, Hyderabad, 1975.

Richard, Bute, *Cambridge History of India*, Vol. IV, Delhi, 1937.

Richards, T.F., *Maughal Administration in Golconda*, Oxford, 1975.

Sarma, A.V.D., *Integration of Andhra and Orissa Cultures,* Delhi, 1986.

Sarojini Regani, *Nizam British Relations, 1724-1857*, Hyderabad, 1962-1963.

Sayana, V.V., *Agrarian Problems of Madras*, Madras, 1949.

Sen, Sunil, *Agrarian Relations in India 1793-1794*, New Delhi, 1979.

Sen, S.P., '*The French in India' (1763-1816)*, Calcutta, 1958.

Siddiqui Abdul Majid, *History of Golconda*, Hyderabad, 1956.

Srikrishna, D., The Vatsavai family of Peddapuram.

Srinivasa Chary, C. S., *Ananda Ranga Pillai*, Madras 1940.

Subba Rao, M.V., *Sri Vijayarama Gajapati*, Vizayanagaram, 1932.

Subba Rao, T., Vizagapatam District Under the East India Company (1682-1858) (unpublished thesis submitted to Andhra University)

Sudershan Rao, Y., '*Andhra between the Empires*', Hanumakonda, 1991.

Sundaram, Lanka, *"The Revenue Administration of the Northern Circars"* Published as series in *J.A.H.R.S.* Vols. VI to XV, Rajahmundry, 1934.

_______, *British Beginnings in the Andhra Desa*, Madras, 1925.

Sweta Chalapati Venkata, '*A Revised and Enlarged Account of the Bobbili Zamindari*', - Ranga Rao Bahadur, Madras, 1907.

Thorson, Edward, '*The History of the British Empire in India*', London, 1841, (6 Vols).

Vadivelu, A., *Aristocracy of Southern India* (2 Vols), Madras, 1903.

Venkata Rangaiya, M. (Ed.), *The Freedom Struggle in Andhra Pradesh*, Hyderabad, Vol. I, (1800-1905).

Wheeler, T., *Early Records of British India*, London, 1878.

Wilson, H.H., *A Glossary of Judicial and Revenue Terms and useful Words in Official Documents relating to the Administration of British India*, London, 1855, (Reprint), Delhi, 1968.

Wilks, Mark, *Historical Sketches of the South India*, Madras, 1860, (3 Vols).

II. TELUGU

(i) Primary sources

Sathagopa charyulu, Komanduri, *Zamindari Committee Report.*

Krsihna murthy sastri, Sripada, *Vijaya Lakshmi Vilasamu,* Rajahmundry, 1932.

Lakshmi Narasakavi, Chatrati: *Padmanabha Yuddham*, Vizianagaram, 1913.

Mrutyunjaya Bahadur, *Hill Zamindarula Charitramu*, Madras, 1887.

Narayana Kavi, Dittakavi, *Rangaraya Charitramu*, Madras. 1917.

Radha Madhava Kavi, *Vishnu Mayaanatakam*, Vizianagaram, 1949.

Rajendra Prasad, H. (Ed.), *Visakhapatnam kaifiyat, Anakapalli Kaifiyat and Doddigallu Kaifiyat*, Hyderabad, 1990.

Satyanarayana Raju, Penumatsa, *Vikramagunadarasamu,* Tanuku, 1951.

Sreerama Sastry, Pattisam, *Vikramadeva Satakam*, Kakinada, 1932.

Surakavi, Adidam, *Rama Lingeswara Satakam*, Vizianagaram, 1931.

Tirupati Venkata Kavulu, *Nana Raja Sandarsanamu*, Tanuku, 1951.

Veera Swamayya, Enugula, *Kasiyatra Charitra,* Madras, 1890.

Venkata Kodanda Rao, Vijjapurapu, *Visakhapatnam Zilla Vruttanta sangraham*, Vizagapatnam, 1886.

Venkata Satyanarayana Murthy, Kavikondala *Visakhamandala Charitramu*, Kakinada, 1927.

Pusapati Vari Vamsavali, Mackenzie Collections, 405- Oriental Manuscript, Library, Madras.

(ii) Secondary sources

Rama Rao, Adidam, '*Vismrita Kalinga-Andhra Kavulu*', Chennapuri, 1953.

______, *Adidam Surakavi Jivitamu*, Chennapuri 1955.

Arudra, *Samagra Andhra Sahityamu*, Vol. III, Hyderabad, 2002.

Donappa, T., *Andhra Samasthanamulu- Sahitya Poshanamu*, Waltair, 1969.

———., *Andhra Desa Samskriti-Vyasavali*, Waltair, 1975.

Gopala Krishna Rao, K., *Andhra Sataka Vanjamayamu*, Hyderabad, 1975.

Govindu, G., *Anakapalli Directory, Anakapalli,* 2005.

Narayana Murthy, B., *Angla Rajya Stapanamu*, Machilipatnam, 1917.

Pratapa Reddi, Suravaram, *Andhrula Sanghika Charitra*, Hyderabad, 1992.

Satyanarayana Murthy, T., *Padmanabha Yuddham*, Hyderabad, 2002.

Subba Rao, Vanguri, *Sataka Kavula Charitramu*, Narsapur, 1957.

Surya Rao, Angara, *Rendu Sutadbula Visakhanagara Charitra*, Visakhapatnam, 2000.

Varma, G.R., *Mailara Deva*, Tadepalligudem, 1973.

______, *Gudi-Gumpaa*, Tadepalligudem, 1974.

Vikrama Deva Varma, *Kalinga Desamu*, 1925.

Veera Bhadra Rao, Ch., *Andhrula Charitra*, 3 Vols, Chennapuri, 1910.

Venkata Appa Rao, Gurajada, *Kanya Sulkam*, Rajahmundry, 1898.

Venkata Rao, N., *Vizianagara Samasthanam Andhravajmaya Poshana*, Hyderabad, 1965.

III. JOURNALS

(i) English:

Journal of Andhra Historical Research Society

Indian Historical Research Society

Itihas

Proceedings of Andhra Pradesh History Congress

Proceedings of Indian History Congress

Proceedings of South Indian History Congress

(ii) Telugu

Andhra Patrika Ugadi Sanchika.

Andhra Sahitya Parishad Patrika.

Bharati

Grihalakshmi

Kalpalata

Telugu

Vrittantini

Appendices

Appendix - I

Genealogical Tables of Some Zamindari Families

GENEALOGICAL TABLE OF THE KAKARLA PUDI ZAMINDARS

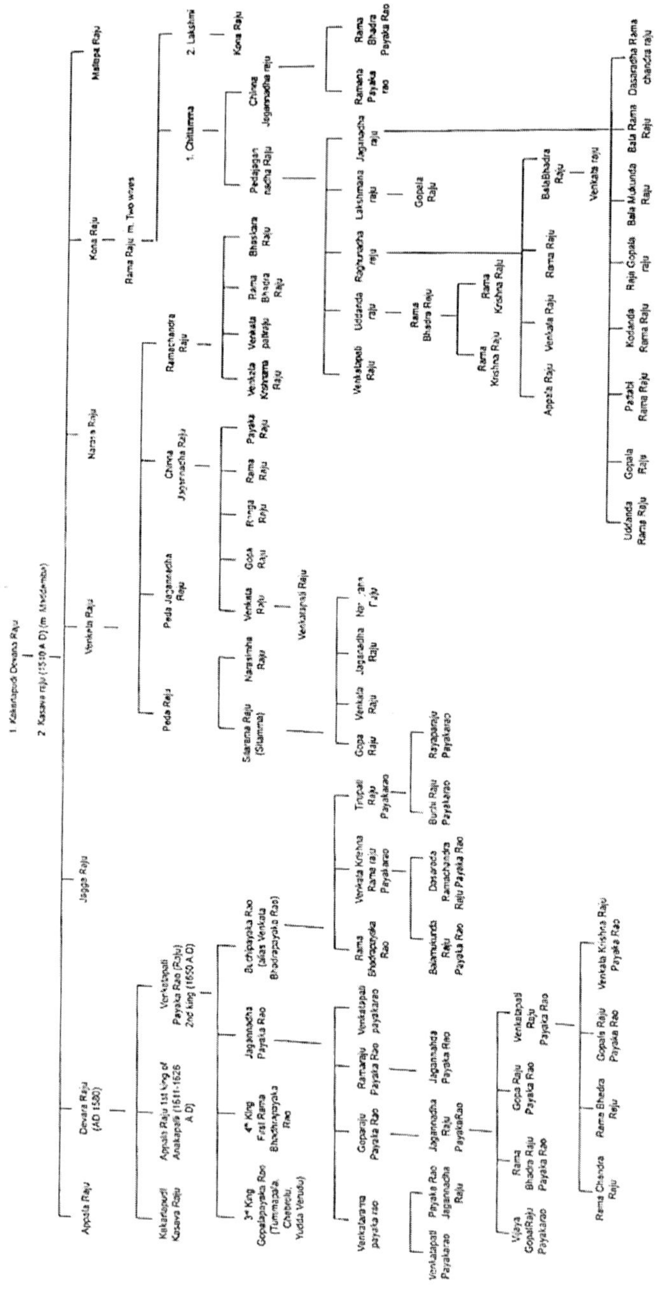

GENEALOGICAL TABLE OF THE MADUGULA ZAMINDARS

- Matsya Vamsa
  - Sri Chola Bhupati (A.D. 721-771)
    - Linga Bhupati
      - Viswa Bhupati
        - Samba Bhupati
          - Linga Bhupati Dev II (1770)
            - Appala Bhupati
          - Krishna Bhupati Dev-I
            - Jagannadha Bhupati Dev-I (m. Ramayamma)
              - Appala Bhupati III (1817-1831) (m. Ramayamma
                - Jogi Mani Devi (m. Mukundadev of Jeypore)
                  - Krishna Dev (m. Neela Devi) (The Estatedar of Kalyana Singapore at Jaypore)
                    - Adopted Mukunda Dev (1905) m. Chandra Mani Maha Devi)
              - Hari Hara Bhupati (1832-53)
              - Krishna Bhupati Dev-II (1853-1875) (m. Two wives) 1875-89 court of words
                - Sitapatta Mahadevi
                  - Adopte Son Vikrama Dev (1876) (Son of the Brother of Rama Chandra Dev of Jeypore)
                - Nilamanipatta Maha Devi (1886)
                  - Ammi Maha devi (1895) (m. Viswambhara) Dev Younger brother of Rama Chandradev of Jeypore)
                    - Rajendra Mani Devi (A.D 1901)
              - Gopala Bhupati
                - Jagannadha Bhupati-II
                  - Prabhavati Devi

GENEALOGICAL TABLE OF THE GOLCONDA ZAMINDARI

Nilakanta Bhupati

|

Vira Bhupati (A.D. 1772-1783)

|

Bairava Bhupati (A.D. 1783-1785)

|

Malla Bhupati (A.D. 1785-1805

|

Chinna Bhupati (A.D. 1785-1796)

|

Krishna Bhupati (A.D. 1805-1812)

|

Ananta Bhupati (A.D. 1812-1833)

|

Chinna Bhupati (A.D. 1845-1848)

Sanyasi Bhupati (A.D. 1856)	Santa Bhupati (A.D. 1891)

GENEALOGICAL TABLE OF THE GODE ZAMINDARI

- Giri Raju
  - Siddi Raju
    - Janya Raju (Chinna Mall Bhupati
      - Akkama Bhupati
        - Bhupati
          - Surana (Namely Pedda Surya Rao) (m. Gumpamma)
            - Upanna
            - Sarvesa
            - Jagga Rao (m. Ankamba)
              - Surya Rao (m. Subhadramma)
                - Pedda Jagga Rao (m. Chellamma, Krishnamma
                  - Subhadramma (1781-1840) m. Mediney Suranna
                  - Banga-ramma
                  - Surya Prakasa Rao (m. Janakkamma)
                    - Son
                    - Son (died at Childhood
                    - Ratnayamma (m. Gudivada Lakshmi Narashimha Rayulu)
                      - China Janakamma (m. Narayana Gajapati Rao)
                  - Lakshmi Narasamma
                  - Bhaskara Rao
                  - Suryanarayana Rao (1818) (m. Achchyamma, Sitayamma, Nilayamma)
                    - Chinavenkata Jagga Rao (1817-1856) (m. Bangaramma)
                      - Achchayamma (m. A.V. Narasimha Rao)
                    - Narayana Gajapati Rao (1820-1903) (m. China Janakamma)
                      - Sitabai (Rani Saheba of wadhwan)
                      - Lakshmi Narsamma Rani & Kurupam)
                        - Narayana Gajapati Raju
                        - Janaki Ratnayamma
                        - Suryanarayana Raju
                  - Chengal Rao (A.D. 1798)
                - Appayamma (m. Mediney Family)
                - Sitayamma (m. Chevala Family)
            - Bhupati
            - Gopal
          - Rama Chandra

Appendix - II

Texts of Inscriptions of the Zamindars

VIJAYARAMA GAJAPATI

S.I.I. Vol. V	SRIKURMAM
No. 1286	Undated
A.R.E. No. 373-W	
of 1896	

1. Sri Kalinga desa parabhidanasya
2. Sri Vijayanagara rajyasya Mahara-
3. Jyasya Sri Paramesvara Prasadena Pala-
4. Kah Sri Suryavamsa Sambhavah Pusha-
5. Patikula Pradipo His Hainessu
6. Sri Maharajadhiraja | Vijayara-
7. Magajapati Maharaju Manyasultan [II *]

GODE CHENGALVARAO

S.I.I. Vol. VI	SIMHACHALAM
No. 1192	S. 1720
A.R.E. No. 365-XXV	(A.D. 1798)
of 1899	

(On a Pillor in the mukhamantapa in the Sri Varaha Lakshmi Narasimhanatha Temple)

1. Svasti Sri [II*] Salivahana Sakavarshambulu
2. || agunetic || Pingala Samvatsara
3. Kartika ba|| || nadu Paddakon [du]-
4. ghadiyala vyala dhanurlagnaman-
5. du suvarna Sri sathagopam Sri simha
6. chalamlo Sri Varaha Nrisimha svami-
7. vari Sannidhini Gode Jaggarayudu Ko-
8. marulaina Chengalvarayanim garu Samarpinchi-
9. nadi || Tu

GODE SURYANARAYANA

S.I.I. Vol. V
No. 1159
A.R.E. No. 279-A
of 1896

SRIKURMAM
S. 1750
(A.D. 1828)

1. Svasti Sri [||*] Salivahana
2. Sake Gatabdah
3. kaganu Vartamana Sarva-
4. dhari Samll Chaitramasa Vasanta Nava-
5. ratramula Vratam Sanganganu
6. Visakhapatnam Kaparastudai-
7. na Gode Suryanarayana
8. rayudu Yisthalaman-
9. du besinadu ||

KRISHNA CHANDRA DEV

(SON OF VIKRAMA DEV)

S.I.I. Vol. V
No. 1192
A.R.E. No. 311 of 1896

SRIKURMAM
S. 1780
A.D. 1866

1. Salivahana sake gatabde agu
2. neti Krodhana nama Samhvatsara a-
3. sivija Suddha mi Soumyavasara-
4. mandu Sri Sri Sri Kurmanatha-
5. Svami Vari Charana Sannidhiki Jaya-
6. puram Letu Jamidaru garu en nu-
7. Sri Vikrama Devu Maharajulu
8. m gari dvitiyya Putrulam-
9. Yina Sri Krishna Chandradevu Maha
10. raju lumgaru ane memu ha-
11. jaru lamai sevisthimi ||

Appendix - III
Photographs

Gateway of Sher Muhammadpuram

Mahal at Sher Muhammadpuram

Kurupam Market

Turner Choultry

Kurupam Tomb

Sri Rajah V. Veeraphadra Raju

Nookalamma Temple

Nookalamma

Sher Muhammad Khan

Gode Narayana Gajapati Rao

Bronze Status of Queen Victoria

Ankitam Venkata Narasinga Rao

Misses A.V.N. College

Collectorate of Visakhapatnam

King George Hospital

Glossary

Adalat	:	A Court of Law
Agraharam	:	Village or Part there of resided by brahmins and held on quit rent or free of assessment.
Amin	:	A Native Surveyor of Land
Ashtakams	:	Eight verse eulogy
Bhasha	:	Language
Bhupati	:	King
Cist/ Kist	:	Land rent
Cowle/ Kowle	:	A Document in writing given by the Proprietor to the Cultivator, defining the terms of lease on which the lands are to be held by him.
Sircar/ Circar	:	Government, a Province or a District.
Desa	:	Country
Dewan	:	The Minister of the King, a Minister
Faujdar	:	Army Officer
Firman	:	Order, Mandate. A real grant or character
Fasli	:	The harvest year a mode of computing time in India from July 1st. By adding 590 to the Fasli year, one may gain a rough calculation the year Annomini (A.D.).
Gramya	:	Colloquial
Hawamahal	:	Place of Breeze
Inam	:	Grant of land held in rent-free and in Hereditary and Perpetual-Occupation

Jama	: A 'gathering' or collecting
Jama Bandi	: The Annual Settlement made under the Ryotwari System
Jagir	: Service lands, a tenure common under the native Government in which the public revenues of a tract of land are made over to a Servant of State
Kaifiat	: Statement, Description, Deposition, Report, Account of Particulars, story
Manyam	: Land held free of Assessment by Village Servants as Emoluments for Service
Mannem	: Agency (hill and forest) area
Mansubdar	: Revenue/Administrative in-charge of a particular area
Maharaja	: King
Muttadari	: Rentier of the Villages
Pesh Cush	: Tax, Tribute
Podu	: The Practice of Setting fire to the forests for the purpose of Agriculture to which the aboriginals on the hills were accustomed
Polligar	: Head of a District
Pituries/ Fituries	: Uprisings
Patrika	: Journal
Raja/ Rajah	: King
Raja Dharma	: Duty of the King
Ryot	: Cultivator
Ryotwari	: According to or with ryots, applied to Revenue Settlement
Sanchika	: Number or volume
Savara	: A hill tribe
Sibbandi	: Personal attendants
Stotram/ Stavam	: Different forms of eulogy
Sangeetam	: Music
Sahitya	: Literature
Subha	: A Province

Subedar	:	The Viceroy or Governor of a Province
Samantas	:	Feudal lords/ Subordinate rulers
Taluq	:	Subdivision of a District
Vamsa	:	Lineage
Zamindar	:	A proprietor directly responsible to the state the Revenues of the land he possesses
Zamindari	:	The Office and right of a Zamindar; the tract of Land Constituting the Possession of Zamindar
Zilla	:	District

Index

H

I

J

K